Legal Pluralism and Governance in South Asia and Diasporas

Legal Pluralism and Governance in South Asia and Diasporas contributes to the already heated debate about legal pluralism but it shifts the attention from the ontology of law to what is treated as law and its impact on governance, with a special focus on the *fora* of dispute resolution. This book addresses sensitive issues such as gender rights and alternative dispute resolution in India, Hindu and Muslim personal laws in South Asia and in Europe, cross-border white violence, the change to Islamic legal traditions under Western domination, women's inheritance in Pakistan and in the partially disputed territory of Gilgit Baltistan, indigenous rights and resistance at the India-Bangladesh border, and customary laws of nomadic groups in India. The authors deploy a variety of views that point at the pros and cons of legal pluralism and also integrates its opponents. They show how constructions of identity, religion, and power have historically informed the conceptualisation of secularism which may be an ideal, sometimes able to provide for perceptions of accountable governance, but also generating dividing worldviews.

This book was originally published as a special issue of *The Journal of Legal Pluralism and Unofficial Law*.

Livia Holden (MA and MPhil - Paris 10, PhD - School of Oriental And African Studies, University of London) is an Anthropologist of Law with long-term experience of fieldwork in India and in Pakistan. She is the author of *Hindu Divorce: A Legal Anthropology* and the editor of *Cultural Expertise and Litigation*. Currently she is Dean of the Faculty of Humanities and Social Sciences at the Karakoram International University and Honorary Senior Research Fellow at Durham University, Department of Anthropology.

Legal Pluralism and Governance in South Asia and Diasporas

Edited by
Livia Holden

Routledge
Taylor & Francis Group
LONDON AND NEW YORK

First published 2015 by Routledge

2 Park Square, Milton Park, Abingdon, Oxon, OX14 4RN
605 Third Avenue, New York, NY 10017

Routledge is an imprint of the Taylor & Francis Group, an informa business

First issued in paperback 2020

British Library Cataloguing in Publication Data
A catalogue record for this book is available from the British Library

ISBN 13: 978-1-138-81239-0 (hbk)
ISBN 13: 978-0-367-73943-0 (pbk)

Typeset in Times New Roman
by RefineCatch Limited, Bungay, Suffolk

Publisher's Note
The publisher accepts responsibility for any inconsistencies that may have arisen during the conversion of this book from journal articles to book chapters, namely the possible inclusion of journal terminology.

Contents

Citation Information vii

1. Introduction 1
Livia Holden

2. Religious personal laws as non-state laws: implications for gender justice 5
Archana Parashar

3. Legal monism and white violence in South Asia 24
Stig Toft Madsen

4. Governance and governability in South Asian family laws and in diaspora 42
Werner Menski

5. In pursuit of the pagans: Muslim law in the English context 58
Prakash A. Shah

6. The "women's court" in India: an alternative dispute resolution body for women in distress 76
Sylvia Vatuk

7. Daughters' inheritance, legal pluralism, and governance in Pakistan 104
Livia Holden and Azam Chaudhary

8. Harmony ideology revisited: spatial geographies of hegemony and disputing strategies amongst the Santal 124
Fauzia Shariff

9. Legal pluralism in discourse: justice, politics and marginality in rural Rajasthan, India 144
Tommaso Sbriccoli

Index 167

Citation Information

The chapters in this book were originally published in *The Journal of Legal Pluralism and Unofficial Law* volume 45, issue 1 (March 2013). When citing this material, please use the original page numbering for each article, as follows:

Chapter 1
Introduction
Livia Holden
The Journal of Legal Pluralism and Unofficial Law, volume 45, issue 1 (March 2013)
pp. 1–4

Chapter 2
Religious personal laws as non-state laws: implications for gender justice
Archana Parashar
The Journal of Legal Pluralism and Unofficial Law, volume 45, issue 1 (March 2013)
pp. 5–23

Chapter 3
Legal monism and white violence in South Asia
Stig Toft Madsen
The Journal of Legal Pluralism and Unofficial Law, volume 45, issue 1 (March 2013)
pp. 24–41

Chapter 4
Governance and governability in South Asian family laws and in diaspora
Werner Menski
The Journal of Legal Pluralism and Unofficial Law, volume 45, issue 1 (March 2013)
pp. 42–57

Chapter 5
In pursuit of the pagans: Muslim law in the English context
Prakash A. Shah
The Journal of Legal Pluralism and Unofficial Law, volume 45, issue 1 (March 2013)
pp. 58–75

Chapter 6

The "women's court" in India: an alternative dispute resolution body for women in distress
Sylvia Vatuk
The Journal of Legal Pluralism and Unofficial Law, volume 45, issue 1 (March 2013) pp. 76–103

Chapter 7

Daughters' inheritance, legal pluralism, and governance in Pakistan
Livia Holden and Azam Chaudhary
The Journal of Legal Pluralism and Unofficial Law, volume 45, issue 1 (March 2013) pp. 104–123

Chapter 8

Harmony ideology revisited: spatial geographies of hegemony and disputing strategies amongst the Santal
Fauzia Shariff
The Journal of Legal Pluralism and Unofficial Law, volume 45, issue 1 (March 2013) pp. 124–143

Chapter 9

Legal pluralism in discourse: justice, politics and marginality in rural Rajasthan, India
Tommaso Sbriccoli
The Journal of Legal Pluralism and Unofficial Law, volume 45, issue 1 (March 2013) pp. 144–165

Please direct any queries you may have about the citations to
clsuk.permissions@cengage.com

Introduction

Livia Holden

Department of Anthropology, Lahore University of Management Sciences, LUMS, Lahore

Legal Pluralism and Governance in South Asia and in the Diasporas focuses on the networks that act as referents for the settlement of justice in South Asia and in the South Asian diasporas. Specific attention was directed to the elaboration of arguments in the legal process and the choice of the *fora* for dispute resolution. We have addressed the local and translocal dynamics that have affected the settlement of justice and their conceptualizations; the colonial and post-colonial instances that have informed the conceptualization of the sources of law and the implications of their recognition by the state; and the modalities of formalization and perpetuation of legal practices. Most of our contributions look at the language of the law by exploring the socio-legal formulations and scrutinizing arguments within the patterns of litigation. But we also look at the ways South Asian laws have been theorized both in South Asia and in the Euro-American socio-legal contexts. We have taken up the challenge of including papers respectively engaging in legal, socio-anthropological, and feminist analysis and sometimes from a multidisciplinary perspective in order to attempt a dialogue among different standpoints.

This special issue went through several hurdles and took almost two years to be finalized. Academic politics and circumstances of life hampered our project to meet and present our papers in Pondicherry. We succeeded to convene a panel on non-state jurisdictions at the Law and Society Conference 2012 in Honolulu. However, the initial funds allocated to this project were withdrawn and only a few papers could be presented at that occasion. In the meantime the authors had sent me their papers, and I realized that they were all highlighting aspects of legal pluralism in spite of the fact that we were talking different languages and some of us very loudly. As editor I found that my task was not to reach a unique and common voice; it was instead to voice those different positions and to point at their socio-legal implications. Interesting dynamics ensued that may deserve separate account but suffice it to say here that some contributors found unsettling the multidisciplinarity of our ensemble and left to pursue the same *foci* elsewhere. More authors joined. Carrying out long term research in Pakistan I was also observing how development organizations that have for a long time pursued the implementation of the global rule of law intended exclusively as state law, seemed now keen to increasingly draw attention to local and non-state practices of dispute resolution. Significant Euro-American investments were put into the implementation of human rights and democracy not anymore through state-law only but non-state law as well. New arguments mobilizing the needs for context-savvy social engineering were developed as a result (Tamanaha 2012). I found all these events confirming the fact that the interaction between legal pluralism and governance resonates as a priority in the socio-legal domain. It also appeared evident that there was a pressing need for a re-contextualization of legal pluralism, in particular regarding the modalities of its performance. Our papers show that depending on how law and law practices are seen and theorized by the state and the social actors bear implications in terms of governance. In spite of the fact that the authors of this special issue have a wide range of positions regarding what is and should be law and how it should be theorized (legal pluralism and legal monism being at the two ends of the spectrum), our contributions show that legal pluralism as a *de facto* phenomenon cannot be ignored.

It seems now a long time since the legal pluralism conceived by Pospisil (1979) in his study of Kapaku Papuans and the study of the relationship between law and social institutions in Western societies by Foucault (1979) and Fitzpatrick (1983).[1] Both the legal pluralism characterized in opposition to legal centralism (Griffiths 1997) and the legal pluralism as multiplicity rather than a unique sovereign system (Baxi 1986; Chiba 1986) have been challenged on several accounts. Criticism revolves around the fear that the equal acknowledgment of the diverse practices of law would irremediably inflate the notion of state law (Tamanaha 1993) as including forms of resistance to it (Fuller 1994) and furthermore blurring the supposedly necessary boundaries between state and non-state law (Tamanaha 2007). While Woodman (1998) and de Sousa Santos (2002) have responded by questioning the ontological nature of the opposition between state and non-state law others have concentrated on models of plurality of law as well as on the examples of integration of counter-hegemonic instances within the state (Benda-Beckman and Benda-Beckman 2006). The need for an opposition between state and non-state law, however, was hardly tackled. By pointing out the ideological framework within which law is designated as state or non-state law *Legal Pluralism and Governance in South Asia and in the Diasporas* overcomes the impasse and shows that legal pluralism does not concern the law as it should be but instead the practices of law as observable phenomena.

Specific questions have been developed here as follows: Where and how do social actors initiate their claims? Do the theorizations of law affect access in terms of gender, religion, power, and ethnicity? What makes social actors to decide in their forum shopping? Our papers show that contexts of non-state law co-exist, intersect, and overlap with those of state law. They are sometimes but not always antithetic and conflicting in spite of the fact that the term non-state law is now acquiring a negative connotation because it is increasingly perceived as law against the state, and thereby threatening.

The first half of this special issue poses the terms of the conflict between legal pluralism and legal monism. It opens with the papers that are skeptical regarding legal pluralism and plurality of laws and provides historical and pragmatic examples of the limitations of legal pluralism. Parashar argues that personal laws exist only when allowed or at least tolerated by the state and alert us to the dangerous implications for gender rights when misconstructing religious laws in terms of personal laws. Madsen discloses how South Asian personal laws are increasingly relevant at the level of global governance for cases involving not only South Asians but also Euro-American litigants. The following two papers focus on European South Asian diasporas and both highlight the urgency of finding ways to substantially accommodate South Asian laws in the European legal setting. Menski indicates the dangers of alienating entire diasporic communities when blindly insisting on European state-centered legal theories and poignantly argues for the need of a responsible acknowledgment of the role of South Asian laws. Shah proposes new ways of looking at law and legal theories arguing that religion should be taken into account as a factor informing the law. He also shows that underlying Christian frameworks have distorted personal law, Muslim law, and *shari'ah* by superimposing the opposition between state and non-state law.

The second half of this special issue outlines four South Asian settings in which legal pluralism and plurality of laws – within and beyond the state – have an impact on the interactions between the state and social actors. Vatuk shows that the Indian state has integrated modalities that have been so far rather viewed as belonging to non-state law and this has generated further variety: new state jurisdictions that inspired from non-state law propose to cater better for women. Holden and Chaudhary describe how from the perspective of the users non-state and state jurisdictions are not necessarily antithetic and can be seen as a continuum since they both impact on governance in Pakistan. The same paper also shows that custom is not *per se* equivalent to personal law and interreligious fields (as practices relating to more than one religion) may deserve further exploration. Shariff explains that the strategies of dispute resolution among the Santals in Bengal are constantly readjusted following the ways social groups position themselves vis-à-vis the hegemonic instances of the state. Sbriccoli describes how law in Rajasthan, if apprehended as discursive practice, is neither limited to the state nor constituted by a linear plurality of jurisdictions intended as mere juxtaposition of *fora*.

As an editor who is skeptical of monolithic views I accepted one paper openly criticizing another contributor on the condition that criticism would not be an attack and communication would be attempted. The readers will realize that an agreement was not reached and perhaps not even a dialogue. This is not the place to go in any depth in the further discussions that resulted when the time came to bind the papers together but I am grateful for the patience of the involved authors and of the chief editor, Professor Melanie Wieber. By taking up the challenge to combine the variety of our views, my suggestion is that instead of seeking unisons, it is far more interesting to make the efforts to understand how different disciplines, backgrounds, and experiences can contribute to understanding and theorizing the practices of law. By not shying away from academic divergences and related politics as well as by integrating multidisciplinary analysis – I think – the authors of *Legal Pluralism and Governance in South Asia and in the Diasporas* have succeeded to flag up the terms for legal pluralism to account for the contextually finite circumstances of law that both within and beyond the state are likely to impact governance in South Asia and in the diasporas.

Note

1. For a non-exhaustive list of authors elaborating on similar vein see Allott and Woodman (1985), Collier and Starr (1989), Comaroff and Roberts (1981), Fitzpatrick (1983, 1984, 1992), Galanter (1981), Gillissen (1960), A. Griffiths (1997), J. Griffiths (1986), Harrington and Yngvesson (1990), Holden (2004, 2008), Lazarus-Black and Hirsch (1994), Menski (2006), Merry (1988), Morse and Woodman (1988), Roberts (1979), Sarat and Silbey (1987), Vanderlinden (1998) and Woodman (2002).

References

Allott, Anthony, and Gordon Woodman, eds. 1985. *People's Law and State Law*. Cinnaminson: Foris Publications.

Baxi, Upendra. 1986. "People's Law in India: The Hindu Society." In *Asian Indigenous Law in Interaction With Received Law*, ed. M. Chiba, 216–256. London: KPI Publishers.

Benda-Beckman, Franz, and Keebet Benda-Beckman. 2006. "The Dynamics of Change and Continuity in Plural Legal Orders." *Journal of Legal Pluralism* 53–54: 12–14.

Chiba, Masaji, ed. 1986. *Asian Indigenous Law in Interaction With Received Law*. London: KPI Publishers.

Collier, June, and Jane Starr, eds. 1989. *History and Power in the Study of Law: New Directions in Legal Anthropology*. Ithaca: Cornell University Press.

Comaroff, John, and Simon Roberts. 1981. *Rules and Processes: The Cultural Logic of Dispute in an African Context*. Chicago: University of Chicago Press.

de Sousa Santos, Boaventura. 2002. *Toward a New Legal Common Sense*. Cambridge: Cambridge University Press.

Fitzpatrick, Peter. 1983. "Marxism and Legal Pluralism." *Australian Journal of Law and Society* 1–2: 45–71.

Fitzpatrick, Peter. 1984. "Traditionalism and Traditional Law." *Journal of African Law* 28: 20–27.

Fitzpatrick, Peter. 1992. *The Mythology of Modern Law*. London: Routledge.

Foucault, Michel. 1979. *Discipline and Punish: The Birth of the Prison*. New York: Vintage.

Fuller, Chris. 1994. *Legal Anthropology, Legal Pluralism, and Legal Thought*. London: LSE Research Online. http://eprints.lse.ac.uk/538/ (accessed February 27, 2013).

Galanter, Marc. 1981. "Justice in Many Rooms: Courts, Private Ordering and Indigenous Law." *Journal of Legal Pluralism and Unofficial Law* 19: 1–47.

Gillissen, J. 1960. *La Redaction des Coutumes dans le Passe et dans le Present* Bruxelles: Les Editions de l'Institut de Sociologie.

Griffiths, John. 1986. "What is Legal Pluralism?" *Journal of Legal Pluralism and Unofficial Law* 24: 1–55.

Griffiths, A. 1997. *In the Shadow of Marriage. Gender and Justice in an African Community*. Chicago: The University of Chicago Press.

Harrington, Christine, and Barbara Yngvesson. 1990. "Interpretive Sociolegal Research." *Law and Social Inquiry* 15: 135–148.

Holden, Livia. 2004. "Official Policies for (un)Official Customs: The Hegemonic Treatment of Hindu Divorce Customs by Dominant Legal Discourses." *Journal of Legal Pluralism* 49: 47–74.

Holden, Livia. 2008. *Hindu Divorce: A Legal Anthropology*. Aldershot: Ashgate.

Lazarus-Black, Mindie, and Susan Hirsch. 1994. *Contested States: Law, Hegemony, and Resistance*. New York: Routledge.

Menski, Werner. 2006. *Comparative Law in a Global Context: The Legal Systems of Asia and Africa*. New York: Cambridge University Press.

Merry, Sally Engel. 1988. "Legal Pluralism." *Law and Society Review* 22: 869–901.

Morse, Bradford, and G.R. Woodman, eds. 1988. *Indigenous Law and the state*. Dordrecht: Foris Publications.

Pospisil, Leopold. 1979. "Legally Induced Culture Change in New Guinea." In *The imposition of law*, ed. B. Burman and E. Harrell-Bond, 127–144. New York: Academic Press.

Roberts, Simon. 1979. *Order and dispute*. New York: St. Martin's Press.

Sarat, Austin, and Susan Silbey. 1987. "Critical Traditions in Law and Society Research." *Law and Society Review* 21: 165–174.

Tamanaha, Brian. 1993. "The Folly of the "Social Scientific" Concept of Legal Pluralism." *Journal of Law and Society* 20: 212.

Tamanaha, Brian, Sage Carline and Michael Woolcock. eds. 2012. *Legal Pluralism and Development: Scholars and Practitioners in Dialogue*. New York: Cambridge University Press.

Tamanaha, Brian Z. 2007. "Understanding Legal Pluralism: Past to Present, Local to Global." *Sydney Law Review* 29: 600.

Vanderlinden, Jaques. 1998. "L'utopie pluraliste, solution de demain au problème de certaines minorités?" *Minorités et organisation de l'État*: 665–675. Bruxelles: Bruyant.

Woodman, Gordon. 1998. "Ideological Combat and Social Observation: Recent Debate About Legal Pluralism." *Journal of Legal Pluralism* 42: 48.

Woodman, Gordon. 2002. "Why There Can Be No Map of Law." in Rajendra Pradhan ed., *Legal Pluralism and Unofficial Law in Social, Economic and Political Development. Papers of the XIIIth International Congress of the Commission on Folk Law and Legal Pluralism* 383–405. Kathmandu: ICNEC.

Religious personal laws as non-state laws: implications for gender justice

Archana Parashar

Macquarie Law School, Macquarie University, Sydney, Australia

This article examines the concept of religious personal laws as used in Indian legal discourse. This concept is used to denote religious laws of various communities that are claimed to be upheld but not modified by the secular state and also to refer to the religion related rules followed by communities outside of state regulation. This existence of various 'religious' laws is increasingly being described as legal pluralism. The ambiguous status of religious personal laws serves to legitimize the continued denial by the state of gender equality to women in family law matters as it creates a space for rules or laws to operate that do not conform to the Constitutional requirements and yet are enforced by the state. When legal scholars deploy this concept un-reflexively they participate in the discourse formation about religious personal laws as exceptional laws or as (progressive) examples of legal pluralism. In this way they assist the state in using the concept as a mode of governance. In this article it is argued that the legal scholars need to accept responsibility for the significant power they wield as discourse formers and acknowledge the power of naming legal practices. They are the scholars who can and should deconstruct the concept of religious personal laws. This is necessary for a serious engagement with the issue of what kind of family law would be truly non-oppressive.

This article examines how the concept of religious personal laws is used in Indian legal discourse to create a space for laws to operate that do not conform to the Constitutional requirements and yet are enforced by the state. Religious Personal Laws are used as a mode of governance where their ambiguous status serves to legitimize the continued denial by the state of gender equality to women in family law matters, for example in succession rules. The main focus of my argument is the role of legal scholars in the discourse formation regarding religious personal laws as the most suitable or the least desirable vehicles of gaining gender justice in the context of family laws in India. It aims to analyze the use of the conceptual tool of legal pluralism by legal scholars in this area and argues for the legal scholars to accept responsibility for the significant power they wield as discourse formers. The argument below relies on Hindu law as the example but it could be extended to all Religious Personal Laws.[1]

There are three broad parts to this article and the argument is developed as follows: the first part explores the meaning of the term Hindu law as understood by lawyers and other scholars. This will be the background context to explain how the misunderstandings about the nature and scope of Hindu law had metamorphosed into the concept of Religious Personal Laws in colonial India. The concept of Religious Personal Laws (RPLs) has continued after independence and the adoption of a constitution that guarantees equality. In the next part the extant analyses that explain the continued existence of RPLs as inevitable are analyzed. The courts have declined to declare the RPLs as unconstitutional, and at the same time the legislatures have reformed Hindu law to the extent of having almost rewritten it but have retained the concept. In this discussion I wish to deconstruct the discourse around RPLs to challenge the implication that the current Hindu laws enforced by the state are religious rules and to question the view that the continued existence of Hindu laws outside of state enforcement constitutes legal pluralism.

In the third part I explore the implications of taking seriously the postmodern insight about the power of discourse as constitutive of social realities. Scholars must acknowledge their role in knowledge production and in legitimizing ideas with consequences that follow from those ideas. Primarily it is the discourse of RPLs and how it is deployed that normalizes the inevitability of RPLs and the accompanying inequalities. It is important to steer the discourse in the direction of asking how family laws may be constructed so as to not condone gender discrimination.[2] The state law can and should strive to create norms of gender justice in family laws. This is not a call to uphold universalism in law and nor is it antithetical to the postmodern celebration of differences. In the present context, this necessitates state laws recognizing religious/cultural differences only when they do not disadvantage any section of the community.

Part 1: What is Hindu law?

This question becomes a relevant question in the context of a worldview that sees religion and law as separate phenomena. It has been asked primarily from the perspective of western scholars and colonial administrators. Therefore it is no surprise that invariably the answers have focused on the religious nature of Hinduism and implicated Hindu law as a kind of an exception to the modern and dominant understanding of law as separate from religion (Menski 2002). However, it is also commonplace to keep repeating that law and religion have a lot in common as social institutions and religious phenomena (Lubin, Davis and Krishanan 2010, 1). Yet analyses always proceed to test how far Hinduism offers a concept of law that is understandable to the western scholar. For example, Lubin et al. explain that the concept of 'dharma' and law are different but then proceed to show that just like law in the west, Hindu law also knows similar institutions (Ibid, 5).

This is a particular issue for any comparative lawyer who is trying to compare different laws. However, the comparison posits law as what exists in the west; that is, it is secular, separate *inter alia* from religion, and emanates from the state. Thus the first issue in studying Hindu law is to unravel its dependence on Hinduism. Lubin et al. make a distinction between the concepts 'Hindu Law' and 'Hinduism and Law' as they say that the former term is applicable to any legal order or legal tradition that has a connection to *Dharmashastra* as its textual canon.[3] It is nevertheless the case that the concept of Hindu law is often used to refer to any practices that Hindus follow.[4] It is this conceptual confusion that further plays out in analyzing the relationship between state and non-state legal systems in the form of state laws and RPLs.

The concept of RPLs

The concept of RPLs is a peculiar legacy of colonialism in many parts of the world. However, the particularities of the concept are formed in specific geographical, political and historical situations.[5] In the Indian subcontinent the British colonists gradually moved from being traders to political rulers and imposed their laws incrementally. While it is possible to say that they left the religious laws of the populations unregulated the actual picture is much more complex. This is a widely discussed topic but for the present purposes I will only briefly narrate the broad contours of the developments because they help explain the connection between religious and customary rules in Hindu law. It is widely accepted now that there was no universal body of rules, scriptural or otherwise, that governed all Hindus and this only complicated the task for the administrators (Randeria 1999).

The colonial administrators in India ruled with a combination of mutual political agreements or treaties and conquest. The developments in provincial and Presidency towns took place differently but initially the British established the courts and provided that these courts could exercize judicial authority. It was the Warren Hastings plan of 1772 that set the stage for the development of the concept of RPLs. It is article 23 of Regulation II of the 1772 plan that 'saved' the right of Hindus and Muslims to be governed by their respective religious laws in the matters of inheritance, marriage, caste and other religious usages or institutions (Ilbert 1907). Other regulations, charters and legislation followed and in varying language and detail authorized the courts to use religious laws of Hindus and Muslims in determining disputes about matters that came to be defined as personal matters (Parashar 1992, 61–76; Parashar 2008).

It is important to remember that before the British arrived in the sub-continent, the population of Hindus and Muslims considered themselves bound by their respective religious laws. Even though the Muslim rulers had established themselves firmly as the political authority by the thirteenth century and Shariat was the law of the land, there is academic opinion that the Hindus were generally left free to be governed by their religious laws except in matters of crime (Pearl 1979, 21; Sarkar 1959). Neither religion made a division between personal and other matters for the purposes of identifying the rules that regulated behaviour. This idea of personal laws was introduced by the colonial administrators and reflected the widespread European distinction between personal and territorial laws. Moreover the ecclesiastical laws governed these personal matters and thus the British authorities easily made the link between personal matters and religious laws.

It is this link that needs to be emphasized when studying the successive regulations in British India that 'saved' the rights of Hindus and Muslims to be governed by their religious laws in 'personal' matters. It is easy to overlook the obvious point that before the arrival of the colonial rulers all aspects of laws were religious laws for both communities. It is the peculiarities of governance needs of the British that created a small island of laws that were designated as RPLs. It is also important to reiterate that the exact contours of what constituted personal matters (and thus personal laws) changed from one regulation to another.

Further the artificiality of the construct of RPLs becomes even more evident when one examines how these rules were ascertained and in how they were applied by the judicial authorities. For example, it is widely accepted that when the religious laws of these communities were mentioned it is not evident whether the administrators meant their scriptural laws, customary usages or both. In the case of Hindu law it is well documented that the colonial rulers had to find ways of determining what was the substantive content of Hindu law on the areas to be governed by the religious laws (Rocher 2010; Dhagamwar 1989; Agnes 1995). The early British administrators tried to get the *Dharmashastras* translated with the help of local experts the Hindu pandits. The courts in addition sought the help of Brahmins or pandits to tell them the substantive law in any dispute.

However, the expectations of these administrators to find fixed and invariable rules came undone frequently and over time the courts, in the true tradition of common law judges, started relying on precedents created by themselves. In addition the courts soon realized that the religious laws of the communities were not necessarily the scriptural rules and started giving effect to the customs of peoples. The so-called religious rules of Hindus (and Muslims) were thus modified in various ways through their interaction with the British judicial system. As explained above the British trained judges relied on precedents they themselves had helped create. In addition, over time the judges started supplementing the rules with the application of the equity formulae of 'justice, equity and right' and 'justice and right' and thus provided direct channels for introducing English law into the 'religious' laws of Hindus (Derrett 1963). The effort to apply the customs rather than the scriptural laws introduced a certain level of artificiality into personal laws, as to be recognized by the courts these customs had to meet the standards set by English law. Once recognized by the courts these customs ended up becoming a part of the state legal system and, as precedents they tended to become fixed and unable to adapt to the changing conditions of society.[6]

These judicial incursions into the religious laws were later supplemented by legislative actions by the British authorities. The legislative authority of the colonial rulers (unlike the judicial authority) was unrestricted (Jois 1984: vol. I, 265, 282). However, initially they refrained from making laws only on 'personal matters' while imposing newly crafted civil and criminal laws in every other area. In this way the construct of personal laws as religious laws retained currency but gradually many areas that were previously considered personal and thus under religious laws came to be legislated upon. A few random examples include: The Caste Disabilities Removal Act, 1850, The Hindu Widows Remarriage Act, 1856, Hindu Inheritance (Removal of Disabilities) Act, 1928, The Child Marriage Restraint Act, 1929 and the list can go on. There is considerable debate about the possible explanations for these enactments (for details see Parashar 1992, 66–76) but for the present purposes I only wish to focus on the undeniable fact that towards the end of the colonial period the so-called religious laws of Hindus stood modified in substantial ways through judicial and legislative activities of the colonial administrators.

Part 2: Constitution's promise of equality but the exception of RPLs

The newly independent state of India set about the task of governance by enacting a Constitution. The Constituent Assembly debated the issue of RPLs at various stages in the process of enacting the fundamental rights and directive principles. The main contentious issue was whether the state in enacting social reform measures would be able to modify the RPLs of any community, given the guarantee of freedom of religion as a fundamental right. The Constituent Assembly did not resolve the issue decisively and, rather than articulating whether RPLs had to conform to the Constitutional guarantees and any social reform legislation enacted in accord with these guarantees, it made the promise of a Uniform Civil Code a directive principle (Ibid 222–227; see also B Shiva Rao 1968, Vol. II: 56 ff.).The courts and the legislature have ever since followed suit in maintaining the ambiguities of state powers with respect to RPLs. The following analysis demonstrates that state institutions are not acting in a uniform or concerted fashion. Their conduct can probably be described as a juggling match where efforts are made to juggle interests as needs arise and it is too difficult to stop the game.

The Supreme Court of India has repeatedly declined to declare RPLs as unconstitutional because they contravene the guarantee of sex equality. This is despite the fact that all RPLs manage to discriminate against women to varying degrees and in different areas. To compound the difficulties the Supreme Court has not taken a consistent stand on the relationship between the Constitution and the RPLs. For example, in *State of Bombay v Narasu Appa Mali*[7] the Supreme Court controversially said that personal laws are not 'laws in force' under Article 12 of the Constitution and therefore it was not necessary for the court to decide whether they should conform to the Constitution. However in a later decision in *C. Masilamani Mudaliar v Idol of Sri Swaminathaswami Thirukoil*[8] it has said that personal laws are laws in force and must conform to the Constitution. In the case of *Mary Roy v State of Kerala*[9] the Supreme court said that in accordance with the Constitutional provisions the federal law prevailed over state succession laws for Christians, yet in *Daniel Latifi v Union of India* it upheld the Constitutional validity of the Muslim Women's Act, 1996 when that legislation took away from Muslim women only the very limited right to ask for maintenance under the federal Criminal Procedure Code.[10]

The legislative reform of Hindu laws was one of the major activities undertaken by the newly independent Indian state (for details see Parashar 1992). In the earlier reforms of Hindu law had converted a Hindu marriage into a monogamous marriage for men and brought the legal position of women and men in the matter of marriage all most on par. It had also allowed the marriage to be dissolved in certain circumstances and thus modified its nature as a sacrament. Most recently the 2005 amendment to the Hindu Succession Act has fundamentally altered the nature of coparcenary by making daughters coparceners with the brothers and other male members (Agarwal 2008).With this reform the federal law has caught up with the changes introduced by various state legislatures in giving daughters equal property rights as the sons or abolishing the concept of Hindu joint family and taking away a major site of inequality in law.[11] Significantly, the federal Hindu Succession Act has not abolished the concept of a Hindu coparcenary or joint family (Agarwal 2008, 306–354).[12]

In the context of these legislative changes it is appropriate to reconsider here the earlier question of what is Hindu Law. As explained above the definition of Hindu law as one *ultimately* based on Dharmashastras presents as a problem. For argument's sake, if one takes the latest reform as the illustration, any one would be hard pressed to show a connection between the Act's definition of a coparcenary and the Dharmashastras definitions. However, when the state claims to be enacting 'Hindu' law it has the responsibility to articulate 'Hindu' in what sense and why in that particular sense.[13] The legislative definition of a Hindu in all Hindu law Acts is itself in need of explanation. Similarly, the legislative process of the 2005 amendment of the Hindu Succession Act shows that the reforms were not informed by any theological concepts or by the actual social practices of any section of the Hindu communities.

Moreover, there is not even a suggestion in the entire legislative process that the law reformers were molding a 'Hindu religious' concept. It is of course taken for granted that the secular legislature can enact 'Hindu' law. Thus the categories 'Hindu' and 'Hindu law' are conflating religion with cultural/community identity. If the label 'Hindu law' is being deployed not as a marker of religious affiliations but of cultural identity and invokes the majority status of the community it becomes that much harder to justify lesser rights for women. Yet this is what the state has done in the radical legislative reform of the Hindu Succession Act in 2005 to make daughters coparceners in the Hindu joint family. This is amply illustrated by the 2005 amendment of the Hindu Succession Act, which is path breaking by any account, but it still manages to give women/daughters lesser rights than men/sons. For example, it contained a provision that denied the daughters a right to question the validity of a partition that had already taken place. It included a proviso that nothing in this Act shall affect or invalidate a partition or other alienation of property that had taken place prior to 20 December 2004. Significantly, among the brothers and sisters, the limitation only applies to sisters. If a brother wishes to question the validity of a partition or alienation nothing in the Act prevents him from doing so, whenever the partition had taken place.[14]

That said, the progressive aspirations of the 2005 Act are undeniable and one can also not overlook the practical necessities of implementing change.[15] The state is making an effort to reform the law despite it being classified as RPLs. This is not the place to engage in a discussion about the capacity or otherwise of law to achieve gender justice. The significant point for the purposes of the present article is that a choice is being exercized by the state agencies whether to modify any law and how to do so.[16] Moreover, this kind of differential legislative treatment of men and women would not have been acceptable without the availability of the concept of RPLs. Legal scholars ought to bring this issue into the public domain and create the necessary discursive space for asking what is 'Hindu' about this succession law?

It is plausible to explain the continued use of the category RPLs as an indicator of cultural identities and may explain how it gets used differently for different communities. While 'reforming' Hindu law extensively the state has refrained from doing so in the case of Islamic law. A common explanation is that Muslims are a minority community and a democratic polity has to protect minority rights.[17] An obvious implication of this argument is that the relevant difference is that of majority or minority status rather than that of religious inviolability of any rules. Even though never articulated so, if it is the majority status of Hindus that allows the state to modify its RPLs, the sanctity of RPLs surely becomes disassociated from the religious aspect of Hindu Law.

At the very minimum it is implausible to explain this conduct by the two main legal institutions as upholding the religious inviolability of RPLs. It is therefore, disingenuous to keep deploying the concept of RPLs as a special category of law. It deflects attention from the very different responses these institutions make to very similar questions and juggle competing interests but in an unpredictable way. When legal scholars still persist in using this concept, it can only be deconstructed, as an exercize in helping maintain the hegemony of the state in deciding when to grant or withhold equal rights from women, and this is the subject for analysis in the following section. If the analogy of the juggling act of the state is emphasized, one can readily see that the changes are informed by many factors other than the religious nature of the rules. However, the state does insist on designating this law as Hindu and it needs to be explained why. If legal scholars continue to deploy the category of RPLs when actually discussing the cultural practices of the community, they are responsible for obfuscating the reality that these laws are not about religion but about one's identity and specifically identity derived from one's interpretation of religion. Just as there is no one form of religion, the same can be said, even more intensely, for cultural identities. Should the state decide (how and) which identities to uphold or enforce through laws? In the absence of any questioning by the legal scholars, the Indian state continues to perpetuate the ambiguous concept of RPLs and retains the right to decide which aspects of these laws are modifiable.

If it is not the religious nature or the majority or minority status of the religious communities that matters, another explanation for the existence of RPLs is that they are an expression of legal pluralism. There are two broad senses in which the idea of legal pluralism can be used – as non-state law or as the lived practices of people with no connection to the state laws. Both of them function to legitimize a gender discriminatory regime and therefore need to be examined.

The assertions of legal pluralism often conflate the state institutional arrangements of upholding RPLs and the sociological fact of living laws (but whether they should be classified as 'laws' is the very issue of contention as discussed below).State institutional responses with respect to Hindu law have been briefly discussed above and it is the second issue of actual practices or the so-called living Hindu law that is the focus of the following analysis. I argue that a reliance on the discourse of legal pluralism can create a false sense of complacency that invokes the status of law for many practices and thus legitimize unfair outcomes primarily for women. Moreover, the use of this concept by legal scholars and by scholars in the disciplines of anthropology, sociology and critical studies differs significantly and should be the subject of greater inter-disciplinary dialogues (Moore 1978; Teubner 1992). All of them answer the question of when a system of rules is entitled to be designated as law, differently (Mundy 2002; Freeman 2009; Allot and Woodman 1985; Galanter 1981; Griffiths 1986; Merry 1988, 1997; Beckmann 2002; Tamanaha 2000). Legal thinkers by no means have a monopoly in this task but the dominant disciplinary understandings of the concept within the legal discipline carry substantial weight (Griffiths 2002). The following discussion aims to emphasize that as long as the dominant understanding of the concept of law within legal discourse remains unchanged it is misleading to suggest the existence of legal pluralism.[18]

Since the discourse of legal pluralism is deployed in many ways, for the development for my argument, I wish to focus attention on the simultaneous rise of the concepts of the modern state and state law. A brief recapitulation of the interconnections between the development of the modern state, the rise of the concept of sovereignty as well as positivist ideas about law and eventual transfer of these ideas to the colonized countries will be used to suggest that the concept of non-state law becomes a meaningful concept only in the presence of the concept of state law. The latter is in turn dependent on the emergence of the modern state in Europe. The modern state is characterized by the centralization of political power in a manner that saw the state become the only source of law. In the process of centralizing political power the modern state replaced different kinds of law with the state law in Europe. The concept of sovereignty and state law thus came together in the definition of a modern state (Poggi 1990; Gill 2003).

A parallel development and in part an effect of enlightenment thought saw the ascendance of the positivist views about law. Together these developments resulted in the hegemonic ideas about law as state law and more importantly as secular law because in positivist view law was separable inter alia from religion. The European colonizers carried these ideas with them to their colonies and inevitably measured the pre-existing systems of law in these countries against their understandings. It is no surprise that most of the 'other' systems fell short of their definition of law and were variously described as primitive, customary, indigenous or religious laws. In every instance the difference was mapped against the state law and it was the prerogative of the political power to decide whether and to what extent to accommodate these systems of rules (for introduction to literature see Hooker 1975).

For example, the spectrum of colonial state responses spans the complete denial of status of law to the indigenous Australians' laws to the 'saving' of religious laws on the Indian subcontinent discussed above.[19] Even when the religious laws of the colonized peoples were 'saved' and ostensibly left alone by the colonizers they were not accorded the same status as state laws. In every instance the state law was law proper and other systems were placed along an evolutionary continuum. Thus the anthropological accounts of primitive societies tied up with the views of legal thinkers that these societies would come to acquire legal systems as they developed. Therefore, it is important to acknowledge that the concept of legal pluralism only becomes relevant with the rise of the centralized authority of the modern state. Before the advent of the modern state, the concept of a singular source of law did not exist (Tamanaha 2007). Paradoxically, once the modern state becomes the singular source of law, other systems of rules whether religious or customary need to be classified and the scholars make these claims of a similar status as law. With the close of European colonialism, at least in the formal sense, the discourse of development of primitive societies has given way to the ostensibly more enlightened stance of postmodernism that sees diversity everywhere and eschews essentialist definitions. Thus the study of legal pluralism now mostly refers to the efforts of scholars to define law in non-essentialist and thus multiple ways.[20]

Within the discipline of law, the dominant ideology of law continues to be positivist and legal positivist philosophy does not have the capacity to define as law rules that do not have the right pedigree. So, too, by definition religious rules cannot be state enacted rules and thus it is difficult to describe them as legal in the technical, positivist sense. The dominance of legal positivist philosophy is a disciplinary reality despite there being in existence a robust challenge from critical scholarship of many kinds. Therefore, the question whether the multiplicity of systems of rules can be described as legal pluralism is a difficult question to answer, and in part depends on whom one is talking to; e.g. within legal scholarship itself there are efforts at conceptualizing legal pluralism with expansive or non positivist definitions of law (Macdonald and Kleinhans 1997; Davies 2006; Melissaris 2006). Griffiths makes a distinction between 'juridical legal pluralism' and 'empirical legal pluralism' and explains that the former refers to a particular sort of legal arrangement while the latter refers to a social state of affairs (1986). In the context of the argument in this essay that is concerned with the discourse formation about RPLs as non-state laws, Griffiths' distinction does not help conceptually. For even the most traditional legal thinkers will have no problem accepting that people organize their lives by reference to many systems of rules.[21] However, these and legal rules are distinct to a greater or lesser degrees. It is not clear what is gained conceptually by designating all of them as laws whether state or non-state. In fact such description inadvertently functions as a further bolstering of the status of state law as 'real' law.

Moreover it is important to acknowledge that in the mainstream legal scholarship the 'concession' of describing certain rules as non-state laws is available primarily in legal discourses of the non-dominant varieties.[22] That is, the prevailing mainstream ideas about law continue to be the positivist ideas and even though the alternatives exist, they do so as marginal discourses in the discipline of law.[23] This observation is in no way meant to privilege the positivist definitions of law but simply to describe an existing disciplinary state of affairs.[24] Thus, when legal sociologists or legal anthropologists talk about law and when the mainstream lawyers do the same they are operating in parallel universes.[25] This different emphasis is in turn present in their respective understandings of legal pluralism as well (Moore 1986; Pospisil 1971). My main concern here is that the discourse of legal pluralism sanitizes the continuing dominance of the state legal system and makes it look like there is actual parity among various 'laws'. Moreover, this kind of discourse of social scientists does nothing to alter the lawyers' understandings of law.

Therefore it is important to analyze how the concept of legal pluralism is used by social scientists and some legal thinkers as well. The disciplinary reality within the discipline of law needs to be acknowledged as the dominant discourse maker of law. As long as the mainstream definition within the legal discipline does not change, the social science definitions function to create a false impression that plural legal systems are operating. It is necessary to remind ourselves that all laws are not equal in any legal pluralistic situation. An apt example is available in the Australian state response to the issue of acknowledgement of indigenous laws. Starting from its use of the doctrine of terra nullius and the consequent idea that there were no indigenous peoples or laws, the Australian state has come a long way in the landmark decision of the High Court in Mabo No2,[26] the enacting of the *Native Title Act 1993* (Cth) and the national apology to the indigenous peoples delivered by the nation's then Prime Minister (Rudd 2008). However, neither of these events has moved the discourse about recognizing indigenous laws even a little bit (Anker 2008). The state law continues to be the only system of rules that is defined as law and even though it is up to this system to recognize the indigenous laws – that is, the criteria for recognition are those of the state system – there is no inclination to do so.

There is ample evidence of contemporary indigenous Australians living by reference to their laws as understood by them. It would be rare indeed for legal scholars to challenge the existence of such rules and systems of governance. However, in this situation the existence of indigenous laws, even though outside of the state legal system, cannot meaningfully be described as legal pluralism. If it is argued that for the indigenous peoples their laws continue to be laws irrespective of state response, the problem remains that state laws can and do override these laws at any time and in any situation. Therefore, the proponents of legal pluralism have to address this fundamental issue of defining the legal systems that exist in plurality. The fact that people organize their lives by reference to various systems of rules is undeniable but when and how those systems become entitled to be defined as legal systems is as yet an unresolved matter. Definitional problems are of course not a peculiar problem only for defining legal pluralism but are present in every non-traditional area of a discipline. However, it is a matter of importance as it helps focus attention on the power of naming and explains the function of legal scholarship in creating a discourse of happy coexistence of various laws.

When legal scholars (rather than social scientists) claim the existence of legal pluralism, primarily it is the unarticulated but nevertheless significant claim to be providing a better or more accurate knowledge about the legal systems. The aspirations of authors in the post structural mode are no different than others in that every scholar is interested in establishing the correctness of their view about knowledge. The claims about extant legal pluralism, while the hegemony of state legal systems is intact, create a false sense of inclusiveness when in reality there is an urgent need for changing the status quo. This is not to suggest that the dominant legal discourse is impervious to change but as yet I see no evidence that leads me to believe that genuine co-existence of multiple laws is imminent. In this context the authors who herald legal pluralism create a make believe world but to the detriment of the non-dominant sections of society. For, the description of extant community practices as peoples' law is made by the scholars and not by the state or even by the peoples themselves.

If in the true spirit of post structuralism one could resist claiming authenticity of one's definitions or theory it becomes possible to examine another important issue: when and why any definition or theory finds acceptance and is used widely. For example, in legal feminism and other feminist literature the concept of voice is used to demonstrate how only the views or ideas of the relatively privileged and powerful members of society find acceptance in the official discourses of the state and law (Bassel 2010, 157).

Part 3: Power of discourse

In this part I will rely on Menski's (2003) argument about the existence of 'real' Hindu law as lived practices of people in order to ask whether this may be understood as legal pluralism. In his closely argued book Menski says that there is not one but many Hindu laws. In his view it would be a 'fundamental mistake to start with the presumption that in Hindu law it is the state that is central as a lawmaker, or even law enforcer' (Ibid, xix). Instead, he says that Hindu law has been an open system, a matter of concern for everyone at all levels since at no stage did religion or the state or ancient sages regulate people's daily lives. He argues that the phenomenon of self-controlled order explains the role of Hindu law in regulating people's lives rather than any positivist principle that depends on rules, lawmakers, or the state. This legal system is thus unlimited and consists of open-textured legal informality and legal pluralism and represents a culture-specific form of legal arrangements. It follows that Hindu law exists as people's lived practices and legal and other scholars make a mistake when they try to understand it only as state-enacted or -supported legal rules.

Could this be Menski's way of saying that Hindu law is primarily non-state law in so far as people organize their lives without resorting to state laws? For the purposes of the present discussion, the relevant specific issue is in what sense is it (non-state) law, which is also Hindu (law)? I suggest that this question shows the necessity of prior agreement about the definitions of the concepts of Hindu law and non-state law. If for example, Hindu law, to be called that, must have some eventual connection to Dharmashastras as discussed above, most contemporary practices of Hindus would not meet this standard. It is widely accepted that Hindu law, even prior to colonization, varied in different regions and it was further localized in the form of different local customs. However, this plurality does not obviate the need for a definition. Therefore, it remains to be established that any particular contemporary customary practice is 'Hindu' in a meaningful sense, that is, something more than the fact that certain Hindus claim it to be in conformity with Hindu dharma.

In a more formal application of the rules of Hindu jurisprudence the hierarchy of four sources of dharma at least requires some reflection on when custom may be an acceptable source of rules. However, Menski says that this ranking of sources of rules does not operate in practical contexts.[27] If so, the question remains as to why simply following customs is distinctly Hindu? In the context of my argument here about the relationship between RPLs and state laws such conflating of Hindu law with any customary practices of Hindus raises a number of difficult problems. This use of the term 'Hindu law' makes a very different argument from the claim that Hindu law is religious law that is the subject of RPLs discourse. If, however, it is accepted that RPLs are actually the customary practices of Hindus, how may they be examined for perpetuating gender discrimination? If the constitution and other laws were creating spaces for customs to operate unchecked it would amount to discrimination perpetrated by law. A further issue is whether people are choosing to be governed by such customs or are compelled to resort to them. I will discuss the implications of these questions below.

If the claim about legal pluralism is simply acknowledging the existence of different customary practices it raises issues that not all of these evolving customs are uncontroversial either in their existence or in their content. For a start, it has to be accepted that in contemporary India, whether in the rural or urban settings, society is complex and fragmented rather than simple and harmonious. If a section of any population claims that they have a certain custom it is not an automatic conclusion that everyone else will agree. I make this point specially to illustrate the dangers that lurk for women in romanticizing community practices as collective agreements or as Hindu law.

Vasudha Dhagamwar (2003) has made a persuasive argument that the practices that go in the name of custom can be inhumane. It is not only that certain customs operate but also the transgression of such customary practices has to be dealt with. Moreover, the bodies in the non-formal system like the Caste Panchayats get to decide what constitutes transgression.[28] Dhagamwar gives examples of horrific punishments in the non-formal system, sometimes made on the spot by those present. Generally, these customs and practices are not widely known or documented but 'punishments in the non-formal system fall heaviest on women of any age whether she be a toddler or a grandmother' (Dhagamwar 2003, 1489). The existence of these so-called customs is not simply equatable to non-state law, as it's the state law that permits the continued operation of customs in many instances. The Hindu Marriage Act 1955, enacted by the Indian state, regulates the creation and dissolution of Hindu marriages but it also leaves open the option to follow customs if community customs exist in these matters. It would be at least problematic to describe the operation of these customs as outside of the state legal system (Holden 2008).

So too it would be equally contentious to describe as Hindu practices, those imposing the penalties for transgressing specific customs. For almost certainly those imposing the penalties would have a different perspective than those subjected to the harsh penalties. It would be a mockery of justice to say that it is sufficient that the majority acceptance constitutes the specific practice as customary. In this stance the lower caste men and most women stand in a precarious position, as they are the ones likely to be subjected to arbitrary and harsh punishments by these non-formal bodies. Dhagamwar notes that most of these penalties would normally constitute criminal offences but the curious relation between the state enactments and customs creates this zone as free of state law. Thus it is one state law, e.g. the Hindu Marriage Act, that is allowing another state law, e.g. criminal law, to be ignored when the Marriage Act allows the operation of customs, and when any of such customs is allegedly broken the 'community' decides the punishment that would be a criminal act otherwise. I argue that this is not an example of non-state law in operation but state law choosing selectively to create islands of immunity from state law regulation.

It is this fact of choosing that needs to be brought to the fore in legal discourse. Thus the earlier arguments about religion and identity as the explanations for creating the concept of RPLs stand uncovered for what they are – political choices made by the political actors. Furthermore, people who decide to live by Hindu law principles often are also making choices whether to use the state mechanisms or community mechanisms for dispute resolution.[29] The choice to invoke community rather than state machinery for enforcement of rules has many layered explanations and should not be treated as straightforward evidence of 'living' law. In a different context Holden (2003, 128–129) makes a pertinent point that traditional panchayats operate with an underlying Hindu system of thought, but it is erroneous to understand their jurisdiction as purely religious as it would amount to a disregard of the social and financial implications of the same. It is important also to keep in view the empirical reality that even in the state legal systems of the industrialized societies a very small fraction of disputes reach the courts. Most of the disputes that do manage to reach the official system are also resolved informally (Galanter 2010, 118). There is no serious suggestion that this is an example of legal pluralism. Thus the legal realist observation about the separation between the official and living law could be equally applicable in describing the practices of Hindus without designating it legal pluralism.

It is the responsibility of scholars engaged in discourse formation to be reflexive about the importance of naming a system of rules as religious and/or law. The designation has definite implications for the status they gain as a consequence. When in the context of Hindu law Menski says it is his professional duty to provide a detailed analysis of Hindu law as it presents itself today, he is participating in discourse formation that is not neutral and can be dangerous for women in particular (Menski 2003, xv). By designating as Hindu law all practices of Hindus he is conflating religion with cultural practices and, even if inadvertently, further merging religious power with legal power.

It is this power to name that needs to be acknowledged and then exercized self reflexively. In the following discussion, I rely on Himani Bannerji's (2000) arguments about the definitional power of discourse, although made in another context, to challenge the celebratory viewing of RPLs as legal pluralism. She examines the multiculturalism-diversity discourse in Canada as manifest in the official celebration of diversity and the attendant material practices in the name of multiculturalism to argue that this discourse has the definitional power over the lives of non-white women in Canada. This diversity discourse manages to convey the idea of Canadian society as a progressive society but in the process there is no theoretical or analytical space left for analyzing relations of power and ruling. Moreover, this discourse is not new or *sui generis* but constructed by the opinion makers by relying on the liberal notion of plurality. That is 'by reading the notion of difference in a socially abstract manner, which also wipes away its location in history, thus obscuring colonialism, capital and slavery' (Ibid, 555).

The main function of this celebration of diversity is that it deflects attention from political and historical as well as continuing realities of power differentials and creates a picture of happy co-existence by focussing on a few particularities of people's cultures. The ethnic cultural issues become the short hand for managing differences and multiculturalism becomes 'a matter of co-existence of value-free, power-neutral plurality, of cultural differences where modernity and tradition, so-called white and Black cultures, supposedly hold the same value' (Ibid). The effect of this discourse is that conceptually difference can be understood and celebrated without any reference to the political and cultural content. Thus discourse becomes focussed on neutral diversity rather than uncomfortable differences of social class, gender, race or sexuality. She goes on to argue that difference is a much better heuristic device if not exactly an analytical concept to tackle situations that imply and call for politics. The discourse of liberal plurality has a depoliticizing capacity as it divests the political from the social.

I wish to extend this insight to the construction of the discourses of legal pluralism[30] and more particularly of depicting all customary practices as Hindu Law. The issue here is one of political naming and agency.[31] As legal scholars each one of us must acknowledge that constructions of analytical categories carry material consequences for real people. When academics celebrate Hindu law as postmodern law in all its diversity or propose non-essentialist definitions of legal pluralism they do so without having to consider the very real cost for women who may need to resist the validating label of law for gender oppressive practices.

The long history of RPLs giving women lesser rights even in state enacted laws should be a reason for anyone to pause and consider the consequences of depicting them as religious laws or non-state laws. As I have argued above they are neither religious nor laws in the mainstream sense of those categories. They are state actions that manage to justify selective gender discrimination in the guise of upholding religious/cultural autonomy of any community. In this discourse, the question about the necessary dependence of one's identity on state enforced religious laws is not a topic of serious analysis. When legal scholars repeat these claims as inevitable markers of identity they engage in the creation of authoritative discourse of law, which is functioning to deny women equal legal rights yet claiming to be progressive as it is inclusive of diversity. However, I do not agree with the analysis of Okin that multiculturalism is bad for women as the problem is not with differences but lies in not examining, which differences are worth recognizing (Okin 1999; cf. Anthias 2002). It is undeniable that there is a value judgment involved in such an examination but no discursive position is a value neutral position. Thus, legal scholars endorsing the continuation of RPLs need to justify the possibility of consequent gender discrimination, whether because it is more important to maintain community identity or religious identity.

Thus legal analysts must explain what is religious about the RPLs in the absence of any analysis, in theological terms, of the claims made in the name of religious rules/laws. Whether it is the Hinduttva movement leaders (Kapur and Cossman 1993) or the ultraorthodox Mullas, they make claims as political rhetoric rather than based on any serious study of religious doctrine. However, they are political actors invoking the aid of religion to legitimize their claims and can hardly be criticized for that. It is an altogether different matter when the legal scholars simply repeat or endorse these claims. At the very minimum, they need to be aware of their role in creating an authoritative discourse about law, including RPLs. So too when it is claimed that minority cultural identity is jeopardized by granting legislative equality to women something more than mere assertion is required.

Scholars who create the discourse of legal pluralism to describe this situation are also not really broadening the disciplinary horizons to reconceptualize law to make it more inclusive. Rather when they append the label law to very many social practices, they are enabling institutional discrimination by invoking the legitimizing power of the label law. The power of naming certain practices as law primarily belongs to legal scholars. If this was not the case, the sociologists and anthropologists could keep pursuing their studies of societal phenomena without having to bother about naming them as laws. Moreover, the contemporary anthropological, sociological or critical ways of understanding laws are not the dominant discourse of the discipline of law. The power of naming becomes even more evident when combined with the fact that the existing hierarchies of knowledge within the discipline of law determine that 'law and . . .' studies are definitely the marginal discourses. Despite the existence of extensive legal scholarship in the critical/post structural genre, the dominant disciplinary understandings of law continue to be the positivist or modernist understandings. The extensive critiques of law by feminists and post-structuralists as yet have not managed to displace the dominant disciplinary views (For an introduction, see Fineman 2011; Ward 2004). The 'real' view of law continues to be that which the professors and judges who are very far away from any critical views uphold. In common law countries this is easily substantiated by examining the content of legal education that primarily focuses on legal doctrine.

While it is essential to challenge the hegemony of the mainstream and modernist discourses of law it needs to be acknowledged simultaneously that in the contemporary state of affairs the appending of the label 'law' carries a message of the authoritative nature of whatever is designated as law. In this situation, what is being achieved by calling all customs Hindu law? This labelling is achieving the status of law and thus an implied immunity from questioning of those practices because they are law. The irony is that the dominant disciplinary view does not agree with this nomenclature so the institutional view remains unchanged. At the same time in the community a discourse can be floated that all these social practices are 'laws' and therefore authoritative. As a Hindu woman, I could probably transgress social customs more easily but when I am told that these are legal rules, they automatically appear non-discretionary. Thus, neither the dominant discourse of law changes nor do the individuals attain greater autonomy under legal pluralism discourses. I wish to emphasize that this is not an endorsement of essentialist definitions of law but neither is it acceptable to endorse pluralism without self-reflexive awareness of how that discourse can disadvantage the marginalized peoples.

Moreover, the efforts of legal scholars to define legal pluralism[32] are not even what the community leaders are seeking. The communities asking for the 'protection' of their RPLs want their laws to be recognized, and applied by the state institutions. There the aim in the name of cultural identity is state recognition for their RPLs rather than being told that their practices of not coming to the state institutions is also now seen as law.[33] Elsewhere, Nancy Fraser (2000) has eloquently argued that the politics of recognition is functioning to displace concerns of redistribution and reifying cultural or group identity. According to her it is more important to strive for a politics aimed at overcoming subordination by enabling a person to participate in society on par with every one else (Ibid 113). I wish to extend this idea to the present context of legal pluralism.

The discourse of legal pluralism is displacing any discussion of the state power exercized through law. By designating community practices as law this discourse is not actually creating a possibility for the co-existence of state and non-state laws as equal entities or as mutually recognizing each other. The hierarchies remain and the mis-description of this state of affairs as legal pluralism creates a false sense of achievement. However, this sense of achievement is only ever available to the legal scholars in the academy.[34] The subjects of non-state laws must always remain prepared for the state regulation to be extended to them any time. In Fraser's terms, our focus should be on the possibility of eradicating institutionalized relations of social subordination. It means that in conceptualizing legal pluralism we cannot ignore the institutionalized superiority attributed to the state legal systems. Nor should it be that anything that is labelled non-state laws is beyond scrutiny for its capacity to deliver a fair or non-oppressive regime of rules. It is here that the contributions of anthropologists and socio-legal scholars have a real potential to play a role in creating a discourse of fairness and non-oppressiveness.

In conclusion, extending these ideas to the specifics of RPLs in India means that we need to consider seriously the consequences of conceptualizing them as some sort of 'special' laws. It is no more progressive to refrain from questioning the problematic aspects of legal pluralism discourse than to claim that it is for the minority women only to decide whether they wish to live by their (sometimes, misogynistic cultural practices). Feminist scholars have grappled with these issues for a long time and haltingly come to the stage where critical reflexivity in arguments is accepted as more important than the desire to appear non-imperialist.[35] I suggest that in RPLs discourse it is imperative that legal scholars discharge their responsibility to create the space for articulating what would constitute gender just laws for all women. This is not to distract from the valued contributions by scholars in other disciplines but is meant to bring home the responsibility to legal scholars to be ever vigilant about the conceptual categories used in their discipline.

Notes

* An earlier version of this article was presented at the 2012 International Conference on Law and Society, Honolulu on Non-State Law and Governance in South Asia and in the Diasporas.

1. I anticipate an objection that Islamic law is divine in its origin and thus cannot be modified by human agency. Without going into this controversy my stance is that all religious laws make a

similar claim and none of them have been able to oust state jurisdiction to legislate. Many Islamic states have legislatively modified aspects of shariah rules.

2. Gender just family laws would at the very minimum give equal legal rights to men and women during the continuation of marriage and at its dissolution. For instance, during the existence of a marriage these rights would include the guardianship rights of husband and wife, the ownership of property and at the end of a marriage by divorce rules about the custody of children and division of property. At the end of marriage by death they would include rules of succession and testamentary powers.
3. They explain that the term 'Hinduism and Law' refers to Hinduism's relationship to legal ideas and institutions etc. as a separate or separable matter from Hindu law (Ibid, 6).
4. For example Werner Menski uses the concept of Hindu law in this manner. I will discuss this usage later (Menski 2003).
5. All legal systems deal with plural laws but in very different ways. Therefore it is important to pay attention to the specific details in each situation (Grillo, Bollard, Ferrari, Hoekema, Maussen and Shah 2009).
6. In another context see Chanock (1985) for the argument that such customary rules have no realistic relation to peoples' practices; see also Snyder (1981).
7. AIR 1952 Bom 84; in this case, a Hindu male asked the SC to declare Hindu Marriage Act 1955 unconstitutional as a law that contravenes Art 14. He argued that Muslim men are treated differently and allowed the right to polygamy while Hindu men are denied the same right. The court rejected the argument but said that personal laws are not 'laws in force'.
8. (1996) 8 SCC 525.
9. AIR 1986 SC 1011.
10. (2001) 7 SCC 125.
11. See The Kerala Joint Hindu Family System (Abolition) Act, 1975 The Andhra Pradesh Hindu Succession (Amendment) Act, 1985; The Tamil Nadu Hindu Succession Amendment Act 1989, The Maharashtra Hindu Succession (Amendment) Act, 1994; The Karnataka Hindu Succession (Amendment) Act, 1994.
12. For a critique of this amendment in failing to give women complete parity with men see Parashar and Nagarajan (2012, forthcoming).
13. It is undeniable that there is no one or singular form of Hindu religion, just like any other religion but if the category is to be used it has to be delimited also.
14. This provision was subsequently declared unconstitutional because it differentiated between the rights of coparceners on the ground of their sex; see *R. Kantha v Union of India* AIR 2010 Karn 27. For further details see Parashar and Nagarajan (2012 forthcoming; see also Saxena 2011, 285ff).
15. The explanation presumably for thus restricting the rights of daughters was that they were the 'new' owners of property and they should not cause earlier property settlements to be disturbed.
16. For an analysis of the effects of law reforms in Hindu succession laws see (Basu 2001); see also Majumdar (2003) who argues that women gaining increasing property rights but then not claiming them are not contradictory developments.
17. The more common argument is that Islamic laws are un-modifiable because of their divine nature. It is a topic of extensive debates but one I will not address here.
18. It is salutary to pay attention to the argument of Greenhouse that scholars must make a distinction between legal pluralism and cultural pluralism (Greenhouse 1998).
19. I wish to emphasize that the mainstream definition of law has been used to the detriment of indigenous peoples and their laws but it would be naïve to suggest that ifonly the colonizers had accepted the situation as one of legal pluralism it would have led to a different outcome or power relations.
20. One consequence of this shift in scholarly focus has been that writings about legal pluralism are no longer dealing with the after effects of colonialism in formerly colonised societies. However, as the postcolonial literature has made evident the analysts of postcolonial societies necessarily have to reckon with dominant discourses and in legal pluralism discourse this means dealing with celebratory discourses of multiplicities of law; see Santos (2002); for essays on Indian law and pluralism see Eberhard and Gupta (2005) and various articles in volume 31 of *Indian Socio Legal Journal.*
21. Fiske and Ginn (2000) suggest that it is more useful to talk about plural legalisms. This phrase better describes the discursive formations that co-exist within a single legal order.

22. Brian Tamanaha makes a distinction between legal pluralism and normative pluralism (1993) Cf. Voyce (2007) for an observation that different approaches to legal pluralism raise the question of whether these parallel laws were accomplished by cooperation, subservience or resistance.
23. For example, Cotterrell (2008) could describe the contemporary critiques of law as in his seminal *Politics of Jurisprudence* as varieties of skepticism; that things have not changed that much is evident in the continuing debates about the nature and scope of legal education in common law countries where the prioritizing of legal doctrine is a manifestation of the continuing dominance of positivists' view of law but this is too big a topic to be discussed here.
24. It is of course extremely important to challenge the dominant disciplinary discourse and the contemporary, innovative scholarship in law is overwhelmingly critical in genre. However, the point I wish to make here is that there is a very wide gap between this scholarship and the mainstream views about law. I will return to this issue later.
25. This definitional disconnect is evident in for example, Van den Bergh (1986).
26. *Mabo* and Others v Queensland (*No. 2*) (1992) 175 CLR 1.
27. It is of course undeniable that Hindu law has always included customs (sadacara) as a source of rules and Menski's main argument in this book is that the central theme of Hindu law is the phenomenon of self-controlled order rather than being subject to top down rules of law. But as Davis (2003, 741–743) argues even then it is a big leap of faith to suggest that formal enforcement of law is superfluous or unnecessary; see also Michaels (2010); Lariviere (2004).
28. Caste panchayats are different from the statutory panchayats and are more unaccountable in an official sense, see Galanter and Baxi (1989).
29. Solanki (2012) argues that shared adjudication between state and other bodies can enhance gender justice; cf. Basu (2012) who argues that feminists should strive for substantive rights rather than accept that mediation is a better alternative.
30. See also Fisk and Ginn (2000, 115–120) for a discussion of how to analyze discourse formation in legal writings.
31. I am borrowing this phrase from Bannerji, note above, 556.
32. See Roberts (1998) for the argument that the concept of legal pluralism is primarily constructed by legal academics.
33. This is more evident in India in the case of Muslim law and the demands for state recognition made in the name of the community. Flavia Agnes is the well-known proponent of the view that any changes in their law must be acceptable to the Muslim community and there is no suggestion that the state institutions should stop upholding these laws.
34. For example, Tamanaha (2000, 318) argues that a non-essential conceptualization of legal pluralism means no form of law is placed in a hierarchy above any other but surely this is not the experience of Indigenous Australians. The scholar no doubt has the freedom to conceptualize thus but in the process the politics of change should not fall out of the picture.
35. See for a collection of essays on this matter the journal Ethnicities, 2008 (8); also see Phillips and Saharso (2008).

References

Agarwal, Bina. 2008. "Bargaining, Gender Equality and Legal Change: The Case of India's Inheritance Laws." In *Redefining Family Law in India*, edited by Archana Parashar and Amita Dhanda, 306–354. New Delhi: Routledge.

Agnes, Flavia.1995. *State, Gender and the Rhetoric of Law Reform*. Bombay: SNDT Women's University.

Anker, Kirsten. 2008. "The Law of the Other: Exploring the Paradox of Legal Pluralism in Australian Native Title."In *Dealing With the Other: Australia's Faces and Interfaces*, edited by Pierre Lagayette. Paris: Sorbonne University Press. Available at http://ssrn.com/abstract=1606967. Last accessed on January 31, 2013.

Anthias, Floya. 2002. "Beyond Feminism and Multiculturalism: Locating Difference and the Politics Of Location." *Women's Studies International Forum* 25 (3): 275–286.

Bannerji, Himani. 2000. "The Paradox of Diversity: The Construction of a Multicultural Canada and "Women of Color"." *Women's Studies International Forum* 23 (5): 537–560.

Bassel, Leah. 2010. "Intersectional politics at the boundaries of the nation state." *Ethnicities* 10: 155–180.

Basu, Shrimati. 2001. *She Comes to Take Her Rights*. New Delhi: Kali for Women.

Basu, Shrimati. 2012. "Judges Of Normality: Mediating Marriage in the Family Courts of Kolkata, India." *Signs* 37 (2): 469–492.

Beckmann, Franz von. 2002. "Who's afraid of legal pluralism?" *Journal of Legal Pluralism and Unofficial Law* 51: 37–82.

Bergh, Van den. 1986. "The Concept of Folk Law in Historical Context: A Brief Outline." In *Anthropology of Law in Netherlands: Essays on Legal Pluralism*, edited by Keebet von Benda-Beckman and Fons Strijbosch, 67–89. Dordrecht, Netherlands: Foris.

Chanock, Martin. 1985. *Law, Custom and Social Order: The Colonial Experience in Malawi and Zambia*. Cambridge: Cambridge University Press.

Cotterrell, Roger. 2008. *The Politics of Jurisprudence: A Critical Introduction to Legal Philosophy*. Oxford: Oxford University Press, 2nd Edition.

Davies, Margaret. 2006. "Pluralism and Legal Philosophy." *Northern Ireland: Legal Quarterly* 57: 577–596.

Davis, Donald R. 2003–04. "Traditional Hindu law in the Guise of "Postmodernism": A Review Article." *Michigan Journal of International Law* 25: 735–749.

Derrett, Duncan. 1963. "Justice, Equity and Good-Conscience." In *Changing Laws in Developing Countries*, edited by J. N. D. Anderson, 114–153. London: George Allen and Unwin.

Dhagamwar, Vasudha. 2003. "Invasion of Criminal Law by Religion, Custom and Family Law." *Economic and Political Weekly* 38 (15): 1483–1492.

Dhagamwar, Vasudha. 1989. *Towards a Uniform Civil Code*. Bombay. N. M. Tripathi.

Eberhard, Christoph and Nidhi Gupta. 2005. "Legal Pluralism in India: An Introduction." *Indian Socio Legal Journal* 31: 1–10.

Moore, Sally Falk. 1986. "Legal Systems of the World: an Introductory Guide to Classifications, Typological Interpretation, and Bibliographical Resources." In *Law and the Social Sciences*, edited by L. Lipson and S. Wheeler, 11–62. New York: Russel Sage Foundation.

Moore, Sally Falk. 1978. *Law As Process: An Anthropological Approach*. London: Oxford University Press.

Fineman, Martha A. 2011. *Transcending the Boundaries of Law: Generations of Feminism and Legal Theory*. London: Cavendish-Routledge.

Fiske, Joe Anne and Patty J. Ginn. 2000. "Discourse and Defiance: Law, Healing and the Implications of Communities in Resistance." *Journal of Legal Pluralism* 45: 115–135.

Fraser, Nancy. 2000. "Rethinking Recognition." *Left Review* 3: 107–120.

Freeman, Michael and David Napier. 2009. *Law and Anthropology*. Oxford: Oxford University Press.

Galanter, Marc. 2010. "Access to Justice in a World of Expanding Social Capability." *Fordham Urban Law Journal* 37: 115–128.

Galanter, Marc. 1981. "Justice in Many Rooms: Courts, Private Ordering, and Indigenous Law." *Journal of Legal Pluralism and Unofficial Law* 19: 1–48.

Galanter, Marc and Upendra Baxi. 1989. "Panchayati Justice: an Indian Experiment in Legal Access." In *Law and Society in Modern India*, edited by Marc Galanter, 54–92. Delhi: Oxford University Press.

Gill, Graeme J. 2003. *The Nature and Development of the Modern State*. Basingstoke: Palgrave Macmillan.

Greenhouse, Carol. 1998. "Legal Pluralism and Cultural diFferences: What is the Difference? A Response to Professor Woodman." *Journal of Legal Pluralism* 42: 61–71.

Griffiths, Anne. 2002. "Legal Pluralism." In *An Introduction to Law and Social Theory*, edited by Reza Banakar and Max Travers, 289–310. Hart: Oxford.

Griffiths, John. 1986. "What is Legal Pluralism?" *Journal of Legal Pluralism* 25: 1–55.

Grillo, Ralph, Roger Bollard, Alessandro Ferrari, Andre J. Hoekema, Marcel Maussen, and Prakash Shah, eds.2009. *Legal Practice and Cultural Diversity*. London:Ashgate.

Holden, Livia. 2003. "Custom and Law Practices in Central India: Some Case Studies." *South Asia Research* 23 (2):115–134.

Holden, Livia. 2008. *Hindu Divorce*. Aldershot: Ashgate.

Hooker, M. B. 1975. *Legal Pluralism: An Introduction to Colonial and Neo-Colonial Laws*. Oxford: Clarendon Press.

Ilbert, Courtenay. 1907. *The Government of India: A Brief Historical Survey of Parliamentary Legislation Relating to India*. 2ndEdn Oxford: Clarendon Press.

Jois, Rama. 1984. *Legal and Constitutional History of India*. Bombay: N. M.Tripathi.
Kapur, Ratna and Brenda Cossmani. 1993. "Communalising Gender/Engendering Community: Women, Legal Discourse and Saffron Agenda." *Economic and Political Weekly* 28 (17): WS35–WS44.
Lariviere, Richard. 2004. "Dharmasastra: Its Present Value and Relevance." In *Dharma; Studies in its Semantic, Cultural, and Religious History*, edited by Patrick Olivelle, 611–627. Special double issue of the Journal of Indian Philosophy.
Lubin, Timothy, Donald R Davis, and Jayanth K. Krishnan. 2010. "Introduction." In *Hinduism and Law: An Introduction*, edited by Timothy Lubin, Donald R. Davis and Jayanth K. Krishnan, 1–14. Cambridge: Cambridge University Press.
Macdonald, Roderick and Martha-Marie Kleinhans. 1997. "What is Critical Legal Pluralism." *Canadian Journal of Legal Studies*. 12: 25–46.
Majumdar, Rochona. 2003. "History of Women's Rights: a Non-Historicist Reading." *Economic and Political Weekly* 38 (22): 2130–2134.
Melissaris, Emmanuel. 2006. "Perspective, Critique, and Pluralism in Legal Theory." *Northern Ireland: Legal Quarterly* 57: 597–609.
Menski, Werner. 2003. *Hindu Law: Beyond Tradition and Modernity*. New Delhi: Oxford University Press.
Menski, Werner. 2002. "Hindu Law as a Religious Legal System." In *Religion, Law and Tradition: Comparative Studies in Religious Law*, edited by Andrew Huxley, 108–126. London: Routledge.
Merry, Sally E. 1997. "Global Human Rights and Local Social Movements in a Legally Plural World." *Canadian Journal of Law and Society* 12 (2): 247–271.
Merry, Sally E. 1988. "Legal Pluralism." *Law and Society Review* 22: 869–896.
Michaels, Axel. 2010. "The Practice of Classical Hindu Law." In *Hinduism and Law: An* Introduction, edited by Timothy Lubin, Donald R. Davis and Jayanth K. Krishnan, 58–72. Cambridge: Cambridge University Press.
Mundy, Martha, ed. 2002. *Law and Anthropology*. Aldershot:Ashgate.
Okin, Susan M., Joshua Cohen, Matthew Howard, and Martha C. Nussbaum, eds. 1999. *Is Multiculturalism Bad for Women*? Princeton, NJ: Princeton University Press.
Parashar, Archana. 2008. "The Concept of Religious Personal Laws." In *Towards Legal Literacy*, edited by Kamala Sankaran and Ujjwal Singh, 147–154. Delhi: Oxford University Press.
Parashar, Archana. 1992. *Women and Family Law Reform in India: Uniform Civil Code and Gender Equality*. New Delhi: Sage.
Parashar, Archana and Vijaya Nagarajan. 2012. "My Brother's Keeper: Regulation of the Brother–Sister Relationship in the Religious Personal Laws." *South Asia* (forthcoming).
Pearl, David. 1979. *A Text Book on Muslim Law*. London: Croom Helm.
Phillips, Anne and Sawitri Saharso. 2008. "Guest Editorial: The Rights of Women and the Crisis of Multiculturalism." *Ethnicities* 8: 291–300.
Poggi, Gianfranco. 1990. *The State: Its Nature, Development and Prospects*. Stanford: Stanford University Press.
Pospisil, Leopold J. 1971. *Anthropology of Law: Comparative Theory*. New York: Harper Row.
Randeria, Shalini. 1999. "Religion, Politics and Collective Identities in India.' *Internationales Asien Forum* 39: 381–189.
Roberts, Simon. 1998. "Against Legal Pluralism: Some Reflections on the Contemporary Enlargement of the Legal Domain." *Journal of Legal Pluralism* 42: 95–106.
Rocher, Rosane. 2010. "The Creation of Anglo-Hindu Law." In *Hinduism and Law: An Introduction*, edited by Timothy Lubin, Donald R. Davis Jr. and Jayanth K. Krishnan, 78–88. Cambridge: Cambridge University Press.
Rudd, Kevin. 2008. "Motion of Apology to Australia's Indigenous Peoples." *Australian Indigenous Law Review* 12: 1–5.
Santos, Boaventura de Sousa. 2002. *Toward a New Legal Common Sense: Law, Globalization and Emancipation*. 2nded London: Butterworths.
Sarkar, Judanath. 1959. *Mughal Administration*. 4thEdn, Calcutta: M.C. Sarkar.
Saxena, Poonam P. 2011. Family Law II. 3rd Edn, Delhi: Lexis-Nexis.
Shiva, Rao B. 1968. *The Framing of India's Constitution*. The Indian Institute of Public Administration, New Delhi: N. M. Tripathi.

Snyder, Francis G. 1981. "Colonialism and Legal Form: the Creation of "Customary Law" in Senegal." *Journal of Legal Pluralism* 19: 49–90.

Solanki, Gopika. 2012. *Adjudication in Religious Family Laws: Cultural Accommodation, Legal Pluralism, and Gender Equality in India*. Cambridge: Cambridge University Press.

Tamanaha, Brian. 2007. "Understanding Legal Pluralism: Past to Present, Local to Global." *Sydney Law Review* 30: 375–411.

Tamanaha, Brian. 2000. "A Non-Essentialist Version of Legal Pluralism." *Journal of Law and Society* 27: 296–321.

Tamanaha, Brian. 1993. "The Folly of the "Social Scientific" Concept of Legal Pluralism." *Journal of Law and Society* 20: 192–217.

Teubner, Gunther. 1992. "The Two Faces of Janus: Rethinking Legal Pluralism." *Cardozo Law Review* 13: 1443–1471.

Voyce, Malcolm. 2007. "The Vinaya and the Dharmasastra: Monastic Law and Legal Pluralism in Ancient India." *Legal Pluralism & Unofficial Law* 56: 33–65.

Ward, Iain. 2004. *An Introduction to Critical Legal Theory*. 2nd Edn, New York: Routledge Cavendish.

Legislation and Cases

The Andhra Pradesh Hindu Succession (Amendment) Act, 1985;
The Caste Disabilities Removal Act, 1850,
The Child Marriage Restraint Act, 1929
The Hindu Inheritance (Removal of Disabilities) Act, 1928,
The Hindu Widows Remarriage Act, 1856,
The Karnataka Hindu Succession (Amendment) Act, 1994
The Kerala Joint Hindu Family System (Abolition) Act, 1975
The Maharashtra Hindu Succession (Amendment) Act, 1994;
The Tamil Nadu Hindu Succession Amendment Act 1989

State of Bombay v NarasuAppaMali AIR 1952 Bom 84
Mary Roy v State of Kerala AIR 1986 SC 1011
C. MasilamaniMudaliar v Idol of Sri SwaminathaswamiThirukoil (1996) 8 SCC 525
Daniel Latifi v Union of India (2001) 7 SCC 125
Maboand Others v. Queensland (No. 2) (1992) 175 CLR 1 (Mabo No 2)
R. Kantha v Union of India AIR 2010 Karn 27

Legal monism and white violence in South Asia

Stig Toft Madsen

Senior Researcher, Nordic Institute of Asian Studies - NIAS, Copenhagen, Denmark

Reiterating that unified legal systems have emerged historically as ordering devices sustaining the rule of law in societies capable of upholding the state's monopoly of the legitimate use of physical violence, the article takes up a series of cases where legal pluralism obscures and confronts integrated systems of legal monism. The article presents the role of TB Macaulay in the introduction of Western law in India and discusses its application to a white 'interloper' (non-official sojourner) in the early nineteenth century. Contemporary Western interlopers are discussed through an extended analysis of the case of Niels Holck, a Dane accused of airdropping a large consignment of weapons to the Indian sect Ananda Marga for its 'self-defense' against the democratically elected communist government in West Bengal. India's demand for his extradition is analyzed on the background of Danish legal monism and of innovative forms of Indian litigation, including Public Interest Litigation, aiming to infuse Indian law with the spirit of the constitution as in the case of *Nandini Sundar and others versus State of Chhattisgarh*. The encounter between the two legal systems did not bring about a juridical reconciliation, but resulted in a diplomatic crisis that led India to impose unspecified sanctions on Denmark. The article also considers the Raymond Davis case in which the United States succeeded in retrieving an intelligence agent by submitting itself to Pakistani sharia-inspired law, thus allowing legal pluralism to 'cannibalize' US law-ways at high transaction costs.

All cultures strain to achieve a measure of internal consistency, but, according to Jayaram and Saberwal, some cultures develop specialist 'ordering devices' in the shape of integrative ideologies and practices, which enable societies 'blessed with' such devices to deal with conflicts in a more productive and consistent manner than otherwise possible (Jayaram and Saberwal 2011, 502).[1] Legal monism, I posit, is one such ideal-typical ordering device based on the idea of the unity of law. A unified legal order is a logical, coherent and self-referential system encompassed by a hypothetical *Grundnorm* informing the constitution and the laws, while remaining autonomous vis-à-vis the executive and the legislature.[2] Even though legal pluralism may be ever present in the world around us, in the eyes of a legal monist, the law remains such an autonomous entity *an sich*. Coeval with the modern nation-state, legal monism has been underwritten by the development of national legislation, and the emergence of a legal profession (Dalberg-Larsen 1994, 105). By adjudicating social conflicts through official courts with reference to a rationalized system of general laws and rules, the resultant well-ordered societies have often been capable of ensuring the state's monopoly of the legitimate use of physical force which, according to Max Weber, is the defining trait of the modern state (Weber 1964, 154).

Historically, legal monism has superseded myriad forms of legal pluralism reaching back to the time before the invention of the state. Legal pluralism is an expression of what Perry Anderson (1974) has referred to as 'parcellization of sovereignty', and what Shalini Randeria (2003), in a similar vein, has referred to as 'fractured sovereignty' or 'scattered sovereignties'. In the current era of international migration and global integration, pluralism is being reborn academically as 'global legal pluralism' (Tamanaha 2008:10, 60). There is no gainsaying that in today's global settings, legal pluralism is bound to thrive because imperial or national legal traditions from one part of the world interact with their counterparts in other parts of the world, but also because footloose individuals, some of whom we will encounter in this article, take their law-ways with them when they move. While in the past, legal pluralism repeatedly emerged 'orthogenetically' from within, it now increasingly emerges 'heterogenetically' by transfers and encounters.[3] Legal pluralism, therefore, is not exclusively a tribal, feudal, and colonial phenomenon. As Randeria (2003) suggests, legal pluralism may be part of our common pluri-civilizational future.

This article will portray the lineages of legal monism in South Asia by looking at the early era of European expansion and at contemporary settings where sojourners once again produce challenges to legal monism as it exists in South Asia and in the West. I will focus on Westerners who entered the Indian sub-continent without full diplomatic immunity and whose presence raised the issue of whether they should face the same justice as native residents.

First, I will revisit the early-nineteenth century case of James Tickborne, known from the writings of Elizabeth Kolsky, to illustrate the reach of British law during early colonial times. In my reading, the case of Tickborne shows the high degree to which early British Indian law was able to exert a strong and unified grip on erring Englishmen.

The consolidation of codified law in India is associated with Thomas Babington Macaulay who came to India in 1834 as legal representative on the Legislative Council. Eventually enacted in 1860, the Indian Penal Code, largely drafted by Macaulay, remains 'the longest serving criminal code in the common law world' (Yeo and Wright 2011, 3). It is also a body of law in need of systematic revisions in most of the countries where it is currently statutory law.[4] The Indian legal system has sought to reform itself through e.g. Public Interest Litigation (or PIL), a soft form of pluralism that allows for society to reclaim some of the promises inherent in the constitution while leaving unaffected most court work, warts and all.

On this background of an internally divided judicial system, I will discuss the contemporary Purulia Arms Drop case in India in which the Danish citizen Niels Holck sought to arm members of a religious sect for 'self-defense' against the communist-led government of West Bengal. India demanded Holck face justice in India, but in a drawn-out battle, the Danish courts have prevented his extradition. I analyze the ensuing imbroglio as a confrontation between old-school Danish legal monism protecting individual human rights and an Indian stance which is both more innovative and more security-oriented. As an example of how the Supreme Court in India has dealt with the arming of civilians for self-defense, I will also present the recent case of *Nandini Sundar and others versus State of Chhattisgarh.*

Finally, I will discuss the case of the US citizen Raymond Davis, a 'demi-official' intelligence officer accused of murder in Pakistan. This case, which also has high political volatility, confirms that Western states may go to great lengths to protect their citizens accused of crime abroad, but it also shows the degree to which the United States was willing to submit to the sharia principles in Pakistani state law. In the Raymond Davis case, the twain did meet, but at the cost of undermining the state's monopoly of the legitimate use of force.

An early colonial interloper

In British India there were two main classes of Europeans: The officials, who served the British Raj directly, and the non-officials, who did not necessarily do so. The officials were not always paragons of virtue, but it was the non-officials who most often came into direct physical conflict with the natives. This posed a challenge to the courts. The non-officials wanted the privilege of being tried by a British judge in the Supreme Court in Calcutta under British laws rather than be tried by an Indian judge under East India Company laws in the *mufassil* hinterlands, where they often lived.

In her recent book, Elizabeth Kolsky skillfully seeks to dismantle the British claim to have brought the rule of law to India. By focusing 'on crimes committed by a mostly forgotten cast of European characters – planters, paupers, soldiers, and seamen' (Kolsky 2010, 2), she portrays white violence as endemic to British colonial rule. As a staunch post-modernist, she stretches her point to the limit or beyond. I will illustrate one such exaggeration with material from the first chapter of her book entitled 'White Peril: Law and Lawlessness in early colonial India'. It opens up with a story about a white settler called James Tickborne, a timber merchant living in a place called Saran. One day in 1809, he called on his servant. When informed that the servant was ill, he beat up the messengers who then carried the servant along as he was too weak to walk. Cruelly Tickborne confined the servant in a hut without food and water. After two weeks, the servant died. People staged a protest in the court area, but Tickborne was not arraigned. When Tickborne later again confined someone, the judge asked for orders from the Supreme Court in Calcutta to pursue the case. Since 1806, if Europeans were to be prosecuted in Calcutta, the Supreme Court had to give its consent in advance. The Supreme Court decided to prosecute Tickborne. He then beat up the person who came to arrest him, while shouting to his servants to kill that person, but the Indians helped the court's emissary tie up Tickborne. The verdict of the Supreme Court was jail for two times twelve months, plus a fine for the two cases tried in court. After serving his jail term, Tickborne was released but forbidden to leave Calcutta.

White settlers and sojourners – or interlopers as they were called then – like Tickborne were a problem 'equally injurious to the English character and to the peace and happiness of our native subjects' as the Governor-General expressed it (Kolsky 2010, 28). Kolsky's studies show that the interlopers often got away with their crimes, but Tickborne's case actually shows that he could *not* act with impunity. Early in the nineteenth century, the Supreme Court was able to arrest a person living in far-off Saran, get him to Calcutta, convict him and make him serve his sentence.

The example of Tickborne speaks to the enduring problem of controlling settlers and sojourners in conflict with the people among whom they stay and with the laws of the land. Whether a state is able to extinguish the privilege of impunity, which settlers often seek, in fair measure indicates how far that state will be able to retain the monopoly of the legitimate use of violence.

Unification and reform of Indian law

Indigenous law in Hindu India was plural: 'Hindu law did not enjoy the political conditions for unification' (Galanter 1968, 66). The person most closely associated with the unification of law in India was Macaulay who shaped India in three ways: By turning the educational system away from Sanskrit and Arabic learning towards English; by creating an elite meritocracy of generalist administrators; and by contributing to the growth and codification of Anglo-Indian law. He initiated these reforms during his few years in India, but he continued working on the latter two reforms until his death, by which time they were gradually enacted. Already in 1837 Macaulay submitted the first draft of the Indian Penal Code. It was only 67 pages long (Morgan 2011, 84). It did not proceed from one explicit *Grundnorm* or even from an introductory 'General Part' (Yeo and Wright 2011), but it was a precise and comprehensive code in the spirit of Jeremy Bentham's 'universal jurisprudence', yet conforming to Macaulay's moderately monist maxim:

> We propose no rash innovation; we wish to give no shock to the prejudices of any part of our subjects. Our principle is simply this; uniformity where you can have it; diversity where you must have it; but in all cases certainty (Macaulay 1833).

Macaulay produced the code almost absent-mindedly. His real interests lay elsewhere, i.e. in British history and in the Classics. Macaulay's ear for oratory helped him in his endeavor:

> Strengthening his belief that rhetoric is constitutive of society and politics, his engagement with some of the ancients inspired him to adapt them for the future world he was imagining (Sullivan 2009, 139).

As Gertrude Himmelfarb noted in her 1975 essay 'Who now reads Macaulay?' he inhabited the world of letters, not of science. Macaulay auto-poetically dreamt into being a Whiggish structure of law and education for India without recourse to sociology and he did not do any fieldwork. While in Calcutta serving on the Governor-General's council, he preferred studying Greek or Latin at home to any sortie into the city to enlarge his Indian experience. As a legal monist, Macaulay held that Anglo-Indian law should apply to Europeans living in India (Hee 1982, 58), a conviction that did not contribute to his popularity in Calcutta.

Macaulay's father had worked for the mitigation and abolition of slavery and was closely connected with the Clapham Sect, but Macaulay was an agnostic and a skeptic maintaining an outward Anglican facade. He saw a role for religion in the life of nations, but he was not a religious man himself (Sullivan 2009, 43–44, 349, 461). It would, therefore, be risky to explain his work as a legislator by his Christian origins (see Prakash Shah's article in this issue).

Macaulay's code became the basis of criminal law in a number of countries and territories including Pakistan, Bangladesh, Sri Lanka, Malaysia, Singapore, Sudan, Nigeria, Canada, Australia and New Zealand, but not England itself. According to the authors of a recent detailed overview of Macaulay's work, it is still basically sound, but in the spirit of Bentham and Macaulay, the code should be revised (Chan, Wright and Yeo 2011). However, this has generally not happened. In India criminal law has grown by accretion into a very large body of often incongruous law. In effect, India has pluralized its law and practice so that the state now has at its disposal a set of highly repressive laws and practices, while the higher courts intermittently react with ambitious attempts to give flesh to the more liberal promises enshrined in the constitution. Because the law often fails to deliver justice, the courts have been forced to turn activist, cultivating in this process a talent for brinkmanship in a manner similar to neighboring Pakistan.

Public Interest Litigation (PIL) has emerged as a safety-valve to the inordinate delays and the miscarriage of justice endemic to the courts. By taking up cases at the behest of individuals without *locus standi,* the Supreme Court and some state High Courts have been able to reinterpret the fundamental civil and political rights in consonance with the directive principles in the constitution in a manner consistent with the *Grundnorm,* or the basic structure, of the constitution. Since the innovation of PIL in the 1970s, Indians have been able at once to decry parts of the legal and administrative system as 'colonial', while lionizing Article 21 of the constitution guaranteeing a very broadly interpreted Right to Life and Article 14 guaranteeing Equality, thereby securing a series of landmark judgements. This has often been effected by treating non-justiciable social, economic and environmental claims as if they were justiciable political and civil rights, but as the Salwa Judum case discussed below shows, civil rights cases concerning the state's anti-terror campaigns have also been considered as PIL. As Shankar (2009, xiv–xix, 168) observes, these legal innovations (bordering on judicial populism) took place in the aftermath of the Emergency (1975–77) which had undermined the constitution. The courts tried to make up for their weak-kneed response by opening up a new pluralistic space for achieving justice. In the ensuing 'judicialization of politics' (Randeria 2007), law has almost become politics by other means as courts make inroads into the domain of parliamentarians.

After an initial spurt, the number of PIL-cases has declined. In 2008, PIL-cases constituted around 2% of the cases seeking a Supreme Court hearing and very few of them were eventually admitted. Many PIL-cases have been cunningly entertained by the rich and powerful in the name of the poor and dispossessed. Nevertheless, as the Salwa Judum case shows, the Supreme Court may still act as a forceful corrective to the executive in a manner akin to the courageous verdicts passed by Aharon Barak as the President of the Israel Supreme Court.

A contemporary interloper

As the world globalizes, the planters, paupers, soldiers, and seamen are no longer the typical Westerners in India. New interlopers move abroad to shake the pagoda tree or for other 'demi-official' or non-commercial purposes. In the following I will discuss the case of Niels Holck whose foray into India illustrates what Legg (2011, 505) has termed 'the constitutive role of outsiders' inasmuch as his brief sojourn has caused a unique decline in the official relations between Denmark and India.

Niels Holck is a Dane presently living in one of the better cities north of Copenhagen. In 1981, when accused of bank robbery, he escaped from the police on foot earning him the nickname the Barefoot Robber (Holck and Kyrø 2008, 80–87; Hansen 2008). Holck fled abroad, where his activities ranged from development work among the poor in Latin America to gold smuggling across Africa and Asia. In the process he acquired several passports one of which identified him as Kim Palgrave Davy, one of the names by which he is known in India.

Holck's relation to India has been woven around the Ananda Marga.[5] The Ananda Marga – the Path of Bliss – was founded in 1955 by Prabhat Ranjan Sarkar as a socio-spiritual organization. In 1959, Sarkar added the political wing, known as Proutist Universal, where PROUT stands for *Progressive Utilization Theory*. The Ananda Margis share many traits with other Hindu movements, including their dress code, but according to Crovetto (2008), the Ananda Marga core members have subjected themselves to a strict form of institutional and ideological 'totalism' with Indian male renouncers (*sannyasis*) exercising the maximum influence. In pursuance of justice and human development, the sect has established a number of agrarian communities where physical isolation may act to support institutional totalism. Though Sarkar tried to maintain a strong hold on the movement, divisions occurred during his lifetime. The authoritarian ideology prevailing within the movement meant that defectors and renegades were seen as a serious threat to the movement.

Unlike many other Hindu organizations, the Ananda Margis do not direct their anger against Muslims and Islam, but against the state and its regulatory arms, particularly the police and the judiciary. Already in 1967, Ananda Marga *sannyasis* were allegedly attacked by local people, at the instigation of communist party workers, at its Calcutta headquarters. In 1971, Sarkar and some of his disciples were arrested for abetting the murder of several renegades. On his part, Sarkar accused the state of poisoning him while in jail. In 1976, he was convicted despite having obtained some international support. Sarkar was subsequently granted another trial. Cleared of all charges, he was released in 1978.

Like other fundamentalists, Ananda Margis see the world as divided between the forces of good and the forces of evil. According to Sarkar, 'Peace is the result of fight. Peace-lovers of the universe must not keep themselves away from fight' (Crovetto 2008, 38). Peace for Sarkar had two forms: Black static peace implying absence of struggle, and white 'sentient' peace implying active and, if necessary, armed struggle on behalf of the suppressed. Crovetto (2008, 40–41) details the logic behind Sarkar's challenge to the state's monopoly of the legitimate use of force:

> To win the fight against evil in society, Sarkar said *täntrikas* should acquire strength because it was 'impossible for goats to establish sentient peace in the society of tigers.' The real source of people's power might be their spiritual force, but organizing on the material level was indispensable. He observed that arms were more necessary than the drums and cymbals used for worship. Not only should *täntrikas* arm themselves, they should go on inventing ever more powerful weapons as a counter-balance to those society has.... With regard to taking preemptive actions, Sarkar told his followers that one needed to be sure of the enemy's intentions and could then act with impunity.

Holck became a sympathizer of the Ananda Margis, which he saw as a Third World development movement brutally persecuted by the corrupt communist rulers of West Bengal. He reasoned, 'I gradually reached the conclusion that it would be a crime against the poor not to do something illegal, if that would benefit the poor and save human lives' (Holck and Kyrø 2008, 80, my translation). Thus convinced, Holck dropped four tons of weapons over Purulia district in West Bengal for the Ananda Margis from a medium-size airplane in December 1995. According to Peter Bleach, who was on the plane, the consignment included '77 cases of Kalashnikov rifles, Makarov pistols, sniper rifles, anti-tank grenades, RPG rocket-launchers, anti-personnel mines, night-vision binoculars and 25,000 rounds of rifle ammunition' (Scarborough Evening News 2011; The Independent 2000). Many weapons have been smuggled into India by revolutionaries, separatists, *jihadis* and others, and India also has a large illegal arms manufacturing sector, but the Purulia Arms Drop remains unique insofar as it involved white Westerners supplying arms to an Indian religious group (Madsen 2011; India Today 1996; Sharma 2012).

The arms drop was not well executed by the crew consisting of five Latvians and the weapons ended up in the hands of the Indian police. Thus, the Ananda Margis harmed no one with these weapons. After a confusing return trip from Thailand, all were arrested in Bombay airport save Niels Holck, who once again managed to slip off and make his way back to Denmark by drawing, he maintains, on his contacts or accomplices among Indian parliamentarians and police officers. According to Holck, it was Bleach who insisted on returning via India in order to enable the Indian police to arrest Holck: Bleach reckoned he himself would be released, because he had to some extent collaborated with British intelligence agencies when the arms drop was in its planning stage. The Government of India (GOI) faced sharp criticism for not having prevented the arms drop and for letting Holck flee (Baweja 1996).

When India subsequently requested the extradition of Holck, Denmark was initially unable and unwilling to do so, but after the attack on USA on 11 September 2001, Denmark passed a controversial law in 2002 enabling the extradition of Danish citizens accused of serious crimes not only, as hitherto, to the Scandinavian countries but to the EU and to other countries as well (Lov nr 378). India renewed its extradition request in December 2002. After protracted high-level negotiations between the two countries, the Danish government on 9 April 2010 agreed to extradite Holck after having secured a series of very unusual diplomatic guarantees from India specifying how Holck would be treated while in India, how he would be tried, and allowing him to serve any prison sentence he might be awarded in Denmark.[6] The GOI further agreed not seek a death sentence. Thus India bent over backwards – exhibiting its soft underbelly in the process – in order to capitalize on the new situation arising after 9/11. Even though Holck was accorded special privileges not available to other prisoners, the extradition order was challenged by Holck in court. Holck repeatedly asserted that he would certainly be killed, if handed over to India. With the help of an articulate lawyer, Tyge Trier, Holck won the case in the lower court, which quashed the extradition order. Subsequently in June 2011, the Eastern High Court confirmed the decision of the lower court when an unusually large bench of five judges unanimously held his extradition illegal with reference to the poor human rights record as regards treatment of prisoners and undertrials in West Bengal and elsewhere in India. The court based its verdict on Article 3 of the European Convention of Human Rights prohibiting torture and other forms of ill-treatment, and further noted that India had not ratified the UN Convention against Torture and not signed the Optional Protocol to the convention. The diplomatic agreement, which sought to bracket such general issues by focusing on the individual case at hand, was found by the court to be devoid of sufficient muscle to secure Holck's safety if handed over to Indian custody.[7] In effect, the Danish court cast doubts on the guarantees that the GOI and the Government of West Bengal had made, and it refused to lend support to an agreement that the Danish government had signed after protracted high-level negotiations.

After the Eastern High Court decision, the GOI in August 2011 let it be known that it would freeze or slow down an unspecified range of bilateral relations in retribution to the failure to extradite Holck and in anger over the decision of the Danish prosecution not to attempt to appeal the case to Supreme Court. The Indian reaction mostly took the form of veiled threats broadcast through the Indian media announcing that India would insist that all official contact should be routed through the Indian Ministry of External Affairs for (lengthy) scrutiny. In July 2012 further news reports indicated that the GOI had decided to deny visas to Danes, if not to other Scandinavians as well (Hindustan Times 2012). But at the same time, the Indian Embassy in Copenhagen continued to celebrate India's Independence Day with many Danish invitees and to support major cultural programs promoting India in Denmark. This hazy no-peace-no-war situation may be compared to the confrontation between India and Nepal in 1989–90 when India imposed an economic blockade on Nepal for a variety of economic and military reasons, which were not spelled out to the Nepalese. Likewise, Denmark apparently was to be taught a lesson by being subjected to the threat of economic and other losses.

To Danes, the situation was reminiscent of the Muhammad cartoon crisis where several Muslim countries felt slighted and put pressure on the Danish government to 'do more' to prevent the publication of the cartoons.[8] In both cases the Danish government responded that court decisions should be respected, period. But to argumentative Indians, contestation is God. Legal decisions are not necessarily reached by reference to the law in a narrow technical sense but by allowing a plurality of elite and subaltern interests to present their case and a compromise worked out within an expanded constitutional framework. Soft legal pluralism in the form of PIL allows for such contestation even within a single constitutional framework, while legal monism seeks closure by applying Occam's razor. In the Holck case, the Danish courts stuck to an 'adjudicative model' leaving less space for 'litigation as negotiation' (Kidder 1996, 476–477). The diplomatic agreement had guaranteed Denmark that Holck would be treated exceptionally well, but even this high-level agreement between two states to define the exception did not imbue their accord with juridical power.[9] The Danish courts did not trust the guarantee and aborted the process of bringing Holck to justice. This insult to India's honor and/or legal sensitivities led the GOI to blacklist and harass Denmark, thereby contesting the autonomy of Danish law. Initially, Denmark contemplated seeking the assistance of the EU (Bostrup 2011), but the Danish government did not announce any counter-measure. Instead, it expressed its regret over the turn of events. Danish firms, which have reportedly suffered heavy losses of business opportunities, have made known their dissatisfaction with the stalled extradition, but they have sued neither the Danish government, nor the Indian government.[10] More than one year having passed with no party blinking, the stalemate wears on even if intermittently unhinged by renewed saber-rattling from the Indian side and in September 2012 by Holck's statesman-like announcement that he would be willing to stand trial in an Indian court on 'neutral ground' in the greater interest of both nations.

Calibrating global legal monism

Holck bought the weapons because he sympathized with the Ananda Margis whom he felt were persecuted by the West Bengal government and perhaps also by Naxalite armed groups operating in the Purulia area. At the very end of the High Court case, Holck said that he wanted the truth to come out and that he would win a fair trial because the right to self-defense is a valid legal argument. In other words, Holck sought to explore the limits of the state's monopoly of the rightful use of force. His attorney did not pursue this line of argument and the prosecution did not make it a major point to shoot down Holck's argument. In India, the right to exert violence is repeatedly appropriated by non-state actors. Moreover, the Indian state has repeatedly allocated itself a large leeway in its use of force. Here I would like to point out that the Indian state recently has walked a thin line similar to Holck's. In its struggle against the armed uprising of the Naxalites in the state of Chhattisgarh in Central India, the GOI in 2005 raised an armed force of about 6,500 barely literate village youth aged seventeen upwards ordering them to operate as Special Police Officers within the law at a honorarium of IRS 3,000 per month, i.e. much less than the US$ 10 a day that Taliban foot soldiers are said to receive. This force, named Salwa Judum, proceeded to engage in 'mass violations of fundamental constitutional rights' (Venkatesan 2011,44) often in connection with the forced removal of people from Naxalite-infested villages to safe villages under Salwa Judum control. In 2007 anthropologist Nandini Sundar, who is professor of sociology at Delhi University, together with the historian-anthropologist Ramachandra Guha, and EAS Sarma, former Secretary to GOI and former Commissioner for Tribal Welfare in Andhra Pradesh, filed a writ petition in the Supreme Court against Salwa Judum. The court accepted the petition as a PIL case. Eleven judges heard the case for 26 days over several years before delivering the verdict in 2011.

The verdict of the Supreme Court in *Nandini Sundar and others versus State of Chhattisgarh* went in favor of the petitioners and 'directed the State government to prevent the operation of Salwa Judum or any other such group that seeks to take the law into its own hands or violates human rights of any person' (Venkatesan 2011,44). In other words, the court affirmed the state's monopoly of violence specifying that the state can only delegate its right to use force to duly constituted groups. By extension, if the state did not have the right to defend its citizens against the clear and present Maoist threat by raising a motley army in the name of self-defense, it is also not likely that an equally motley crew of non-nationals should enjoy the right to arm a socio-religious group like the Ananda Marga. Niels Holck, the Government of Chhattisgarh, and the GOI seem alike in misconstruing the right to self-defense.

How did the Supreme Court of India arrive at its decision? For a start in section 2 of its order, the court says:

> As we heard the instant matters before us, we could not but help be reminded of the novella, 'Heart of Darkness' by Joseph Conrad, who perceived darkness at three levels: (1) the darkness of the forest, representing a struggle for life and the sublime; (ii) the darkness of colonial expansion for resources; and finally (iii) the darkness, represented by inhumanity and evil, to which individual human beings are capable of descending, when supreme and unaccounted force is vested, rationalized by a warped world view that parades itself as pragmatic and inevitable, in each individual level of command (Supreme Court of India).

The verdict goes on to deride the 'development paradigm unleashed by the State'. Touching on the 'resource curse' and 'developmental terrorism', the Supreme Court verdict posits in section 13 that:

> Policies of rapid exploitation of resources by the private sector, without credible commitments to equitable distribution of benefits and costs, and environmental sustainability, are necessarily violative of principles that are 'fundamental to governance', and when such a violation occurs on a large scale, they necessarily also eviscerate the promise of equality before law, and equal protection of the laws, promised by Article 14, and the dignity of life assured by Article 21 (Supreme Court of India 2011, see also Liang 2011 and Venkatesan 2011, 46).

With the Indian Supreme Court being capable of such bold leaps of imagination, it becomes understandable that the GOI (and many Indians) would find Danish black letter law rather stale. Danish courts may be flexible, but the activism that has taken root in India using PIL as an unorthodox quasi-political tool to intervene as a 'last resort for the oppressed and bewildered' (Robinson 2010) has no counterpart. In Denmark there is a strong *Ombudsmand's* institution. It considers around 50 cases in its annual reports, which the executive often adopts as a guideline for the future. It is rare, however, that ministers are impeached or civil servants tried as a direct result of the findings of the *Ombudsmand* (Elbæk-Jørgensen 2001, 223). Since 1953, Commissions of Inquiry (*Undersøgelseskommissioner*) headed by judges have been charged by the Danish parliament to investigate and report upon specific administrative and political matters. Though such commissions cannot hand down a sentence, they play a central role in political conflict resolution. This judicialization of politics has been criticized by leading judges who, at various points in time, have found the process unduly politicized, cumbersome, and unjust to those at the risk of facing a later trial (Hoffmann-Hansen 2012). Commissions of Inquiry, therefore, do not fully conform to the norm of legal monism and the principle of the division of powers, but not being called upon in the Holck case, legal monism remained in place.

In the Holck case, the prosecutors limited the scope of their arguments to the question of Holck's possible extradition. Noting that Danish law had opened for extradition to any country in the world and detailing how both governments had proceeded correctly into a diplomatic agreement, the prosecution largely left it at that. Had the prosecution painted a detailed picture of the Ananda Marga, it might have reframed the issue from one relating to the legality of extradition *versus* the protection of individual human rights to a question of the duty of one democratic state not to assist, actively or passively, any of its citizens to wage war against another democratic state *versus* the protection of individual human rights. This would have addressed the question that some Danes asked: 'What if Indians dropped weapons over Copenhagen? Would Denmark not demand that such Indians be extradited?' (Information 2007; see also Kyrø 2010; Hansen 2008; Holck and Kyrø 2008, 223). When the frugal prosecution lost twice, the state chose not to seek a final appeal. This, too, would appear strange to Indian eyes because in India appeals all the way to the Supreme Court are common. In 2008, there was a 2.5% likelihood that a case would be appealed from High Court to Supreme Court. In cases originating in Delhi, the likelihood rose to a whopping 10% (Robinson 2010). The result of this easy access to appeal is the 66,569 cases pending in the Supreme Court in January 2013.

The prosecution went to considerable length to gather relevant details about India, but it could have gone further. The prosecutor could have pointed out that India has repeatedly sought the extradition of wanted persons without success. India wanted LTTE-supremo Prabhakaran for the murder of Rajiv Gandhi, but did not get him. India wants Warren Anderson, the former CEO of Union Carbide headquartered in the USA to face trial in the 1984 Bhopal Gas Leaks Case (Expressindia 2010; Misra 2011; Zeenews 2011; Akbar 2010). India also demands the extradition of about a dozen people hiding in Pakistan ranging from Dawood Ibrahim Kaskar for his alleged involvement in the Bombay Blasts in March 1992 to the Lashkar-e-Toiba and the Inter Services Intelligence operatives behind the attack on Mumbai in November 2008. The prosecution could have argued that since India seeks the extradition of others apart from Holck, this increases the likelihood that India would treat Holck according to the agreement reached with Denmark in order to facilitate the extradition of other, more earnestly wanted, persons.

In return, the defense counsel could have mustered a list of persons living in India and hiding from prosecution elsewhere. For example, he could have cited the case of the Vietnamese-Indian confidence trickster and murderer Charles Sobhraj, who took shelter for decades in Indian jails (sic!) to avoid prosecution in Thailand. Sobhraj faced a possible death sentence in Thailand but the Indian authorities refused to let him face trial in Thailand until he had served his sentence in India by which time the Thai case would be nullified. While the case is an example of India's unwillingness to extradite, it would also show the degree to which some criminals are able to get their way in Indian jails (McGirk 1994; Wikipedia). The defense counsel could also have pointed to the case of Haji Mohammed Yaqoob, Minister for Haj and Minority Welfare in the state of Uttar Pradesh who in 2006 promised IRS 51 crore (approximately 10 million US dollars) and the equivalent in gold of the weight of anyone who would chop off the head of Danish cartoonist Kurt Westergaard. It was Westergaard who drew the most controversial of the Muhammad cartoons (Dougal 2006). Indian authorities apparently have not taken the initiative to prosecute this honorable member of the legislative assembly.

Apart from the above possibilities to reframe the issue, the prosecutor could have pursued obvious mistakes on the defense side. For example, Niels Holck claimed that he did not know the true size of the consignment until the crates containing the weapons were reloaded in Varanasi airport. But then he felt helpless to do anything about it because, as he explained in the High Court, the temperature was 55 degrees Celsius.[11] Here the prosecution could have informed the court that in Varanasi the average maximum temperature for the month of December when the airdrop took place is less than 25 degrees Celsius and the average minimum temperature about 10 degrees Celsius. The temperature, in other words, is likely to have been quite pleasant. Or the prosecution could have nullified a string of key arguments the defense counsel made in the Lower Court, and to a lesser extent in the High Court, to the effect that prison conditions and police and army brutality was a particularly serious problem in West Bengal. Several of the sources (International Red Cross, Amnesty International, and Human Rights Watch) which the defense counsel cited to build this argument referred to North-East India and *not* to West Bengal. In effect, the court was led up the garden path when the defense counsel wrongly placed West Bengal in North-East India.

In return the defense counsel could have argued that the court case against Holck could drag on for much longer than visualized in the diplomatic agreement between the two countries. The public prosecutor in the lower court held up the promise that Holck could be back in Denmark in three weeks provided he pleaded guilty, but the diplomatic agreement specified that Holck would not be tried in a Special Court. This meant that the case would be initiated in a court of first instance, *in casu* the Calcutta Chief Metropolitan Court, from where appeals and interventions may be made (by either party or by third parties) to High Court, the Supreme Court and finally as a mercy petition to the President. Mercy petitions with the Indian President regularly take many years to decide.[12] In effect, the case could plausibly have dragged on for years.

Even so the prosecution could have insisted that the issue was properly one of how democracies should relate to each other in a globalizing world. Political science claims that democracies do not wage war against each other. How could a Dane be allowed to do so with impunity? Denmark, as the prosecution did say in the Lower Court, should not become a safe haven for terrorists. Instead, Denmark should honor Security Council resolution 1373 which laid down that "...all States should prevent those who finance, plan, facilitate or commit terrorist acts from using their respective territories for those purposes against other countries and their citizens" (Security Council 2001). As noted by Sasikumar in an article which traces India's route from 'sponsor state' to 'victim state' of terror: 'This resolution has become the rallying point for "victim states" like India. Indian leaders draw attention to the fact that it proscribes *all forms* of support to terrorists' (Sasikumar 2010, 620).[13]

International cooperation is based both on law and on trust. India accorded Denmark exceptionally broad diplomatic guarantees. However, Holck still evaded them because the Danish courts did not want to extradite a citizen to an uncertain fate outside its civilizational orbit. As the defense counsel noted at the end of the High Court case: 'This is a difficult case. It is the first time that a Dane risks being extradited outside the West European cultural area' (Tyge Trier, my translation). Prominent defense lawyers, such as Trier, have tended to plead for the rights of foreign refugees to stay in Denmark. Some of these refugees have been Islamic terrorists, including the Egyptian leader Abu Talal who was eventually kidnapped in Zagreb and disappeared (Seidelin 2012). Unsurprisingly such lawyers also try to protect native Danes from extradition.[14] On the prosecution side, attempts were made to reframe the issue with reference to international law, the common fight against terror, and the importance of supporting an ordered process of globalization. These rather feeble attempts were fruitless as the bench kept its focus on the protection of individual human rights.[15] Holck's argument about the right to armed self-defense against communist misrule – setting aside the state monopoly of legitimate use of violence – was left hanging in the air. Perhaps the prosecution should have shot it down like it was shot down in the Salwa Judum case.

Returning to Jayaram and Saberwal (2011), one may conclude that the increase of complexity on a global scale constrains nations and international organizations to devise appropriate ordering devices. The diplomatic agreement between India and Denmark was an innovative ordering device to overcome this strain, but it was struck down by the Danish courts. It was India's human rights record and not any of a dozen other points that were raised in court which prevented Holck from being extradited. Interestingly, the Calcutta High Court has subsequently upbraided the Indian government for not ratifying the Convention against Torture. Acting on a petition, the Calcutta High Court directed the GOI to ensure that India would ratify the convention because, 'If the U.N. Convention against Torture had been ratified in Parliament, it might have been possible to ensure the extradition of Kim Davy' (The Hindu 2011). However, this may be a vain hope, because the mere ratification of the convention does not mean real change of police practices. Several of India's neighbors, including Pakistan, have ratified the convention, but their police forces have not been reformed and they continue to torture (Asian Human Rights Commission 2011). Nevertheless, such a step would have aligned the two legal systems, thereby contributing to a higher degree of global legal monism.

Innovative global legal pluralism

In January 2011, the American CIA-contractor Raymond Davis was arrested in Lahore after he shot and killed two Pakistanis who followed him on a motorbike. Possibly they were Pakistani intelligence agents shadowing him and Davis apparently reckoned they were about to attack him. Davis was caught on the spot and could have been sentenced to jail or to the gallows according to the Pakistan Penal Code, but the two states reached an ingenious legal solution to free him. The solution was effected through a Pakistani court, but it rested on a diplomatic agreement more secretive and more manipulative than the one made between Denmark and India in Holck's case. It worked to the advantage of the USA, but at the cost of its submitting to sharia principles.

In March 2011 Elizabeth Kolsky published an analysis of this contemporary incident of white violence:

> In the case of Raymond Davis, the Pakistani and American governments are both in a pickle. The Pakistanis don't want their people to think that another foreigner got away with murder and the Americans have no intention of leaving one of their own to rot away in Lahore's central jail.
>
> While Americans and Britons have fuzzy memories about the history of foreign occupation and intervention in South Asia, Pakistanis remain haunted by the past and present legacies of empire. These varied perspectives on the past help to explain the deepening divide between Pakistan and the US in the present. No one disputes the fact that Mr Davis shot dead two Pakistani motorcyclists in broad daylight on the streets of Lahore. The question is: will he get away with it or will a compromise be found so that Mr Davis can be brought to justice? (Kolsky 2011)

After protracted negotiations over whether Davis enjoyed diplomatic status, an out of box solution was devised based on the Islamic provisions of the Pakistan Penal Code relating to retaliation (*qisas*) and blood money (*diyat*) in the case of murder and man-slaughter. This enabled Pakistan to disregard the Vienna Convention on Diplomatic Relations under which Davis sought protection, and the court to release Davis under a sharia agreement where the 18 heirs of the two killed men were bullied into accepting the payment of PKR 206,851,000 (about US$ 2.3 million) as blood money. The money was probably paid by the US government, which, reportedly, also granted US citizenship or residence permits to all the heirs (Ahmed 2011).

The payment of exorbitant blood-money turned out to have dramatic consequences for the benefactors. In 2012, the wife and the mother of one of those killed were shot dead. Apparently, the father had killed them in a dispute over who should marry his widowed, but now wealthy, daughter: Someone from his own family, someone from his wife's family, or someone from the dead man's family? The families were also quarrelling over as to who should have custody over the child of the widowed daughter (Burke 2012; Express Tribune 2012). Meanwhile a group of Sunni religious specialists declared that blood-money received under duress in cases relating to bomb blasts, suicide hits and drone attacks were illegal according to the sharia (Dawn 2011).

The incident shows that a white 'demi-official' interloper in Pakistan may become the object of legal innovations on a scale which even Kolsky did not foresee. Here was a pluralistic innovation emerging heterogenetically through contestation between international law, Anglo-Pakistani law, and the Great Tradition of Islam, endorsed by the USA, and passed through a regular Pakistani court.

In Holck's case discussed above, the Danish courts refused to entertain Holck's claim that he acted justly in defense of the Ananda Margis. The Danish courts, thereby, abstained from undermining the Indian state's monopoly of the right to use legitimate force. Instead, they came down on India's long record of state-condoned human rights abuses. Nonetheless, the gap between the two juxtaposed national jurisdictions was almost bridged. In Davis' case, the cunning solution reached by the two states did bridge the gap, but it opened up the space for legal pluralism in a radical manner as the case dissolved into the cloud of plural law to emerge in the shape of a state-backed sharia decision at high transactional costs to the US tax-payer and to the Pakistani state, and to the chagrin of the Pakistani public who preferred to see Davis sentenced under Anglo-Pakistani law rather than be released with reference to sharia law. Law, it has been said, 'cannibalizes custom' (Kidder 1977, 169 quoting Diamond 1973), but the Raymond Davis case shows that customary and sharia law cannibalizes Anglo-Pakistani law. To judge by the three review articles of legal pluralism by Tamanaha (2008), Michaels (2009) and Griffiths (2011), studies in legal pluralism tend to skirt such issues of sharia law. This is a shame as the close, yet complex, relation between state law, sharia law, military rule, and customary law in countries like Pakistan should be of concern to global legal pluralists.

The Fog of Law

Legal pluralists tend to argue: 'Folk law good, state law bad' (Allott and Woodman 1985, 6 quoted in Michaels 2009, 22), but the mere occurrence of diverse forms of legal pluralism does not elevate legal pluralism to a desirable good. Rather, legal monism is the desirable good, because for a state to deliver the benefits a state may reasonably be expected to deliver in a well-ordered society not based on kinship or tyranny, the law should aim at becoming a unified whole applicable to everyone equally. The existence of plural or parallel legal orders jeopardizes clarity and equality in favor of the acknowledgement of difference. Legal diversity increases the scope for contestation by furthering uncertainty and 'fogginess' within states. Legal pluralism may even undermine the state's monopoly of the use of legitimate violence by creating competing legal orders, often with reference to religious dicta, that may disavow state authority. Because 'legal pluralism challenges a perceived monopoly of the state in making and administering law' (Michaels 2009, 3), legal pluralism has the character of a tragedy of the commons. To paraphrase Garrett Hardin (1968): Freedom in the legal commons brings ruin to all. If India is today a more stable and a more liberal country than Pakistan, it is in no small measure because India has worked harder to maintain the legal uniformity, consistency and certainty inherent in Macaulay's legacy and in the Indian constitution, while the Pakistani legal system suffocates under the Damocles Swords of customary law and sharia law.[16]

Legal pluralism, it could be optimistically interjected, opens up spaces in which complex conflicts may be productively played out. In the interests of pluralistic democracy and peaceful intercourse between nations, states may safely proffer a salad bowl of legal pluralism either under the aegis of their own legal systems or even outside. In this article I have tried to argue that this is not a wise, safe and desirable rule-of-thumb. When it comes to law *'Uniformity where you can have it; diversity where you must have it; but in all cases certainty'* is a better maxim than *'Diversity where you can have it; uniformity where you must have it; and in all cases contestability'*. As this article shows, transnational cases illustrate the need for unification in a stark form because national jurisdictions are by nature diverse.

Notes

1. The article was initially drafted for the Workshop on Non-State Law and Governance in South Asia to have been held 7–12 November 2011 in Pondichéry, India. I would like to thank Morten Hee, Stephen Legg, Kate Toft Madsen, Steen Schaumburg-Müller, Sho Tsubakiyama, Peter Voldby and the two anonymous reviewers for clarifications and suggestions, and Livia Holden for her gritty perseverance in editorial pursuits.
2. On Hans Kelsen and the unity of law, see Dalberg-Larsen (1994), Adamo (n.d.), and Günther (2008).
3. See Redfield and Singer (1973, 340) for the distinction between orthogenetic and heterogenetic cities.
4. See Nielsen (2009) for a recent summary of some of the pros and cons of the legal system in India.
5. The following is a condensed version of Madsen (2010) based largely on Crovetto (2008).
6. Though Macaulay was in favor of applying the law equally to all, he 'called for a special exemption from long terms of imprisonment to be created for convicted European residents, specifying banishment instead.' Imprisonment in India would be too cruel and erode the esteem for the English national character (Wright 2011, 52, note 152).
7. I attended some of the lengthy court meetings in the lower court in Hillerød and some of the meetings in the Eastern High Court in Copenhagen. I also monitored press coverage of the case. See Madsen (2011) for a write-up.
8. In India over 50,000 people were detained under TADA (Terrorist and Disruptive Activities Act) over a period of ten years. Less than one per cent of them were convicted (Shankar 2009, xxi). 'Doing more' in Indian parlance may not mean efficiency from a legal point of view, but incarceration and harassment.
9. See e.g. Legg (2011, 506) on the ability to define the exception as the mark of sovereignty.
10. Foreign investors incurring losses due to actions or in-action of the GOI or the Indian courts have recently found new ways to sue Indian authorities (Ghosh 2012).
11. Bleach apparently has stated that Holck knew what the cargo contained already before arriving in Varanasi (Holck and Kyrø 2008, 237).
12. The appeal procedure was a moot point in the court proceedings. I am referring here to a brief conversation I had with Ijaz Khan, the Indian CBI official present in the court case in Copenhagen. The position also emerges from the High Court verdict, page 4 (Udskrift af Østre Landsrets Dombog 2011).

13. Examples of India as a sponsor state of terror includes India's arming of Sri Lankan Tamils in the early 1980s (Madsen 1996,176; Madsen 2011).
14. See also Kaur (2012) who confounds judicial extradition cases in Denmark with possible extra-judicial instances of extraordinary rendition.
15. See Theils (2012) for ongoing attempts in the UK to extradite 'Tiger Hanif' and others to India.
16. See Karstedt (2011, 115, table 6.1) for Pakistan's failures in a comparative perspective.

Notes on contributor

Stig Toft Madsen is affiliated with the Nordic Institute of Asian Studies (NIAS) as senior research fellow. His recent publications include 'Udupi Hotels: Entrepreneurship, Reform and Revival' co-authored with Geoffrey Gardella in Krishnendu Ray and Tulasi Srinivas (eds.) *Curried Cultures, Globalization, Food, and South Asia*, 2012, and 'Ajit Singh S/O Charan Singh' in Stig Toft Madsen, Kenneth Bo Nielsen and Uwe Skoda (eds.) *Trysts with Democracy: Political Practice in South Asia*, 2011. His interest in the anthropology of law is reflected in 'Being on and being in: Exposure and influence of academic experts in contemporary Denmark' in Livia Holden (ed.) *Cultural Expertise and Litigation: Patterns, Conflicts, Narratives,* 2011.

References

Adamo, Silvia. n.d. "Kontinental retspositivisme: Hans Kelsen og Norberto Bobbio". Available at <http://jura.ku.dk/crs/nyt_retsfilosofisk_netvaerk/Hans-Kelsen-Norberto-Bobbio.pdf/> Last accessed on January 29, 2013.

Ahmed, Aijaz. 2011. "Islamic Law Saves Raymond Davis – Joint Saudi-ISI-CIA Mission Successful! Indus Herald Exclusive Report on Behind the Scene Moves". Available at <http://indusherald.blogspot.com/2011/03/islam-law-saves-raymond-davis-joint.html> Last downloaded on March 16, 2012.

Akbar, Mobashar Jawed. 2010. "Anderson Laughed at Indian Law and State". *Times of India.* Available at <http://blogs.timesofindia.indiatimes.com/TheSiegeWithin/entry/anderson-laughed-at-indian-law> Last downloaded on June 20, 2012.

Allot, Anthony and Gordon R. Woodman. 1985. "Introduction". In *People's Law and State Law: The Bellagio Papers,* edited by A. Allott and G. R. Woodman, 1–9. Dordrecht: Foris.

Anderson, Perry. 1974. *Passages from Antiquity to Feudalism.* London: New Left Books.

Asian Human Rights Commission. 2011. "INDIA: Demoralised Police Force is a Security Threat". Available at <www.humanrights.asia/news/ahrc-news/AHRC-STM-121-2011> Last downloaded on September 16, 2011.

Baweja, Harinder. 1996. "Straining Credibility". *India Today*, 31 March, 34–38.

Bostrup, Jens. 2011. "EU står klar til at hjælpe Danmark mod Indien". *Politiken*, Internationalt, 19 August, 8.

Burke, Jason. 2012. "How CIA Blood Money Led to Family Killing". Available at <http://dawn.com/2012/05/16/how-cia-blood-money-led-to-family-killing> Last accessed August 16, 2012.

Chan, Wing-Cheong, Barry Wright and Stanley Yeo, eds. 2011. *Codification, Macaulay and the Indian Penal Code, The Legacies and Modern Challenges of Criminal Law Reform.* Farnham: Ashgate.

Crovetto, Helen. 2008. "Ananda Marga and the Use of Force". *Nova Religio: The Journal of Alternative and Emergent Religions* 12(1): 26–56.

Dalberg-Larsen, Jørgen. 1994. *Rettens enhed – en illusion? Om retslig pluralisme i teorien og i praksis*, København: Akademisk Forlag. Also available in English: *Unity of Law: An Illusion? Legal Pluralism in Theory and Practice.* Verlin/Massachusetts: Galda und Wilch Verlag, 2001.

Dawn. 2011. "SIC Scholars Say `Forced Blood Money` is Illegal". 21 March. Available at <http://dawn.com/2011/03/21/sic-scholars-say-forced-blood-money-is-illegal/> Last accessed August 17, 2012.

Dougal, Sundeep. 2006. "Off with His Head!" *Outlook*, February 20. Available at <http://www.outlookindia.com/article.aspx?230294> Last accessed on January 29, 2013.

Diamond, Stanley. 1973. "The Rule of Law vs. the Order of Custom." In *The Social Organization of Law*, edited by D. Black and M. Mileski. New York: Seminar Press.

Elbæk-Jørgensen, Thomas. 2001. "En prøvelsesparallel: Folketingets Ombudsmand og de statslige revisionsorganer". In *Staten i forandring*, edited by Petersen, H., Koch Henning and P. B. Koch, 215–231. Det Juridisk Fakultet, Københavns Universitet Årsskrift, København: Jurist- og Økonomforbundets Forlag.

Expressindia. 2010. "Bhopal Gas Tragedy: Case Against Carbide Chief Still On". Available at <www.expressindia.com/latest-news/Bhopal-gas-tragedy-Case-against-Carbide-chief-still-on/631089/> Last accessed on June 8, 2012.

Express Tribune. 2012. "Custody Row: LHC Tells Faizan's Brother to Move Guardian Court". Available at <http://tribune.com.pk/story/422661/custody-row-lhc-tells-faizans-brother-to-move-guardian-court> Last accessed on August 16, 2012.

Galanter, Marc. 1968. "The Displacement of Traditional Law in Modern India". *Journal of Social Issues* XXIV 4: 65–91.

Ghosh, Jayati. 2012. "Worrying Trend". *Frontline*, 10-23 March. Available at <www.flonnet.com/fl2905/stories/20120323290511500.htm> Last accessed August 22, 2012.

Griffiths, Anne. 2011. "Pursuing Legal Pluralism: The Power of Paradigms in a Global World". *Journal of Legal Pluralism and Unofficial Law* 64: 173–202.

Günther, Klaus. 2008. "Legal Pluralism and the Universal Code of Legality: Globalisation as a Problem of Legal Theory". NoFo 5:21. Available at <http://www.helsinki.fi/nofo/NoFo5Gunther.pdf> Last accessed on January 29, 2013.

Hansen, John. 2008. "En Forsvarstale". Review of Niels Holck and Øivind Kyrø, *De kalder mig terrorist*. People's Press. Available at <http://bog.guide.dk/Erindringer/Niels%20Holck/Samfund/Om%20forfatterne/En_forsvarstale_1350977> Last accessed on January 29, 2013.

Hardin, Garrett. 1968. "The Tragedy of the Commons". *Science* 162(3859):1243–1248.

Hee, Edward. 1982. *Macaulay-kommissionens betænkning af november 1854 om engelsk administration i Indien, Historien om en administrativ uddannelsesreform – et tidsbillede med perspektiver, [The Macaulay Commission's Report of November 1854 on the English Administration of India: The History of Educational Reform of the Administration - A Picture of the Times with Perspectives]*, mimeographed essay in private possession, 95.

Himmelfarb, Gertrude. 1975. *Marriage and Morals Among the Victorians*. London and Boston: Faber and Faber.

Hindustan Times. 2012. "Davy Fallout: India Scales Down Ties with Denmark". 12 July. Available at <http://www.hindustantimes.com/India-news/NewDelhi/India-to-scale-down-diplomatic-ties-with-Denmark/Article1-887814.aspx> Last accessed on August 20, 2012.

Hoffmann-Hansen, Henrik. 2012. "Jamen, så må vi have en kommission". *Kristeligt Dagblad*, 27 August. Available at <http://www.kristeligt-dagblad.dk/artikel/475720:Danmark--Jamen--saa-maa-vi-have-en-kommission> Last accessed on September 12, 2012.

Holck, Niels and Øjvind Kyrø. 2008. *De Kalder Mig Terrorist* [*They call me a terrorist*]. København: People's Press.

India Today. 1996. "A Lethal Invasion". Special Report, 15 February, pp. 42–55.

Information. 2007. "Hvad nu hvis det var en inder, der havde kastet våben ned over Nørrebro?" 21 August.

Jayaram, N. and Satish Saberwal. 1996. "Epilogue". In *Social Conflict*, edited by N. Jayaram and S. Saberwal, 495–526. Delhi: Oxford University Press.

Karstedt, Susanne. 2011. "Exit: The State. Globalization, State Failure and Crime". In *Comparative Criminal Justice and Globalization*, edited by D. Nelken, 107–122. Farnham: Ashgate,

Kaur, Ravinder. 2012. "Holck-sagen set med indiske øjne". *Udenrigs* 3: 13–18.

Kidder, Robert L. 1996. "Courts and Conflict in an Indian City: A Study in Legal Impact". In *Social Conflict*, edited by N. Jayaram and S. Saberwal, 474–492. Delhi: Oxford University Press.

Kidder, Robert L. 1977. "Western Law in India: External Law and Local Response". In *Social System and Legal Process*, edited by H. M. Johnson, 155–180. San Francisco: Jossey-Bass Publishers, Special double issue of *Social Enquiry* 47, 3–4.

Kolsky, Elizabeth. 2011. "The Colonial Backdrop". *Dawn*, 13 March. Available at <www.dawn.com/2011/03/13/the-colonial-backdrop.html> Last accessed on January 29, 2013.

Kolsky, Elizabeth. 2010. *Colonial Justice in British India*. Cambridge: Cambridge University Press.

Kyrø, Øjvind. 2010. "Skæbnedage". *Weekendavisen*. 29 April. Available at <www.kyroe.dk/main/idealisten.pdf> Last accessed on January 13 2013.

Legg, Stephen. 2011. "Legal Geographies and the State of Imperialism: Environments, Constitutions, and Violence". *Journal of Historical Geography* 37: 505–508.

Liang, Lawrence. 2011. "A Beacon of Light in the Heart of Darkness: SC Holds Salwa Judum Unconstitutional". *Kafila* Available at <http://kafila.org/2011/07/06/a-beacon-of-light-in-the-heart-of-darkness-sc-holds-salwa-juddam-unconstitutional/#more-8334> Last accessed on July 6, 2012.

Macaulay, Thomas B. 1833. "A Speech Delivered in the House of Commons on the 10th of July 1833 on "Government of India"". Available at <www.columbia.edu/itc/mealac/pritchett/00generallinks/macaulay/txt_commons_indiagovt_1833.html> Last accessed on January 29, 2013.

Madsen, Stig Toft. 2011. "A Dane in Distress". AsiaPortal Infocus, 3 October. Available at <http://infocus.asiaportal.info/2011/10/03/a-dane-in-distress/> Last accessed on February 25, 2012.

Madsen, Stig Toft. 2010. "The Path of Bliss". AsiaPortal Infocus, 29 April. Available at <http://infocus.asiaportal.info/2010/04/29/the-path-of-bliss/> Last accessed on 28 February 2012.

Madsen, Stig Toft. 1996. *State, Society and Human Rights in South Asia*. New Delhi: Manohar.

McGirk, Tim. 1994. "The Lethal Charm of Charles Sobhraj". *The Independent*, Weekend, 7 May, 31.

Michaels, Ralf. 2009. "Global Legal Pluralism". *Annual Review of Law & Social Science* 5, available at <http://papers.ssrn.com/sol3/papers.cfm?abstract_id=1430395> Last accessed on January 29, 2013.

Misra, Savvy S. 2011. "CBI can Seek Anderson's Extradition". *Down to Earth*, 30 April. Available at <www.downtoearth.org.in> Last accessed on January 29, 2013.

Morgan, Neil. 2011. "The Fault Element of Offences" In *Codification, Macaulay and the Indian Penal Code. The Legacies and Modern Challenges of Criminal Law Reform.*, edited by W.C. Chan,, B. Wright and S. Yeo, 59–86. Farnham: Ashgate.

Nielsen, Kenneth Bo. 2009. "Farmers' Use of the Courts in an Anti-land Acquisition Movement in India's West Bengal". *Journal of Legal Pluralism and Unofficial Law* 59: 121–44.

Randeria, Shalini. 2007. "De-Politicization of Democracy and Judicialization of Politics". *Theory, Culture and Society* 24: 438–444.

Randeria, Shalini. 2003. "Between Cunning States and Unaccountable International Institutions: Social Movements and Rights of Local Communities to Common Property Resources". Discussion Paper Nr. SP IV 2003-502, University of Zürich. Available at <http://skylla.wzb.eu/pdf/2003/iv03-502.pdf>. Last accessed on February 28, 2012.

Redfield, Robert and Milton B. Singer. 1973. "The Cultural Role of Cities" In *Peasants and Peasant Societies*, edited by T. Shanin, 337–365. Harmondsworth: Penguin Books. Originally published in *Economic Development and Social Change* (1954) 3: 53–73.

Robinson, Nick. 2010. "The Judiciary: Hard to Reach". *Frontline* 27 (3). Available at <http://flonnet.com/fl2703/stories/20100212270304600.htm>. Last accessed January 28, 2013.

Sasikumar, Karthika. 2010. "State Agency in the Time of the Global War on Terror: India and the Counter-Terrorism Regime". *Review of International Studies* 36: 615–638.

Scarborough Evening News. 2011. "Scarborough's Peter Bleach Tells us His Story". Available at <www.scarborougheveningnews.co.uk/community/local-focus/scarborough_s_peter_bleach_tells_us_his_story_1_3501499> Last accessed on August 31, 2013.

Seidelin, Matias. 2012. *Allahs Danske Krigere i FBIs søgelys*. Copenhagen: Politikens Forlag.

Shankar, Shylashri. 2009. *Scaling Justice. India's Supreme Court, Anti-Terror Law, and Social Rights*. New Delhi: Oxford University Press.

Sharma, Manimugdha S. 2012. "How the Market for Illegal Weapons is Booming in India". *The Economic Times*, 25 November. Available at <http://articles.economictimes.indiatimes.com/2012-11-25/news/35346737_1_illegal-weapons-ak-47s-gun-laws> Last accessed on January 29, 2013.

Sullivan, Robert E. 2009. *Macaulay: The Tragedy of Power*. Cambridge, MA and London: The Belknap Press of Harvard University Press.

Tamanaha, Brian Z. 2008. "Understanding Legal Pluralism: Past to Present, Local to Global". *Legal Studies Research Paper Series* No. #07-0080. Available at <http://ssrn.com/abstract=1010105> Last accessed on January 29, 2013.

The Hindu. 2011. "Kim Davy Extradition: Time Sought to File Affidavits". Available at <www.thehindu.com/news/national/article2453673.ece> Last accessed on January 29, 2013.

The Independent. 2000. "Mission Improbable". Available at <www.independent.co.uk/news/people/profiles/mission-improbable-726033.html> Last accessed February 1st, 2012.

Theils, Lone. 2012. "Grønthandleren kan blive første udlevering til Indien", *Udenrigs* 3: 19–23.

Venkatesan, V. 2011. "A Proven Case". *Frontline*, 12 August, 43–46.

Weber, Max. 1964. *The Theory of Social and Economic Organization*. New York: The Free Press.

Wikipedia. "Charles Sobhraj". Available at <http://en.wikipedia.org/wiki/Charles_Sobhraj> Last accessed on January 14, 2013.

Wright, Barry. 2011. "Macaulay's Indian Penal Code: Historical Context and Originating Principles." In *Codification, Macaulay and the Indian Penal Code. The Legacies and Modern Challenges of Criminal Law Reform*, edited by W. C. Chan, B. Wright and S. Yeo, 19–55. Farnham: Ashgate.

Yeo, Stanley and Barry Wright. 2011. "Revitalizing Macaulay's Indian Penal Code." In *Codification, Macaulay and the Indian Penal Code. The Legacies and Modern Challenges of Criminal Law Reform*, edited by W. C. Chan, B. Wright and S. Yeo, 3–18. Farnham: Ashgate.

Zeenews. 2011. "Why was Anderson Not Questioned, CIC Asks CBI." Available at <http://zeenews.india.com/news/nation/why-was-anderson-not-questioned-cic-asks-cbi_714072.html> Last accessed on June 20, 2012.

Other primary sources

LOV nr 378, Lov om ændring af straffeloven, retsplejeloven, lov om konkurrence- og forbrugerforhold på telemarkedet, våbenloven, udleveringsloven samt lov om udlevering af lovovertrædere til Finland, Island, Norge og Sverige (Gennemførelse af FN-konventionen til bekæmpelse af finansiering af terrorisme, gennemførelse af FN s Sikkerhedsråds resolution nr. 1373 (2001) samt øvrige initiativer til bekæmpelse af terrorisme m.v.) [Act to amend the Criminal Code, Code of Procedure, the Law on Competition and Consumer Interests in the Telecommunications Market, Arms Act, the Extradition Act and the Act on Extradition to Finland, Iceland, Norway and Sweden (Implementation of the UN Convention for the Suppression of the Financing of Terrorism, implementation of the UN Security Council Resolution 1373 (2001) and other initiatives to combat terrorism, etc.)]. Available at <www.retsinformation.dk/forms/r0710.aspx?id=1344> Last accessed February 28, 2012.

Security Council, Anti-Terrorism Resolution; Resolution 1373, Dated 28 September 2001. Available at <www.unhcr.org/refworld/docid/3c4e94552a.html> Last accessed January 25, 2013.

Supreme Court of India (2011) *Nandini Sundar and others (petitioners) versus State of Chhattisgarh (respondents)*, Item No. 44, Court No. 9, Section PIL, Writ Petition, (Civil) NO(s). 250 of 2007. Available at <http://supremecourtofindia.nic.in/outtoday/wc25007.pdf> Last accessed Janaury 25, 2013.

Udskrift af Østre Landsrets Dombog, Kendelse, Afsagt den 30. Juni 2011 af Østre Landsrets 11. Afdeling, kære nr. S-3321-10, [Extract of the Eastern High Court's Decisions, Order delivered on 30 June 2011 by the Eastern High Court's 11th Chamber, Case No. S-3321-10], pp. 18.

Governance and governability in South Asian family laws and in diaspora

Werner Menski

Professor of South Asian Laws, School of Law, SOAS, University of London, UK

This paper, providing one example each from Indian and from Pakistani law, with heavily contested litigation fallouts under English law and in English courts, discusses first why there are significant elements of mistrust in local and particularly translocal relationships that impact on how individuals and whole communities make choices in relation to dispute resolution. Conflicts arise not only over legal processes, costs and delays, but also increasingly in relation to the value systems involved in different types of family law regulation. This may be more so when people cross the boundaries between formal and informal methods of dispute settlement and when non-state jurisdiction and formal governance, in South Asia and elsewhere in the world, are seen to be clashing. South Asians as skilled cultural and legal navigators on a global scale are shown to be more resourceful kite flyers in this regard than states, which may have institutional power, but often do not possess the cultural knowledge and sensitivities needed to inspire trust in bringing about satisfactory resolutions of disputes.

The wider context: Globalized messiness of pluralism and the need for ordering

I must immediately ask for the reader's indulgence, as analysis of the two cases I wish to present here will certainly benefit from an extended contextual framework of analytical tools that I need to lay out first, especially for readers fairly unfamiliar or simply unsympathetic to the emerging methodologies of global legal pluralism. Inspired by recent rethinking of the critical role of legal anthropology in relation to law, I believe this to be a viable way forward, though certainly not a shortcut, to understanding the vast field of what claims to be law in its various forms better than we have done so far.

In today's global world, the difficulties that seem to be caused by people moving around the globe affect not only those individuals who move, but also throw into potential turmoil an often carefully crafted equilibrium – or at least particular kinds of power relationships – between different legal components that may co-exist within any one formal state-centred legal system. We may have thought that such relationships were safely negotiated and somewhat fixed through private international law rules earlier, not only between different state laws but also between state laws and various other types of laws. Upstream and downstream laws, looking at the whole picture from the centre of state regulatory systems, are not set in stone however, and continue to experience multiple negotiations of their relative position within the pluralist field of law.

Today it seems that substantial fragments of whole jurisdictions, in the form of migrants and their families, are moving around the globe. We know that people carry at least fragments of their legal systems in their baggage with them, wherever they go. Shah (2012) has shown that British people in Turkey construct hybrid decision making processes that involve both English and Turkish law. Turks in Europe do the same, wherever they go, in their own way (see Shah in this special issue). Ballard (2007) theorizes in depth how Asians as skilled cultural navigators re-organize the world in their new home on their own terms. In some cases the legal rules that people carry in their baggage will then find themselves presented in whatever fragmented form before entirely new *fora*, causing much consternation and surprise, sometimes even utter disbelief, and now increasingly distrust, if not disgust.

It should also be no surprise at all that this globalizing messiness then sometimes manifests as off-hand rejection to even deal with particular unfamiliar foreign law issues or with foreign law itself on the part of official decision makers.[1] Further research is beginning to uncover convenient strategies of redefining those boundaries of various laws. Neo-positivist scholarship predicted increasingly regulated and uniformized law, but the opposite seems to be happening: Super-diversity clearly also affects the legal sphere and its plural ways of operation. And it does so with totally unforeseen consequences – which were actually quite foreseeable, coming to think of it as a pluralist – but much of this remains unresearched. Regrettably, the benefit of such hindsight comes often too late and does not help hapless litigants in need of a fair decision. The lag between actual legal developments and scholarship that covers it entraps and then often further victimizes many litigants that might have been better off staying outside the official legal regulatory frameworks altogether. However, modern states push us all into more and more surveillance-based processes, so that keeping under the radar itself now increasingly risks criminalization.

The basic and so apparently inevitable scenario of what has been called deep legal pluralism or radical legal pluralism involves the co-existence of competing types of orders and normative systems. These competing forms of laws are inextricably linked, in my present view, to the four focal points of (1) religion/ethics/values; (2) socio-cultural norms and socio-economic arrangements; (3) state-centric laws of different kinds and the political arrangements sustaining them; and (4) various forms of international law and norms that claim predominance in today's world.[2]

To illustrate how this highly dynamic linkage works, one may hierarchize the sequence and intensity of the linkages between these four corners and envisioning rhetoric models. For example, a religious fundamentalist, starting from an ideological position that puts religion at the centre of his/her universe, would consider the various law-making elements in the sequence 1-2-4-3, because s/he probably hates the state, has reservations about 'Western' human rights ideology, and normally starts from a perspective of religious rootedness, which is also typically a very individualistic approach. We see here how decision-making processes are directly connected to what many scholars call now 'legal consciousness'.

Going back to my exercize, human rights fundamentalists in my classes normally tend to start their legal analysis from corner 4, which generates a totally different sequence, probably 4-3-2-1. This happens because of their focus on modern values and individual rights. This appears as a messy patchwork of competing normativities between the local and the global and the tensions between those competing roles cause never-ending agony about decision-making.

It is of course possible to argue, and has in fact been argued by many scholars, that various kinds of pluralism and especially the co-existence of general law systems and personal status laws in many jurisdictions of the world, particularly in the global South, makes the picture even more complicated. So the idea has been that we should simply get rid of personal laws. However, I am certain that abolition of personal laws may work formally, as law manifestly has the formal power to change rules. But this power is also to a large extent a fiction, as the primary legal actor remains the individual, not the state. Formal legal interventions as well as deliberate non-action thus create new forms of reactive plurality, as is so clearly visible in secular Turkey, but also in the UK.[3]

Moreover, it is uncertain that formal unification of personal laws, or even of certain aspects of personal laws, will provide feasible remedies, as the lessons of global legal realism always take us back to the drawing board of 'living laws' and thus the emergence of new deep pluralities. What seems instead possible, and this is increasingly visible now, is the strategy of combining the two competing approaches rather than to see and treat them in opposition or as contradictory forces. In other words, pluralist methodology helps us to understand better state law. This is why new initiatives to revitalize studies in legal anthropology are so very critical to ambitions to make progress in this messy field.

The theoretical underpinnings for such discussions remain globally fuzzied and partly disrupted by sectorial standpoints. A significant example is found in the recent writing by Brian Tamanaha (2010) who appears to differentiate and perhaps antagonize American and European pluralisms. The often highly artificial boundaries between various official laws and unofficial laws may well be shifted by interventions from self-appointed reformers, but there will always be other boundaries arising as a result of such shifts, given that law is everywhere intensely dynamic. 'Living law' is and remains a key concept in that context, but there are many types of 'living law', not just the classic Ehrlich type highlighted by Tamanaha. And, as Hannah Arendt (1958) noted long ago with regard to the human condition of plurality, we are all the same, but every individual is at the same time unique and thus different from everything else. The legal neo-positivism appears just as dangerous as the traditional classic top-down Austinian method. The anti-pluralist stance of dictatorships in the name of one type of law notably needs to be scrutinized.

At an official legal level, it may of course be possible that a formally and often exceedingly well-formulated solution can be found to a particular issue or dispute. But such a formally resolved conflict may not forever settle the issue, which may then continue to simmer below the surface, escaping the radar of official sensors and systems and bypassing formal understandings of law, while still causing havoc in people's personal lives or in other respects. It is useful to remember in this context all the time Sally Falk Moore's wise axiom that all legal interventions are of necessity piecemeal. Maybe it helps, as I shall try to elaborate in the concluding analysis, to view the entire conundrum presented here as a management scenario in which, as pluralists know, the state is not necessarily the only entity in charge of what goes on, in law and in life.

Two case scenarios of distrust and disgust

I shall present here two cases of intense intercultural havoc, asking thereby also to what extent recourse to formal legal systems and official dispute settlement mechanisms is actually viable in certain scenarios that individuals, both men and women, may face in their lives while navigating the pluralities of today's world and trying to cope with their very own personal dramas.

But first still a bit more of background on why and how the selection of material was made. Originally, I had set out to demonstrate how within one particular nation's legal system, that of India, the co-existence of a plurality of legal orderings could lead to surprisingly unpredictable results, both negative and positive. The intended key argument was going to be that the navigation of the boundaries between personal laws and general laws often gives rise to potential conflicts, but these may be resolved if all participants in a dispute play ball and abide, ultimately, by a solution worked out by them or for them. More often than not, such a solution would straddle aspects of formal and informal legal systems and would connect personal law agenda with general law elements, and so on. These would be typical boundary dispute issues of the kind that are popular with family lawyers working on the global South, as the battle between more state involvement (*Verstaatlichung*) and less state involvement (*Entstaatlichung*) continues to rage.

I had in mind to focus on the topic of post-divorce maintenance laws, which has given rise to such amazingly interesting developments in India. But having written quite a lot about this subject,[4] I was readily persuaded to move the analytical searchlight towards private international law scenarios. Thus it was decided that I should rather shift focus to the navigational issues arising between state law and non-state law jurisdictions and governance on a transnational level. The common pattern there would be at first sight that in Western (supposedly uniform and formal) legal systems huge questions arise today over the structure and function of non-Western legal systems, which are by some scholars even challenged as violative of human rights *per se*. Non-Western legal systems are often known to be intensely plural and may consist of an intricate combination of general laws and personal laws. Closer scrutiny shows that there is still much else that awaits analysis, above all a peeling away of several layers of internal conflicts, showing ultimately conflicts within those plural legal systems about the yet deeper pluralities within the minutiae of different components.

I have thus recently come to speak of law as 'pop', a multi-layered plurality of pluralities, and the two cases discussed here illustrate this intensely 'pop'-like nature of laws really well. Thus, we find here firstly a familiar conflict between different types of national legal systems existing in the world today, called private international law or conflict of laws. Secondly, however, one identifies also huge conflicts within the various national legal components involved in a particular case. Both cases presented here may help us to achieve a more sophisticated understanding of how such pluralist conflicts and tensions arise in the first place and why final resolution of such conflicts may often be impossible through recourse to formal dispute settlement *fora* and related mechanisms, more so if the decision makers are foreign judges. The suffering and the chaos will remain present despite a judicial verdict, even if one is given and it does look correct and right. The past cannot be undone, memories of injustices committed will linger. Worse, other people will stumble across the same trip wires, may fall differently and sustain different injuries.

So it does not seem right to simply blame pluralism, pluralities and diversity for the woes of humankind. If Hannah Arendt is right that all humans are unique, we actually have to try and manage this limitless diversity as best we can. Professionals, whether practising lawyers or legal academics of some description, should actually be happy and grateful, for this plural scenario generates never-ending work, especially for those willing to combine theory with practice. A more jaundiced view is also possible: We may reasonably conclude that the presence of such confusions means simply that sharky lawyers will become ever-richer, while poor litigants may be even poorer and more damaged at the end of these convoluted processes. Yet the issue is also on whether state-law alone is indeed able to provide a better and accountable justice. Let us be more positive and hopeful, though, and search for something like 'best practice'.

The cases: Their emergence and their management

The following current cases, conducted largely, though not exclusively, under English law appear to remain unresolved, despite years of legal struggle and despite the fact that one of them is meanwhile officially reported.[5] Concerns of fast and efficient justice seem to fly out of the window when parties fight like proverbial cats and dogs in front of English judges, who may not be amused, and may rightfully ask serious questions about why their valuable time should be taken up with such abstruse litigations over fine points of foreign law, after all. While the official law expects to serve as a dispute settlement forum, it seems that it sometimes pays a rather heavy price for wanting to be in control of how people regulate all or most aspects of their lives. The basic claims of the law may need to be re-examined if the scenario become unmanageable and just too complex to handle. Or should we also comment on the increasing litigiousness observed in many societies and on the opportunity to restrict or at least control it? Maybe some fresh reflections about this are permissible and necessary, too.

These two cases linger on even after many legal actions have taken place to navigate the formal boundaries between the various state laws and non-state laws involved. This would indicate that recourse to courts is not a route to speedy remedies. I am not convinced that this translocal or transnational element is by itself the main reason for such procrastinations of litigation. It appears that the complexities of life and even a somewhat poisonous dose of human deviousness have led us all into a labyrinth of competing and contradictory argumentations called litigation or dispute processing, certainly an attractive industry. The scenarios presented often appear like Gordian knots that judges are then struggling to untie, only to cause new knots and twists.

Actually, in cases of this kind, one generally observes that one or both of the parties (and often the people around them) simply use the various available avenues and dispute settlement *fora* to engage in a battle that ultimately serves hidden agenda, or even no tangible legal purpose.[6] In one of the cases discussed here, indeed in the reported case of *R v. M* of 2011 (see note 10), the learned judge explicitly notes early on, in paragraph 4, 'that nothing turns on this dispute of a practical nature'. So the fight, causing much anguish, huge expenditure and multiple other costs – as we shall see – needs to be scrutinized also as the result of formal legal structures that perhaps unwittingly permit obfuscating arguments, even if they are plain lies, to be paraded as legal evidence. Does this mean that our filtering mechanisms are insufficient? Are we worried that pre-judging an issue will deny justice?

Let me report here also briefly that my experience as expert in court in such cases has indeed been that either of the two parties is lying – but who is it, and why? The expert as a detective may find huge challenges, even to his own professional status and standing, in a formal system that emphasizes adversarial battle, despite struggling to save time and resources. At the end of the day one must still ask, as does another recent paper, whether we really do not know any better how to handle such disputes, or we simply do not want to know.[7]

Finally: The cases themselves

Focusing on the two cases themselves now, we see that the first case, which I shall call N v. P, concerns a frequently encountered problem scenario for Hindu women from India. They frequently marry a man with a foreign passport, move to join him abroad, and then find rather soon that the marriage breaks down and huge unforeseen problems arise because of jurisdictional and intercultural complications. I am not advising against such marriages, being party to one such union myself, but make factual observations of management crises that then land on the desks of British and other judges who may be utterly puzzled and gasping in disbelief about what they are made to read.

In the present case, an Indian Hindu woman, N, had married P, a Hindu male from the UK, in a Hindu marriage ceremony in India. No doubt this was a legally valid marriage under the relevant Indian law. She then came to live in the UK, which is where P is resident, domiciled and working, holding a British passport. P had been married and divorced before, and this was known to N. She obtained entry clearance to the UK on the basis of evidence that there was a legally valid marriage under Indian law, but quite typically, the moment some problems arose in the marital relationship this presumed or actual legal validity was suddenly challenged.

It has become an observable pattern that one of the parties, normally a husband faced with claims for property and other financial entitlements, then suddenly turns round to claim that there was no legally valid marriage. This is not quite what happened here, though, so this particular case introduces yet more twists and turns. Rather than claiming bluntly that the marriage was not legally valid, which was attempted, but did not get the husband very far, when the marital relationship began to crumble, P allegedly tricked N into going to India and then arranged a customary divorce there with the involvement of some caste elders and family seniors. She went along with this process, it seems, not fully realizing (or maybe not wanting to admit to herself) that she was being divorced. P knew Indian law better, he assumed, and thought that he had gotten rid of his troublesome wife who had dared to complain, and he basically abandoned her in India.

P then returned to the UK to resume his business activities, while N stayed back for some time. But soon she got worried about her long-term position, still not having obtained indefinite leave to remain and she managed to get back into the UK. To cut a long and convoluted story short, when she then attempted to resume marital relations or at least co-residence, believing that she was still married, she was basically locked out of the home, became destitute and dependent on the charity of others. The husband, claiming that N had descended from hell to pursue him and his new wife (see below), persisted in denying any responsibility and simply threw N out. In such situations, modern Western welfare states profess readiness to support vulnerable individuals. Yet whatever meagre state support a woman in such a situation in Britain may obtain today depends heavily on whether she even knows where and how to start making such claims. We are not concerned with those aspects of the case here.

The most remarkable twist in this case is, as indicated, that P has meanwhile remarried and has brought another Indian woman to the UK as his wife, while N is still challenging her customary divorce, and does so now in repeatedly aborted proceedings in the English courts. This case appears to indicate, as another case that I encountered earlier, that the right hand of the law may not quite know what the left hand does.[8] Certainly, the cross-jurisdictional navigations in this case are intriguing. Further discussion of this case will be provided below, but it should have become clear that the English courts are going to face claims that a formal decision should be made about the precise nature of N's present marital status and, perhaps, any entitlements to ancillary relief. It goes without saying that the legal status of the purported Indian customary divorce, and the circumstances in which it was procured, will probably be a key element of evidence. But then, quite when and how are people getting married and divorced under Indian Hindu law with its plurality of provisions? In transnational disputes, we now find global messiness and turbulences of the legal kite, as such questions are not decided in the Indian Supreme Court in New Delhi these days, but in courtrooms in faraway places, this time in London.

The second case, which as indicated is by now a reported court decision from the Family Division in London,[9] involved as the petitioner a female Pakistani citizen while the respondent was a British Pakistani who lived in the UK with his parents. It was an arranged marriage, but it does not appear that full and truthful disclosures about the respective parties were made. For example, the wife claims that she was told that the husband was an educated professional, but he turned out to be a driver. The spouses and perhaps even their families did not realize that a match was being made here between two individuals who would clash violently within days of marrying. While the depressing facts are not of direct interest, the fact that the marriage broke down almost instantly after its celebration had important repercussions in terms of formal registration of this marriage, as we shall see.

Other dramatic and complex complications arise because the parties were Ahmadis. The marriage, contracted according to Ahmadi customs in Islamabad on 9 November 2007, consisted of a religious ceremony, referred to as a *nikah* (which may well be an illegal term for this ceremony in Pakistan), followed by a public announcement of the solemnization of the marriage. The husband's claim, however, became very soon that he was only married to the petitioner religiously, not legally. Since in his view there was no legal marriage between the parties under Pakistani law, English law could simply not claim jurisdiction to grant a divorce. The judge was told to close the case and in effect to refuse dealing with the matter. The wife, however, insisted on her claim to divorce under English law, ferociously opposed by the husband and his entire legal team, who collectively argued with much force that the Pakistani marriage had not been a legally valid marriage. There was, however, also some telling evidence that a divorce had been given by the husband, notably under Ahmadi law in the UK. There seem to be no jurisdictional boundaries for the kite journeys depicted in this heavily convoluted case.

This deceptively simple (but only at first sight) case thus asked the English Court as a preliminary issue to ascertain whether there had ever been a legally valid marriage between the parties under Pakistani law. English courts are often faced with such scenarios today, while judges and lawyers alike are regularly out of their depth in such cases and need the assistance of country experts. The added trouble here is, however, that under formal Pakistani law, there is simply no law for Ahmadis, so even the cleverest expert in the world could not just invent such a law to support the wife's claim.

Readers will need to know that Ahmadis have been declared non-Muslims in Pakistan since 1974 and are prohibited by law from calling themselves Muslims since 1984. The galling irony of the matter is that they claim to be better Muslims than the adherents of the mainstream brand of Pakistani Islam. Whatever those religious and sectarian quibbles, Ahmadis as official non-Muslims are also barred from bringing themselves under the provisions of the Muslim Family Laws Ordinance of 1961 in Pakistan, which clearly only applies to Muslims. They simply have no personal law, it seems, because the last thing the Pakistani state would wish to do is to provide a new personal law for Ahmadis. Given that these are probably millions of people, it is highly fictitious to imagine that there is simply a legal void. The case of *R v. M* thus showed in frightening clarity the abyss of utter distrust and disgust, not only between husband and wife, but also between Ahmadis and the Pakistani state. This case therefore shows what happens when there is no formal law and illustrates how the gaps between formal law and informal laws may be and are being filled by people's informal, largely unofficial legal practice. One probably needs the lenses of a psychologist and a legal anthropologist to pick up such evidence, but it could not be much stronger than in the present case.

Involved as the expert for the wife, I had full access to the various documents and pleadings. Not for the first time, I learnt a lot about how Ahmadis as transnational skilled cultural and legal navigators have begun to re-organize their personal law system so as to be able to marry in Pakistan, where many Ahmadis are still living, while there is by now also a global Ahmadi diaspora, with a leadership based in London and with its own agenda of managing such cross-jurisdictional complications.

A marriage document or Nikah Form, dated November 2007, was produced in court, issued by the main Ahmadi organization in the town of Rabwah in Pakistan. The form contains details analogous to a Muslim *nikahnama*, such as details of the parties, the amount of the stipulated dower, names and signatures of the male witnesses and details and signature of the officiant. Another 'marriage certificate' was issued roughly two weeks subsequent to the ceremony and the wife joined the husband in England some time in 2008. Despite the existence of such documents, doubts are in order whether the marriage was formally registered in Pakistan. Of course it is also not universally agreed whether in Pakistani law it is necessary at all to register a marriage to bring about legal validity. Decades of legal involvement on my part have not resulted even in obtaining the agreement of my closest colleagues about this simple matter of law. Does one really need to register a Muslim marriage in Pakistan to obtain full legal validity? The answer appears to depend on what one means by 'law'! While the answer of living law analysis is clearly a resounding no to compulsory registration, as a Muslim marriage contract is valid because God himself is deemed to have listened to the offer and acceptance, positivist and stubborn insistence on sweeping interpretations of legal regulation continues to claim that an unregistered Muslim marriage in Pakistan is not legally valid in spite of the well known published precedents. Such cracks and disagreements are then exploited by devious litigants and their legal advisors, as this case so clearly illustrates, to cause utter havoc in overseas courts and to give even judges sleepless nights.

A related example illustrates this problem further: A few years ago, it was found in a conference on this topic in the Netherlands (the proceedings are unfortunately not reported) that dozens of mature Dutch ladies had been marrying younger Pakistani men, who then presented marriage documents from Pakistan to support their claims for residence in Holland. Someone raised an alarm and the entire legal system looked utterly foolish in trusting official documents rather than understanding the basics of Muslim law relating to marriage. While our sensors about immigration-related abuses are sharp in light of such evidence, the pluralistic safeguards that should have been noticed were not fully called upon: Since when is it the law of Pakistan that a marriage document *per se* constitutes valid evidence of the existence of a legal Muslim marriage under Pakistani law? The gaps between formalistic Western legal systems and the hybrid and thus more culture-sensitive plural legal frameworks of countries like Pakistan are evident here. In the absence of socio-legal knowledge about foreign procedures and processes, such gaps are not even noticed by bureaucrats and lawyers. We see in the case of *R v. M* quite clearly how fuzzily handled key issues in the domestic matrimonial law of another country can lead to serious confusions for judges in a Western jurisdiction that is used to deciding matters on the basis of official documents. But this case highlights two more points: (1) the expert in court is not simply someone acquainted with the positive law of the country of the litigants but more broadly with the socio-legal contexts and law practices of that country; and (2) law practices that become translocal are very often transformed and may acquire contextual validity even if this is sometimes contested in the countries of their origin.

While it made sense to the learned judge that a religious marriage may be legally valid as a matter of custom, the absence of Ahmadi law and the amazingly convoluted arguments over that particular aspect threw spanners into the judicial works. But such money-spinning obfuscations caused immense delay and agony in the decision-making process, because an expert who is challenged by another expert cannot of course just be believed by a court. That then raises the intriguing question of who or what is an expert, again necessarily the subject of another paper.

So the convoluted arguments in *R v. M* carried on. The parties had failed to register the marriage in the UK, as was claimed to have been the original intention. The reason for this failure to register in the UK is evidently the very swift breakdown of the marriage, with more dramatic consequences that do not concern us here. When the relationship had totally broken down, however, and the wife petitioned for a divorce in the District Court, her husband simply denied that there was ever a legally valid marriage between the parties, either in Pakistan or in the UK. On this count, Hindu and Muslim men seem to sing from the same hymn sheet. Totally contradictory positions were taken by the parties, and there was huge confusion over fine procedural details of Pakistani laws on marriage registration, with desperate recourse by the wife's family even to the secular provisions of the Pakistani Special Marriage Act of 1872 as late as October 2009, two years after the marriage. Urgent demands for yet more documentation led to highly risky actions that potentially damaged the judge's trust in the credibility of the claimant and her family. The husband, on his part, was simply unable to provide sufficient proof to support his ardent claim that the marriage was legally invalid. The totally competing positions of the wife, the husband, and their respective experts could form the subject of a lengthy dissertation.

The husband strenuously sought to maintain that the marriage in 2007 had consisted merely of a religious union according to Ahmadi practice. Use of the word 'custom' was vigorously opposed, especially since I had suggested that the case file contained clear-cut evidence of the development of new Ahmadi customs, given the legal void regarding Ahmadis in Pakistani law. The husband's declaration of divorce had been approved by the President of an Ahmadi Board in the UK in July 2009, and was allegedly the only form of divorce necessary in the circumstances. After the three month *iddat* period, the Ahmadi Board had formally confirmed the divorce as effective from 7 October 2009. According to the husband, thus, there was no reason for the English Court to intervene at all.

As indicated, in situations such as this, English law has the facility of using expert evidence on matters of foreign law. The husband relied on the expertise and statements of a senior advocate of the High Courts of Pakistan and a prominent senior member of the Ahmadi community who was also a diplomat. The husband's experts contended that Pakistani Ahmadis, along with other non-Muslim minorities, can and indeed must register their marriages following a religious or customary ceremony under the provisions of Section 5 of the MFLO 1961. Interestingly, these experts not only claimed the law of Pakistan to be what it is manifestly not, but also sought to mislead the Court by reference to another Pakistani Act, the Family Courts Act of 1964. This Act applies indeed potentially to all Pakistanis, but it is merely procedural and contains no substantive provisions regarding compulsory registration of marriages by either Muslims or non-Muslims. While both these experts from the respondent's side adamantly declared the necessity for registration of marriages in Pakistan in order for them to be deemed legally valid, my position was all along that this was a positivism-infected fiction, a myth of law rather than the law itself.

It has subsequently been discovered that there was another case in Pakistan in 2010, *Riaz Javed v. Sheraz Ahmed,* where the learned judge categorically declared that the

MFLO cannot be applied to non-Muslims, including Ahmadis. Information of that case was not presented to the Court in London by the Pakistani experts, evidently for good reason – it contradicts their stance. In addition, as I had shown the Court, the case of *Allah Rakha v. Federation of Pakistan* PLD [2000] FSC 1 held clearly that unregistered Muslim marriages continue to be accepted and legally recognized by Pakistani law. If the majority population of Pakistan does not have stringent rules regarding registration of marriages, it would be safe to assume that minorities are not specifically expected to register their marriages, either. At least this is what I knew to be the situation and thus also argued in Court.

The case file itself and the lengthy proceedings made it absolutely clear that Ahmadis in Pakistan have had to develop their own methods of handling the processes of solemnizing and recording marriages for the benefit of their community members. They had no other option, it appears. This particular case thus intervened in a most dramatic way in the protracted political struggles between the Pakistani state and Ahmadis, a highly sensitive issue, to say the least.

Faced with evidence that Pakistani Ahmadis had no law in their own country, both experts for the husband bypassed the key issue of the case and claimed that Ahmadis from Pakistan would simply register their marriages once they travelled abroad to any other country. Another hidden agenda of choice of law and choice of forum appears here. Indeed, this may well have happened in many cases, but was not possible in the present case, as the marital relationship was probably already seriously strained even before the wife travelled to the UK. The argument about the need for subsequent registration of the marriage abroad raises of course questions how Pakistanis could then travel abroad in the first place as purported spouses if the marriage undertaken in Pakistan did not yet have legal validity in its own right. My pluralist reading of the evidence, thus, from a variety of angles (or corners of the kite, to be clear) provided a sound explanation also for how Ahmadi marriages in Pakistan, while not formally registered with the state, must nevertheless be religiously and legally valid, as otherwise people could simply not travel abroad on spouse visas. To take any other interpretation would also make nonsense of standard rules of private international law.

Case analysis

Analysing these particular cases further, many questions arise and multiple nuances could be identified. The focus for the present paper ought to be the position of private international law agreements and understandings and an examination of the choices that stakeholders make to use particular aspects of legal systems for their arguments. In *N v. P*, there was simply no doubt that the Hindu marriage solemnized in India had created a legally valid union and the dispute rather centres now on whether the customary divorce allegedly conducted in India some years ago means that N is now a divorced woman also for the purposes of English law. The presence of a subsequent wife creates of course intriguing complications: Surely, the English Courts could not simply throw her onto the streets of London?

In both cases, it appears that a barely hidden major purpose of such processes of seeking redress from the English courts is to secure primarily the honour and reputation of the female claimant. Both N and R suffered drastic loss of status and security as a result of the breakdown of their respective marriages. In *R v. M*, the dispute concerned the legal status of the marriage itself, but the ultimate implications for the woman concerned in the litigation are the same as for N. Tellingly, both women chose to approach the English courts, and thus the state, to protect their honour and status, not their own communities, in efforts to maintain their reputation and standing in society as an individual.

It is not that such communities do not exist, but would they be helpful to a woman? In both cases, an aspect of the case concerns allegations of sexual violence that are not the core of the proceedings, but as background facts impact on questions of trust and credibility as much as status and reputation. In choosing to embark on formal legal processes before English courts, or any foreign courts for that matter, such vulnerable women in fact risk further damage to their status and reputation, because their private sufferings enter the public arena and are then likely to be spread out, albeit in closed proceedings, but to a wider public. During the pendency of such protracted proceedings, whether in correspondence between the respective legal advisors or the actual court proceedings, all aspects of the marital relationship itself (of whatever precise status) and its troubled conditions are displayed for almost public viewing. This is certainly not desirable, as the British adversarial system, at any rate, encourages the use of deeply damaging allegations and counter allegations that are designed to be hurtful and probably constitute desperate attempts to make the other side stop pursuing the matter through the courts. In such cases, the marital relationship is regularly shown to have broken down irretrievably, often with graphic detail that may or may not be exaggerated and emotionally embellished.

This display of serious breakdown, sometimes with remarkable clarity, is then consumed with potentially almost voyeuristic involvement on all sides, making me wonder whether concerns of *izzat*, honour and status of individuals fly out of the window in such situations. An alternative reading of such distressing evidence, however, is exactly that such cases are in fact about *izzat*, and sometimes, it seems, really nothing else. Especially in cases where the immigration status of the female party is not ensured yet, however, there may also be huge implications in terms of decisions about where to live, whether to relocate to South Asia, or to what extent reliance on public funds in the UK may or may not be available. That is certainly the key issue in N's case, but not for R. What also struck me is how similar the resulting damage is for such women in comparison to contested hearings about rape claims, where the violated woman is put through harrowing processes of providing intimate details of evidence that more often than not do not assist her in coping with her agonies, but make matters worse.

Dreadfully desperate cases come one's way if one acts as an expert in such cases in the UK. It is a regular feature because of the transnational nature of the relationship concerned that one party argues that the other only came to the UK for the sake of immigration. Viciously damaging submissions are made in such contexts. Long shadows of the dreadful primary purpose phase of British immigration law appear here, and there is frequently much evidence of family force and totally inadequate processes of arranging such marital relationships. People just do not check each other out well enough while contemplating a marriage, it seems. Some readers will simply say that this is a hallmark of South Asian marriage arrangements, clearly identifying that something is wrong with them. Inadequate pre-screening seems a global predicament, though, and is not necessarily restricted to arranged marriage systems.

The particular case of *R v. M* had, however, another dimension that may be of much concern to some of us. I refer here to the wider political implications of such litigation, as the case basically concerns the legal status of an Ahmadi marriage in Pakistan. The key issue was whether there actually is something like Ahmadi law in Pakistan at all. Given that a community of possibly several million people could not really live without any law, hugely important questions fell out of the woodwork of this particular case. The official case report dares indicate the gravity of this highly explosive political scenario – provided the reader understands in the first place that there is this particular problem that many people (and certain states, coming to think of it) would rather not discuss openly, let alone in a court environment.

So one may also need to ask as an analyst why this particular litigation even went as far as it did. There were obvious efforts to stop this private mess from turning into a public disaster, but the efforts made to intervene are themselves highly indicative of how certain processes of handling the tensions of legal pluralism may and do create new legal problems. Why, in this particular reported case, should it be the woman claimant who faces excommunication and fine by her own community if it was the husband, also according to the court decision that we now have, who was the bully and the abuser? If R had given up her case, justice would clearly not have been done. An examination of the gendered characteristics of private international law would drastically change the focus of the present paper at this late stage, but this would be another absolutely important trail to follow in future work. Are state courts sufficiently aware of the potentially hostile intervention in female claimants' cases through threatening sanctions or plain non-action, as seems to be the scenario for N, whose community – both in India and in the UK – has completely let her down, reflecting thus the male-centric reactions to breakdown scenarios that blame the female spouse even when it is clear for all to see that she is a victim rather than the cause of the breakdown. Or do we still argue that Asian women are expected to put up with various forms of abuse merely to stay married? The evidence in these two cases bears closer scrutiny to support a conclusion that nobody may be ultimately entirely blameless. But then, again, this is merely a faithful reflection of the pluralities of human life.

Returning to the political issues raised by *R v. M*, if the Pakistani government tacitly acknowledges Ahmadi marriages as legally valid without openly endorsing them, does this mean that Ahmadi law is in fact part of Pakistani state law, even though this is not officially admitted? Again, the highly sensitive political nature of this litigation was made apparent in the court hearing and informs the decision rendered by Mrs. Justice Parker. Official legal systems and their necessarily political decisions thus run the risk of upsetting diplomatic relationships and causing ripples in circles far removed from the troubled spouses that triggered off the litigation in the first place. Sometimes, thus, a dispute settlement process will also be an exercize in diplomatic damage limitation.

R v. M shows that what English courts – and those of any country with an Ahmadi diaspora – need to be aware of is that some form of Ahmadi personal law is actually in place in Pakistan. Such a law evidently also upholds the validity of marriages amongst this community, confirming that marriage remains a cornerstone of society. In this regard, too, there simply cannot be a legal void for such a large community on such fundamental issues. Fortunately, Mrs. Justice Parker took the step to acknowledge this clearly in her judgement. Due to the Pakistani government's evident disinterest in this matter (which reflects similar problems for the large Hindu minority in Pakistan), this confirms my argument and suggests that Ahmadis have had no choice but to develop their own unofficial methods of dealing with family law matters such as marriage and divorce.

One might thus argue that an Ahmadi personal law has existed in Pakistan since the early 1970s when they were declared non-Muslims, but so far nothing has been written on this matter. After the issue had been raised in court, the reaction of the Pakistani expert present was that Ahmadis were simply following the law as they had done before. Such strategic myopia and stubborn refusal to acknowledge the dynamism of legal pluralist reconstruction is of course symptomatic and reflects the rather deficient and outdated state of knowledge about the themes of legal dynamism and pluralist reconstruction among South Asian lawyers.[10]

This case provides a clear example, then, of how detailed lack of knowledge on the part of English lawyers and the English judiciary about the constitutional and legal framework of South Asian countries, in this case Pakistan, can lead to potentially dire consequences for women. Fighting for her status, if nothing else, R and her family had to suffer huge costs in terms of expense and agony. N has not even got that far, since she has no financial resources to pursue her claim the way R could do. This then indicates and confirms that availability of resources crucially impacts on access to justice, but again, we know that.

If the District Judge or Mrs. Justice Parker in the High Court had decided in favour of her husband, not only would R have been left with no remedy under UK law, but she could even easily have been accused of illicit extra-marital sexual relations (*zina*) under Pakistani law by some legal crook. The issue of her status in society (*izzat*) is certainly a core aspect that cannot be overlooked. The same goes in principle for the case of N with its own culture-specific characteristics. In both cases, then, recourse to English law reflects the helplessness of the immigrant woman who cannot rely on her own family or community to obtain full justice.

Preparing the concluding analysis: Domestic courts as navigators of foreign laws

Having been chosen as a forum, domestic courts have to embark on a journey that is designed to end in resolution of the case brought to court. The kite flying symbolism of my legal model outlined above works well also here, then. But do our courts know what journey they embark on when they open their case files to prepare for hearings? Clearly, the complications raised by cross-jurisdictional cases and the choices of a particular forum demand highly developed skills, which even judges do not have when it comes to detailed matters of foreign laws. So they are in the driving seat, but can they ensure a safe journey. From this perspective, the expert becomes a co-pilot, a sort of NavSat (apparently also known as SatNav) for the Court, with judges retaining discretion to ignore the expert voice in attempts to find the right direction. Kite flyers, this confirms, do not even need a full driving licence, but a co-pilot may be required in certain situations. If there is a cacophony of voices, and the Court is faced with diametrically opposed claims, which is pretty common, I would think, detective work is in order also for our stressed judges.

The present paper has shown that when courts in overseas jurisdictions climb (or should one envisage this rather as being dragged) into the driving seat of a complex transnational legal battle, they risk rather a lot, including their own professional reputation. Faced with such grave risks, a tempting safer strategy might be to refuse to act or to reject the offer of a co-pilot. But telling a litigant to go away does not solve the problem at all.[11] Such an evasive strategy is going to be seriously damaging in the long run for maintaining the status and power of a national court system. Courts, then, to some extent, have no choice about whether to act or not. Also in multicultural and intercultural scenarios, they are being tied into the most difficult scenarios and have to make decisions that people could not find, make or agree upon in their own lives.

I was told earlier this year that Norwegian judges simply use a different method as a matter of routine, namely to pretend that there is no foreign law in existence and to decide the case entirely according to domestic rules, inspired by human rights principles. Readers who understand my kite model and can envisage this will see here recourse only to corners 3 and 4 of the kite, cutting out corners 1 and 2. The convenient but somewhat unpersuasive and remarkably plurality-unconscious argument is that the parties are in the country, the judge is a domestic authority, bound by domestic law, and so one can zoom in and sort out the cancer by shooting x-rays and domestic remedies at the dangerously lurking growth that caused the legal dispute. Such narrow-visioned procedures and dodgy insurance strategies to compensate for lack of licences and absence of driving skills when it comes to foreign laws cannot be healthy in any jurisdiction in today's globalizing world in the long run. When I put it to those judges in one of the most justice-conscious states of the world that then nobody foreign would wish to come to their courts and they would lose control – with cross-reference to the growing evidence of Muslim Arbitration Tribunals in the UK – the penny dropped superfast. In a plural society, also in white-dominated Norway, one cannot just avoid taking notice of foreign laws. That some people may not be happy about this and may do mad things as a result is something not entirely unrelated, of course, as recent events in that same country so cruelly confirmed. Again, elaborating on such connections is another issue for another paper.

Conclusions

While civil law courts are known to deliver fairly cryptic judgments, common law judges often expand on issues of socio-cultural and other relevance to the case before the court. This may then allow us deeper insights into the minds of judges and their approaches to questions of choice of jurisdiction, which I understand to be one of our focal points of interest.

A judge in any particular legal system may be somewhat reluctant to renounce or decline jurisdiction. What may happen rather more often, then, is that such an eager judge will not be able or willing to address finer points of the socio-cultural strains between the parties and will merely make a formally grounded decision in line with known and recorded state law, whether statute or precedent. We know that this can then lead to scenarios of injustice, so that new forms of equity have to step in to offer remedies and justice.[12]

In scenarios such as the present ones, where a domestic court has been asked to decide on a matter of foreign law and has of necessity got to decide such cases based on the judge's interpretation of matters of foreign law, huge additional difficulties arise. These problems can, in some cases, be solved by the involvement of experts. This paper is not, however, a somewhat self-advertising commercial, or a ploy to tout for more business. Rather, I reiterate recent findings and a growing conviction of those who are involved in this complex field that the combination of theory and practice drives us inexorably towards more use of expert evidence in matters of cross-jurisdictional law and intercultural normative navigation.

Here I have sought to emphasize also that the decision-making process concerning choice of forum is not something that could ever be fully regulated by legal intervention. To return to the starting point of this paper, in a globalizing context of superdiverse mixing of jurisdictional elements, we are always bound to find new challenges and problems that somehow never came up before. New combination and constellations of conflicts of law are bound to arise if the nomic din (a phrase borrowed from Andrew Harding) of globalized legal pluralism is intensified. However, in relation to many such cases, there is a considerable wealth of knowledge and expertise available, but it may not be readily accessible. Bottlenecks of justice may be caused here not only by lack of interest or concern, but also by lack of access to relevant information and by the limited availability of skilled kite flyers in the form of experts of foreign laws and fully trained legal professionals who know when and where to ask for additional help.

Finally, one more point, and this is not just an afterthought, but relates to the very core of this special issue. The evidence produced in this paper demonstrates and confirms for all to see that the state in the form of courts is not actually completely in charge of things, as simplistic positivism theories would suggest. More often than not, it is a kind of servient tool of the ultimate aim of ambitions – and let us not forget, official promises – to secure justice. Disputes are brought to the courts and challenge the legal system to come up with answers to questions posed by sometimes really desperate individuals. Solutions to messy scenarios brought about by the complexities of life are sought. Courts as reactive agents are challenged, quite often beyond their official capacity. This of course is why experts are sometimes urgently called for and are basically ordered to be employed for the benefit of the Court as ad hoc temporary assistants. Finding myself acting in such capacity from time to time, I know from first-hand experience the strains and stresses of that process and field of activity. One is required to follow certain formalities, is allowed to say certain things, but advised to keep strategically quiet about others. But silence is not always golden. Experts as skilled cultural and legal navigators have to constantly adjust to the micro-climate of their field of action. Maybe this is why there is so much evidence of misuse of the position of expert in cross-cultural and cross-jurisdictional cases, as the desire to be retained and make profit overrides adherence to 'the truth'. But then, pluralists know that the truth can be looked at from different perspectives and so there may be competing truths.

Regarding choice of forum, the fact that litigants and also their opponents are normally in the UK when English courts are accessed means that recourse to English law and the English forum is not really a choice. It is dictated by circumstance, by jurisdictional rules, and quite often by the complexities of today's globalized life. The resulting turbulences are illustrated by the two cases discussed here. Faced with real and perceived deficiencies in a foreign jurisdiction or normative system, will and should an English Court go as far as refusing to accept what an overseas jurisdiction does and offers? Or is the task of the Court in private international law disputes rather to act as a skilled kite flyer? Is the main challenge to navigate the competing expectations of litigant and opponent, and to avoid a crash scenario?

Notes

1. For a remarkable example, see Werner Menski (2007). Here an English County Court judge refused to deal with a claim relating to a divorce case involving Indian Hindu customary law, basically telling the litigant to go away and give up his claim, which of course did not resolve the issue.
2. See in detail my various recent writings on kite flying and the underlying model of the kite as an illustration of the dynamism within the law and the constant need to make decisions and to navigate the journey of all the kites involved. For example, see Werner Menski (2010a).
3. Ihsan Yilmaz, who wrote his much-cited 2005 PhD under my guidance, has clearly shown how this works in practice. Much earlier, David Pearl and Werner Menski (1998) provided significant evidence, too, inter alia by introducing the hybrid concept of *angrezi shariat*, British Muslim law, which is officially not supposed to exist, but has even been smuggled by dishonest governments into the formal legal structures of English law, specifically in financial matters, adoption laws and in relation to certain divorces.
4. See more recently Werner Menski (2008, 2009, 2010b).
5. See *R v. M* [2011] EWHC 2132 (Fam).
6. The only major study from Pakistan on this subject contains amazingly clear evidence of competing management strategies, so that one may imagine a kite being pulled in different directions by several strings and different kite flyers. See Muhammad Azam Chaudhary (1999).
7. See Werner Menski (2011a).
8. See the article mentioned in note 2 above and now also Werner Menski (2011b).
9. *R v. M* [2011] EWHC 2132 (Fam).

10. On the deficiencies of legal education in India, in particular, see Werner Menski (2011c).
11. See on this again the case and article mentioned in note 2 above.
12. Two examples are prominent in my mind here. Firstly, the decision in *Chief Adjudication Officer v. Kirpal Kaur Bath* [2000] 1 FLR 8 [CA] and then the unreported decision in *Ali v. Ali* in 2000, in which a Bangladeshi woman was given almost the full amount of dower (*mahr*) due to her from the divorcing husband, who had claimed that an English judge should simply ignore the *mahr* agreement as a matter of culture. For details see Werner Menski (2002).

References

Arendt, Hannah. 1958. *The Human Condition*. Chicago: University of Chicago.

Ballard, Roger. 2007. "Common Law and Common Sense: Juries, Justice and the Challenge of Ethnic Plurality." In *Law and Ethnic Plurality: Socio-Legal Perspectives*, edited by Prakash Shah, 69–105. Leiden: Brill.

Chaudhary, Muhammad Azam. 1999. *Justice in Practice. Legal Ethnography of a Pakistani Punjabi village*. Oxford: Oxford University Press.

Menski, Werner. 2002. "Immigration and Multiculturalism in Britain: New Issues in Research and Policy." *KIAPS: Bulletin of Asia-Pacific Studies XII* : 43–66.

Menski, Werner. 2007. "Dodgy Asians or Dodgy Laws? The Story of H." *Immigration, Asylum and Nationality Law* 21 (4): 284–294.

Menski, Werner. 2008. "The Uniform Civil Code Debate in Indian Law: New Developments and Changing Agenda." *German Law Journal* 9 (3): 211–250.

Menski, Werner. 2009. "Indian Secular Pluralism and its Relevance for Europe." In *Legal Practice and Cultural Diversity*, edited by Ralph Grillo, Roger Ballard, Alessandro Ferrari, André Hoekema, Marcel Maussen and Prakash Shah,. 31–48. Aldershot: Ashgate.

Menski, Werner. 2010a. "Fuzzy law and the boundaries of secularism.' December 3, 2010 *Potchefstroom Electronic Law Journal* 13 (3). Available at SSRN: http://ssrn.com/abstract = 1752910.

Menski, Werner. 2010b. "Law, State and Culture: How Countries Accommodate Religious, Cultural and Ethnic Diversity. The British and Indian Experiences." In *Cultural Diversity and the Law. State Responses from Around the* World, edited by Marie-Claire Foblets, Jean-François Gaudreault-Desbiens and Alison Dundes Renteln, 403–446. Brussels: Bruylant and Ėditions Yvon Blais.

Menski, Werner. 2011a. "Islamic law in British courts: Do we not know or do we not want to know?" In *The Place of Religion in Family Law: A Comparative Search,* edited by Jane Mair and Esin Őrűcű, 15–36. Mortsel: Intersentia.

Menski, Werner. 2011b. "Life and law: Advocacy and expert witnessing in the UK." In *Cultural expertise and litigation: Patterns, Conflicts, Narratives*, edited by Livia Holden, 151–172. London and New York: Routledge.

Menski, Werner. 2011c. "Flying Kites in a Global Sky: Teaching New Models of Jurisprudence." *Socio-Legal Review* 7: 1–22.

Pearl, David and Werner Menski. 1998. *Muslim Family Law*. London: Sweet & Maxwell.

Shah, Prakash and Derya Bayir. 2012. "The legal adaptation of British settlers in Turkey." Queen Mary School of Law Legal Studies Research Paper No. 97/2012.

Tamanaha, Brian Z. 2010. "Understanding legal pluralism: past to present, local to global." In *Legal Theory and the Social Sciences*, edited by Maksymilian Del Mar and Michael Giudice. Aldershot: Ashgate.

Yilmaz, Ihsan. 2005. *Muslim Laws, Politics and Society in Modern Nation States. Dynamic Legal Pluralisms in England, Turkey and Pakistan*. Aldershot: Ashgate.

In pursuit of the pagans: Muslim law in the English context

Prakash A. Shah

GLOCUL Centre for Law and Culture, Queen Mary, University of London, London, UK

A reconfiguration of law is taking place in the contact between Western and Muslim law. While Muslim law is itself a complex, pluralistic amalgam of different legal 'bricks,' in the context of the struggle for Islam to be acknowledged as a legitimate source of value pluralism in the Western context, the religious aspects of Muslim law, with their doctrinal justifications, are brought into sharper relief. The English case shows that customs among Muslims are suppressed in this process of 'shariatization.' Beyond that, even Muslim doctrines are being placed under the spotlight in various ways. These changes are taking place not simply because Muslims are living as non-dominant communities in Europe, where they are under the gaze of the dominant culture and seen as potential or actual violators of human rights and the rule of law. Relying on the 'dynamic of religion' as theorized by Balagangadhara (*'The heathen in his blindness...' Asia, the West, and the dynamic of religion*, 1994, Leiden, E. J. Brill), these processes are seen as outcomes of the collision between two religious cultures, the Islamic and the Western, and they tell us more about the nature of religion itself.

Introduction: the return of the pagans

There is much emphasis on religion now in Europe and elsewhere, and this is also where the minor resurgence in the academic research on unofficial law is focused. American research still seems very preoccupied by the constitutional wall of separation erected in the country's early years. While the Muslim factor is changing this somewhat (Moore 2010), the very religious freedom that was to be enjoyed behind the constitutional wall is now questioned as being impossible, constraining legal decision-makers to doing a form of protestant theology (Sullivan 2007). Although differently arranged in various European states, the freedom of religion guaranteed in, say, the European Convention of Human Rights also carries with it similar problems for legal decision-makers. European concerns with respect to religious freedom certainly have been generated by the Muslim factor but that has sparked off a competitive assertion of religious rights among others. Modood (2012, 132) points to this when he says, "Insofar as the dominant religion, Christianity, exhibits a new political assertiveness, it is primarily in reaction to the minority presence and politics and in a context of continuing decline in Christian religiosity and church membership." This brings back to European minds some of the old, and often fierce, intra-Christian struggles about religion that the Americans wanted to avoid, but also the historical hatred and fear of Muslims whose current manifestation has been given its own 'phobia.'[1]

In this scenario, with millions of Muslim immigrants and their offspring (some 18 million in 17 West European countries, about 4.5% of the population in 2010: Pew Research

Centre 2011), not yet as many as in India though (Indian Muslims number nearly 10 times that at 180 million, about 15% of the population: Pew Research Centre 2011), the legal and other apple carts were bound to be upset. Having proclaimed the "disenchantment of the world" (Gauchet 1999) or the arrival of "a secular age" (Taylor 2007), some prominent non-legal commentators have not helped much in the analysis, effectively universalizing Christian theological presuppositions and Euro-American experiences. Some European commentators now comment that the activists in the 'Arab Spring' are indicating their wish to become part of 'universal history,' reflecting a classic Eurocentric "appropriation of the multiple pasts and histories of peoples on earth within the framework of one past of one people" (Balagangadhara 1994, 56). Still, the dogma of unidirectional progress toward secularity and uniformity of law are being challenged by the large-scale presence of Muslims, and a fight-back now seems in play at many levels, most radically demonstrated by the massacre by Anders Breivik in Norway in July 2011.

For understanding the quality of contemporary intercultural and interlegal encounters between the West and its Muslim diaspora, I have drawn assistance from the work of Balagangadhara (1994) and the research program he established on the Comparative Science of Cultures (see also de Roover, Claerhout, and Balagangadhara 2011; de Roover 2011). While not yet used much within circles of legal scholarship, I have preferred Balagangadhara's work in comparison to Asad's much acclaimed account of the 'secular,' 'secularism,' and 'secularization,' which is partly useful and yet somewhat unsatisfactory (Asad 2003). In particular, Asad's discussion of European identity and the place of Muslims in relation to it is very useful, especially as he underlines the fact that European identity is very much tied up with Christianity, as is the concept of 'minority' (Asad 2003, 159–180). However, he discusses all three terms primarily in relation to 'modernity.' Asad also overlooks Balagangadhara's work, which could have provided a challenge for Asad's framework, especially as Asad does not make sufficiently clear whether he refers to the above three terms or to 'religion' (also Asad 1993) in definitional or theoretical terms.[2] Balagangadhara (1994) examines religion as a phenomenon in the world and proceeds to provide an original theory of what religion is (which Asad does not), and he shows that the distinction between 'religion' and the 'secular' is made by and within a religion. Going further, Balagangadhara shows that Western culture has experienced various phases of 'secularization,' which is one of two ways in which Christianity has spread, the other being proselytization.

Building on Balagangadhara's earlier insights, de Roover, Claerhout, and Balagangadhara (2011) have recently argued that 'secularization' can be seen as the extension of Christian ideas into the general or commonplace attitudinal framework of a society, which then function as heuristic tools (*topoi*) for the development of theories. As those ideas spread, they lose their specific and ostensible Christian character, and mix in various ways. The Christian theology that informed them moves more to the background and becomes invisible. Christian commonplace attitudes are also extended to other societies according to what is assumed to be a universal framework. While there may be a number of agencies for effecting secularization in this manner, legal mechanisms appear to provide key tools for generalizing Christian *topoi* in a secular guise. Secularized concepts within Christian theology such as the freedom of religion, secularism, and *laïcité* are encoded into legal instruments, used for building legal theories, or taken up by academics, law reformers, and others to argue for legal change.

It may be observed that such processes of secularization, despite their source in Christian teachings, also affect the status of *specific* religions, including the Christian churches and believers, because of the demand of universalization that the specific rules of any particular religion must give way to general secular rules. While secularization predates the

Reformation, Protestant critiques of Catholicism and mutual Protestant accusations of idolatry gave a major fillip to secularization (de Roover 2011, 46–51). Roy (2010, 143) refers to Protestant thinkers according to whom "secularization was not only inevitable, but positive, to the point where religion must merge with the secular; in a post-secular world values are no longer conveyed by religion in itself. In this theology of secularization the religious marker was obliterated."[3] The religious conflicts debated in European courts and other legal fora are often rooted in this dynamic and can range from banning Christian prayers at formal local authority meetings[4] and obliging Christian employees to provide official services to homosexual couples[5] to seeking the cleansing of schools of Christian insignia,[6] and so on.

Christian battles for religious rights can also be set against the prominent attention to Muslim concerns. This was recently revealed sharply in the aftermath of the lecture given at the Royal Courts of Justice in February 2008 by Dr Rowan Williams, the Archbishop of Canterbury, in which he highlighted the question of Islamic law and the prospects for the recognition of a Muslim supplementary jurisdiction within English law (Williams 2008).[7] Dr Williams' own explanation for taking this position was that it is part of the responsibility of his office to speak out on behalf of all faiths in Britain and that it is theologically right to think in pan-religious terms (Milbank 2010, 54–55).[8] Dr Williams' speech was greeted by a mixed and sometimes hostile reaction by commentators in Britain (Milbank 2010, 43–46).[9] As Roy (2010, 157–158) points out, within the Anglican Church, Dr Williams' approach was criticized by leading Asian and African bishops on the ground that it was too tolerant of Islam.[10] Governments and politicians took a somewhat backseat position and publicly distanced themselves from any institutionalization of legal pluralism, and in 2011, the British government decided not to publish a study on the operation of *shari'a* councils that had been commissioned by the Ministry of Justice under the previous Labour Government. A campaign group, One Law for All, has been particularly vocal about the negative effects of *shari'a* councils. It is dead against any formal recognition of *shari'a* principles, argues for a cessation of the councils' activities, and has supported the introduction of a Bill in the British parliament to curb the activities of *shari'a* councils.[11]

Some exceptions should also be noted. Views published in journals catering to legal practitioners were fairly moderate and even supportive in their reaction (Shah 2009, 79). Lord Phillips, now President of the UK Supreme Court, gave a widely reported lecture at the East London Muslim Centre a few weeks afterward on 3 July 2008 (Lord Phillips of Worth Matravers 2008). He ostensibly spoke in support of the Archbishop, but was rather more emphatic in highlighting the tolerant history of the United Kingdom and, in a minor passage, the possibility of religious dispute resolution subject to civil law. More recently, the British Academy's Policy Centre commissioned Prof. Maleiha Malik to write a report *Minority Legal Orders in the UK* (Malik 2012). Also, since 2008, a number of lower profile closed-session discussions have been taking place in select academic and legal practitioner circles about how to actualize any accommodation for Islamic law *within* English law. The general tenor of all these relatively milder responses has nevertheless been to advocate only a limited scope for concessions within official English law and to emphasize the possibility of *shari'a*-based dispute resolution *outside* of the official legal order. The discussions have carefully steered away from any substantial concessions to, for example, the recognition of unregistered marriages. Dr Williams' rather more open invitation therefore subsequently collapsed into a more conventional exclusion of explicit legal concessions to *shari'a*.

There is, without doubt, a multiplicity of voices taking differing positions with respect to the legal integration of Muslims in the United Kingdom. In the process, we see a number of views as to how Muslims should be positioned within the prevailing dominant legal order, and which parts of their cultures they should carry on with, transform, or reject. In this article, I want to make a number of claims with respect to unofficial dispute resolution carried on by Muslims.[12] With the English case as the main focus, I argue that a reconfiguration of unofficial law is taking place in the contact between Western and Muslim law, with two distinct elements. First, Islamic doctrines are being placed under the spotlight in various ways and pushed into conformity with the dominant Western culture. These changes are taking place where Muslims are living as nondominant communities in Europe, under the gaze of the dominant culture and judged as potential or actual violators of human rights and the rule of law. Second, taking as a given that Muslim law is itself a complex, plural amalgam of different legal 'bricks' (Menski 2006, 279–379; Hallaq 2009), I argue that in the context of the struggle for Islam to be acknowledged as a legitimate source of value pluralism in the Western context, the *religious* aspects of Muslim law, with their doctrinal justifications, are foregrounded and, conversely, that customs among Muslims are suppressed because they are seen as remnants of paganism within a religion. I refer to this process as 'shariatization.'

Relying on Balagangadhara's explanation of the 'dynamic of religion,' I present these processes as an outcome of the collision of two religious cultures, the Islamic and the Western. The image of a Huntingdonian sort of clash is inadequate because the important thing here is the manner in which the structuring of legal experience results in changes and distortions when contact is made with another religious legal culture.[13] We thus need to draw upon certain features of Christianity and Islam to explain the trajectory of Muslim law in Europe. To that end, I have picked on a key insight offered by Balagangadhara's reading of the role of the 'secular' within the West. As he explains, the 'secular,' as a theological construct, marks the absorption of the pagan world by early Christianity through the purging of the former's idolatrous practices:

> As western Christianity expanded, so did the Christian-religious world. The earlier civic, pagan world contracted and marginalised in this process. 'Idolatry', a theological concept, drew the boundaries. After having gone through purgatory and neutralised of its sin, once a practice was admitted into the Christian world, it could find a place in this world. It is thus that a 'secular' world was to emerge later, but within the Christian world. It is a Christian-secular world that came into being, as generated within a religious world. That is why the secular world is in the grips of a religious world. (Balagangadhara 1994, 444)

Coming to the contemporary picture, Balagangadhara (1994, 445) writes:

> In other words, I suggest to you, the western experience of other cultures . . . is no different from that of the early Christians. It is not called 'idolatrous', to be sure, but that is because the 'secular' world of ours is also a de-Christianised religious world.

According to this reading, Christianity preserves a space for the secular that is the realm of false, pagan religions cleansed of their idolatrous elements.[14] Customs or ancestral practices became a key battleground for the identification and elimination of idolatrous elements within a culture since the early period of Christianity.[15] With the elaboration and spread of the canon law especially after the Gregorian reforms, the effects of which have been described elaborately by Berman (1983), customs began to be subordinated to other sources of law in Christendom.[16] Modern, post-Protestant Western law takes the realm of the secular as a vastly expanded space, as reconfigured through the rhetorical arsenal of human rights and the rule of law, thereby losing its character as belonging to a specific religion, and becoming universal in character. Islam has been considered a pagan and false religion in the sense described here and its fate is to be cleansed of those elements.[17] The cleansing process continues apace, and is renewed with respect to the diasporic communities in multicultural Europe. There is consequently a recurrent struggle to identify and root out the pagan practices seen as embodiments of false religions; only that they are not now referred to as pagan, idolatrous, or false but, in secularized form, as violators of human rights, individual autonomy, gender equality, the rule of law, and so on.

Islam shares some of these tendencies of Western culture as it also conceptualizes a framework of heathendom and idolatry outside the true religion.[18] While some space is preserved for the revelation-based religious cultures – Judaism and Christianity – which are nevertheless regarded as deficient (see Waardenburg 1999, 2003), its mission is yet to cleanse all cultures of their idolatrous elements. Islam has not, however, created a realm of the secular in the way that Western Christianity identified, even though there are some undertheorized conceptual contenders for that role. In a recent contribution, An-Na'im (2008) attempts to consider the place of Islamic law in a secular state context, arguing that Muslims can, within the terms of their own doctrines, accept a secular state. With particular reference to Turkey, Indonesia, and India, An-Na'im assumes that something like a 'secular state' is intelligible to Muslims, and indeed argues that it is necessary for contemporary Muslims. However, in failing to account for the fact that the secular state emerged within Christian theology, he misses a crucial step in his argument. He does not take into account Asad's observation that words in Arabic for the 'secular' – notably *almaniyy* and *dunyawiyy* among others (as well as their derivatives) – only began to appear in lexicons from the nineteenth century with deeper Western contact, and notably in legal contexts. Although both Asad (2003, 208) and Roy (2007, ix) locate secularism within Europe and Western culture, they nevertheless suggest that such a lack is not conclusive as to whether the 'secular' or 'secularism' do not exist within Islam. Asad's and Roy's accounts suggest that they assume that the 'secular' should be intelligible to Muslims and ask to be convinced that it is not. A different position is taken by de Roover, Claerhout, and Balagangadhara (2011), who argue that Christian theology provided 'conditions of intelligibility' for ideas such as the 'secular state'; when such constructs are transplanted into a country like India, the lack of such conditions presents fundamental obstacles to their interpretation and elaboration, and they get distorted in the process.[19]

As with the examples of reconfiguration being discussed in this article, Asad links the appearance of the neologisms he identifies to a reconfiguration of legal bricks in Egypt produced by Western influence. The reconfiguration being discussed here is therefore hardly unique and has precursors elsewhere at points of Muslim and Western contact. Apart from the example of Egypt discussed by Asad, one can refer to the passing of the Muslim Personal Law (Shariat) Application Act 1937, of which Pearl and Menski (1998, 41) remark:

> We have seen that there was a desire by the religious leadership of the Muslim community to reduce the role of local, Hindu-influenced custom. As a direct result of appeals by the Muslim community, the Muslim Personal Law (Shariat) Application Act 1937 was enacted in British India in order to reduce the instances where custom would become the rule of decision.

Whether or not we agree with Asad, Roy, or An-Na'im about the intelligibility of the 'secular' within Islam, these examples demonstrate that contact between Western and Islamic ideas provokes reconfiguration in the latter. In the diasporic context, the pressure upon Muslim cultures grows in the shadow of Western culture and law. As we see, Muslims remain identified as followers of a deficient culture, their *doctrines* being liable to contestation within a dominant Western context. Even when their *practices* are opened to examination, it is done with the assumption that they are founded on an aspect of Islamic doctrine. This is consonant with the general tendency within Western culture of assuming that belief or doctrine founds practices within a culture, and that the study of a practice will yield its 'meaning.' In the process, Muslims are compelled to declare the doctrinal justifications for their practices and, where that is not possible or acceptable, are obliged to expunge their cultures of idolatrous elements embodied in customs, exacerbating a tendency that is already latent within Islam.

Aspects of Muslim legal reconstruction in diaspora

When the Archbishop of Canterbury, Dr Rowan Williams, made his speech in February 2008, it was already becoming known more widely that alternative Muslim institutional structures for dispute resolution had been operating across Britain at least since the early 1980s (Pearl and Menski 1998, 74–80; Shah 2010). Since their emergence, their work has tended to concentrate on matrimonial issues and, notably, the issuance of divorces for Muslim women (Badawi 1995; Shah-Kazemi 2001; Bano 2007). Such bodies are established according to the various segments of Islam represented in Britain, including Barelwi, Deobandhi or Salafi, Ahmadiyya,[20] and various Shia groups,[21] and are often linked to mosques that may refer questions to those bodies which mosque personnel do not feel able to handle. Not all such bodies may refer to themselves as *shari'a* councils, although that is the most generally used designation in the literature (the more popular press has tended to use *shari'a* law courts, *shari'a* courts, or Islamic courts). Some have taken on a more formalized structure with established and evolving procedures, websites, record-keeping, form-filling, and a panel of *ulema* (learned men, scholars) who can consult each other, sometimes across *maddhab* (school of law) lines, before making decisions.

Research at Cardiff University, led by Prof. Gillian Douglas, studying the procedures of case handling and decision-making by the Birmingham Shari'a Council, the London Beth Din and the Catholic Tribunal for Wales was reported in 2011 (Douglas et al. 2011). It confirms the above observations, although the findings cannot necessarily be generalized for other Muslim bodies (see, e.g., Bowen 2010). *Shari'a* councils tend to be run on a voluntary basis and charge minimal fees, especially when compared with the costs involved in going to official courts. Besides lawyers and official courts being seen as too expensive, they may also not necessarily be regarded by the clients as capable of understanding or responding to their problems. This is particularly so if a marriage is not registered or it is a case of enforcing the terms of a *nikah* (Islamic marriage contract) that the English courts do not regard as binding. Similar reasons are reported by Bunting (2009, 84–89) for Canadian Muslims opting out of official family law.

The establishment of a network known as the Muslim Arbitration Tribunal (MAT), just some months prior to Dr Williams' speech, excited some additional interest. Some reporting in the European press has mentioned that the MAT is recognized as capable of delivering *shari'a*-compliant decisions enforceable in English law,[22] while some legal scholars have also received the same impression. In a recent article, American scholars, Witte and Nichols (2010, 123), provide a similarly exaggerated reading of the accommodation of unofficial tribunals under English law:

> English courts have regularly upheld the arbitration awards of Muslim tribunals in marriage and family disputes, so long as all parties consent to participate and so long as all arbitration takes place without physical coercion or threat. The same deference is accorded to the marital arbitrations of Jewish, Christian, Hindu, and other peaceable religious authorities.

According to English law, if the parties to a dispute want to agree to a binding arbitration, it could be enforceable under the Arbitration Act 1996. This practice is already well established among the Jewish *Batei Din*, and appears to be in use among the Ahmadiyyas and Ismailis.[23] However, such agreements only apply to nonfamily disputes (the exception being inheritance[24]) and is better known in business rather than family practice. So, in fact, English law mirrors the situation in Ontario *since* its passing of the Family Statute Law Amendment Act, 2006, requiring that only family arbitration decisions that are made in accordance with Ontario and Canadian laws be enforced in courts (Bunting 2009, 80–84).[25] Meanwhile, anecdotal evidence suggests that the MAT is largely consulted on family casework, and its bid to become a hub for settling business disputes has not yet borne much fruit. In practice, therefore, in terms of the types of cases it mainly refers on to its network, it appears to be not so different to the other *shari'a* bodies. However, press and academic reporting to the effect that *shari'a* dispute resolution is now recognized in English law could be explained by the fact that the MAT's own website announces that "any determination reached by MAT can be enforced through existing means of enforcement open to normal litigants."[26]

The emergence of *shari'a* councils is seen by Menski (in Pearl and Menski 1998, 74–80) as part of the rise of *angrezi shariat*, which is a wider concept incorporating the whole range of unofficial legal practices among British Muslims, and which has even been taken note of in the British parliament.[27] Since previous demands for the official recognition of *shari'a*, made as far back as the early 1970s (Nielsen 1993), had been met with rejection by the government,

> [l]ike the communities themselves, these semi-official Muslim bodies are pursuing a strategy of operating *angrezi shariat*, aspiring for its eventual official recognition without claiming this as a definite right at the present time and lobbying vigorously for it. In other words, by the creation of social facts, a quiet process of legal restructuring is being achieved from within the community. . . . (Pearl and Menski 1998, 80)[28]

While there is little doubt that, as in Britain, elsewhere in Europe too there have been individual processes of reconstruction and adjustment, a problem that remains difficult to assess is why the pattern of institution-building has occurred in Britain to the extent that it has. A possible explanation is provided by Bowen (2010, 417–418), who distinguishes French and British postcolonial arrangements, influenced by the backdrop of their respective colonial settings. In the French case, the civil law tradition has remained influential among postcolonial North Africans.[29] The British case, notably in India but also elsewhere, was characterized by a policy of recognition of religion and personal status law, and this finds echoes in the British post-colonial diasporic context (also Rohe 2007, 93).

A possible extension of this argument can be made with respect to migrants originating in Turkey, and their descendants, who constitute a substantial proportion of the ethnic minority and Muslim population in Western Europe today. As is well known, Turkey already has a fairly long history of living with civil law in family matters, once *shari'a* was officially 'abolished,' and that may mean that *shari'a* is seen as an ethical issue to be dealt with by oneself or within one's social circle, but which one does not expect to be recognized in the courts of the state. Further, political parties in Turkey running on a platform for the resurrection of personal law have been closed down, which has probably meant a much more cautious strategy being followed by the proponents of reform along Islamic lines. The decision of the European Court of Human Rights in the *Refah Partisi case*[30] is well known and much discussed in European legal circles. It followed the closure of the political party by Turkey's Constitutional Court on the ground that the party's program of establishing a plurality of legal systems in which each group would be governed by a system in conformity with its members' religious beliefs was in conflict with the constitutional principle of secularism (*laiklik*). The less widely known case of *Fazilet Partisi*,[31] in which that party had been closed down by the Turkish Constitutional Court on the ground that it offended against the secular nature of the Turkish Constitution, was formally struck out by the European Court after the party withdrew the case alleging bias of the Court in *Refah*. Meanwhile, Rohe (2007, 93–94) has noted: "The Turkish Republic, being the state of origin of the Muslim majority in many parts of Europe completely abolished the *Shari'a* rules, and the vast majority among Turks would reject the re-introduction of such rules in European countries." Admittedly, Turkey plays a crucial role in the affairs of its European diaspora, but for other Muslim populations, politically led secularization in countries of origin may not prove to be as strong a factor.[32]

An additional explanation for why other European countries remain relatively shielded from the kind of semi-public profile of *shari'a* in Britain is provided by Rohe (2007, 19), who says:

> As it comes to the areas of family law and the law of succession, the application of legal norms in Germany and in other European countries are often determined on the basis of nationality of the persons involved rather than by their domicile. In this respect it may generally be stated that Islamic law has a strong position especially within these areas.[33]

And Rohe (2007, 19) immediately thereafter notes, "Furthermore, a powerful lobby obviously tries to preserve this area as a stronghold due to religious convictions as well as for reasons of income and exercise of power." Therefore, the maintenance, through the principles of private international law, of the rule that the law of one's nationality is to be applied in court cases, which often means a version of *shari'a*, could have meant a more diminished perception of the necessity for *shari'a* fora than in Britain. In that sense, the assumptions of courts in many continental European countries may effectively be more legally pluralistic than the British application of the *lex loci* or the Swiss application of the law of residence.[34] As Rohe (2007, 115) notes further, "the application of Islamic family law – within the limits of public policy – has become everyday business in German courts." I do not mean to suggest that there are no other considerations playing on the minds of European judges to avoid the application of *shari'a* or other 'foreign' rules. In fact, European courts regularly have recourse to rules of public policy/*ordre public*, e.g., to avoid recognizing the effects of the *talaq* (unilateral Islamic divorce issued by a man: Fulchiron (2010) for France; Rohe (2007, 115–125) for Germany). Since the 1970s, British private international law rules have also moved steadily to prevent reliance on overseas laws (Pearl and Menski 1998, 86–104), often creating havoc for the recognition of transnational family relations with confusions among lawyers, judges, and the individuals caught up between laws (e.g. Menski 2011; Shah 2011).

Pursuing the pagans

The formal gap between *shari'a* fora, and *shari'a* principles in general, on the one hand, and English law, on the other, does not mean that there is no interaction and mutual accommodation in practice. The resulting complexity defies easy theorization. Aina Khan, a London-based solicitor specializing in advising Muslim clients on family law issues, suggests some measure of success in getting courts to enforce *mahr* agreements, and this is the kind of claim that the official courts might find even more difficult to resist in future, given that the UK Supreme Court has accepted that pre- and postnuptial contracts are enforceable.[35] A further gap opens up, however, when marriages are not registered officially and the courts do not want to generously apply the presumption of marriage to afford recognition to such marriages, with a wide range of potential implications.[36] As noted, it is in such kinds of cases where the practice of *shari'a* councils comes into its own; unwittingly or otherwise, English law has been ceding ground to Muslim fora in such cases. At the same time, subtle and not so subtle processes of reform are taking place to bring Muslim law and dispute resolution fora within the framework of 'secular' English law. We can take two examples of such processes to illustrate the ways in which reform through secularization takes place. The first instance is a more explicit process of reform taking place through 'external' legislative proposals aimed directly at curbing the activities of *shari'a* councils so that they cannot operate without heed to Western secular law and its principles. The other could be described as 'internal' reform but instigated under the influence of Western secular law and its principles.

An important recent development is the proposal to legislate against certain activities of *shari'a* councils and similar bodies by the introduction of a Private Member's Bill by Baroness Cox in the House of Lords. The Arbitration and Mediation Services (Equality) Bill had its second reading in the House of Lords on 19 October 2012. As is the fate of many private members Bills, it may not eventually pass into legislation. Although the title of the Bill is not specific to *shari'a*, the fact that *shari'a* councils, the MAT, and similar bodies are the targets of such legislation is evident from the surrounding debates and public statements made on behalf of those who support the Bill, including members of the campaign groups One Law for All and the National Secular Society, as well as by Baroness Cox.[37] Among the things the Bill seeks to do is to amend the Equality Act 2010 (general antidiscrimination legislation) so as to make unlawful, in the provision of arbitration services, discrimination, harassment, or victimization on grounds of sex, and it includes within that

(a) treating the evidence of a man as worth more than the evidence of a woman, or vice versa,
(b) proceeding on the assumption that the division of an estate between male and female children on intestacy must be unequal, or
(c) proceeding on the assumption that a woman has fewer property rights than a man, or vice versa.

Another relevant provision of the Bill, seeking to amend the Arbitration Act 1996 with respect to similar concerns, states that:

> No part of an arbitration agreement or process shall expressly or implicitly provide –
>
> (a) that the evidence of a man is worth more than the evidence of a woman, or vice versa,
> (b) that the division of an estate between male and female children on intestacy must be unequal,
> (c) that women should have fewer property rights than men, or vice versa, or
> (d) for any other term that constitutes discrimination on the grounds of sex.

The Bill also aims at making it a criminal offence where a person "(a) falsely purports to be exercising a judicial function or to be able to make legally binding rulings, or

(b) otherwise falsely purports to adjudicate on any matter which that person knows or ought to know is within the jurisdiction of the criminal or family courts."

These provisions amply demonstrate that the target is *shari'a*-based dispute resolution now widely practiced in the United Kingdom, and covers any dispute resolution conducted under the Arbitration Act 1996. If it is passed into law, *shari'a* councils will be subject to legal action on the basis that they have breached one or another provision (of which the above are illustrations) of the legislation. It could bear down further on their activities or drive them out altogether, which seems to be the intended aim of at least some of the proponents of the legislation. At a broader level, this development signals the fact that while *shari'a* dispute resolution takes place in parallel to the framework of the official English law, there is further pressure to bring English law to bear upon it. The kind of step we see in the Bill is far from being a unique development in Western legal systems. Mention has been made of the Ontario legislation passed in 2006 that sought to remove official imprimatur from family arbitrations which were based on religious law. In Oklahoma, an initiative seeking to amend that state's constitution stated in part: "The courts shall not look to the legal precepts of other nations or cultures. Specifically, the courts shall not consider international law or Sharia Law." On 10 January 2012, a Federal Appeals Court concluded that by singling out Islam for unfavorable treatment in state courts, the law was likely to violate the Establishment Clause of the First Amendment, and it upheld a preliminary injunction against the bringing into force of the amendment.[38] The Oklahoma initiative is, however, part of a wider campaign also being pursued in several other states to prevent *shari'a* rules from being considered by courts in the United States.[39] Although these efforts by countries in the 'Anglosphere' limit *shari'a* from being invoked within official legal contexts, they cannot eliminate the existence of Muslim law or disputes about it altogether. As Balagangadhara (1994, 371–373) shows, the transmission of world views, which are best exemplified by religions, requires doctrinal and organizational authorities to constrain such transmission and to resolve interpretive disputes. Indeed, the efforts in these countries could be interpreted as countermeasures designed to preserve the domain of 'secular' Western law in the manner Balagangadhara describes, also seeking to constrain transmission and limit interpretive possibilities.

The Arbitration and Mediation Services (Equality) Bill is notable in the present context because of the manner in which it attempts to reform or eliminate *shari'a* dispute resolution practices. It is like the Ontario and Oklahoma legislation in that it attempts to do away with practices that do not conform to principles upheld within Western jurisprudence generally or upheld within a particular Western country. However, it is notable how the proponents of the legislation do not appear very much interested in the details of the practice within *shari'a* councils, and to the extent that they are, their various statements and publications usually provide stereotyped impressions of practice.[40] Rather, a reading of the Bill demonstrates that it is concerned primarily with making practices unlawful in so far as they are assumed to be founded on offending principles. Typically, it is presupposed that (religious) principles, and the beliefs to which they give rise, provide a foundation to practices. The 'battleground,' so to speak, shifts very much to principles, while practice shifts to the background: English courts therefore may routinely grant residence orders to mothers, but since they are presumed to act on the basis of legal equality or the best interests of the child principles, the practice is not regarded as morally deficient. Among the other effects the pressure generated by such (semi-) official nudging has is to persuade Muslims to abjure from endorsing those very same principles on the grounds that they are 'not Islamic,' to attribute errant practices to ignorance and a lack of Islamic education, and to advocate reform of those practices.[41]

Another illustration of the reconfiguration occurring within Muslim law in England, and one that more sharply illustrates the marginalization of custom and practice within Muslim communities, is provided by the case of *Uddin v. Choudhury*.[42] This case reached the Court of Appeal from the Islamic Shariah Council, in Leyton, East London, via the county court. It concerned a very short-lived unregistered and unconsummated marriage between two British Bangladeshis. The groom's father wanted back mainly some jewellery said to be worth over £25,500 that the bride and her mother had taken from the groom's family. The *shari'a* council dissolved the marriage at the instigation of the bride. The groom had agreed to the *shari'a* council being asked to do so on the condition that the jewellery and portion of the *mahr* (dower) already paid be returned, although the bride claimed that none of the promised £15,000 *mahr* had been paid. But the *shari'a* council made no decision as to the return of either. Then, at the county court, a single joint expert, Faiz ul Aqtab Siddiqi, one of the scholars behind the establishment of the MAT (also an English barrister), was appointed by the court to advise on the position in *shari'a* law, but significantly not on the customary practices followed in the community of the parties. Sheikh Siddiqi stated, and the court accepted, that unless mentioned in the contract, the gifts were just that – gifts – and, further, that the *mahr* was due, given that the marriage had been broken off at the groom's instigation. The court ruled that the contract was enforceable and that the wife was also due *mahr* of £15,000. When the groom's father, representing himself, applied to the Court of Appeal for permission to appeal and an extension of time for preparation, the court refused and said that it accepted the county court's findings.

For present purposes, an important feature is that the proceedings went ahead on the assumption, at least on the part of the bride, the *shari'a* council, and the expert, Sheikh Siddiqi, that the principles of *shari'a* were applicable and, conversely, that customary practices and understandings were of no relevance. Bowen (2010, 430) cites an interview with Sheikh Siddiqi where the latter states, "*Nikah* is a contract and should be entered into through education and not based on cultural background, for example on Pakistani or Indian ideas." The *Uddin* case therefore illustrates a more or less consistent thread running through the discourse around Muslim law – the prioritization of the doctrines of *shari'a* and, conversely, the marginalization of or lack of attention to customary practices and conventional understandings. One could take the view of the conduct of the legal proceedings that at least the *nikahnama* (or *kabinama*, a written marriage contract) was given effect by the courts. Marriage is, after all, understood as a contractual arrangement in Islamic law and that sits well with a Western 'secular' understanding of contract. On such a reading, one may say that there is a 'conversion' of the Islamic norm to the Western norm on the basis of similitude.[43] On a different reading, however, it could be said that the wife's family were unjustly enriched by having gone through a short, unconsummated marriage, but how can such arguments obtain a fair hearing in the current trend to *shariatization* in the context of flirtation between official law and British Muslim law? What has happened to custom, *adat*, *riwaj*, and *urf*?[44]

The relative lack of academic analysis of the fate of this type of unofficial law (see however Ballard (2006) strongly arguing for the importance of custom) typifies other discussions of Muslim legalities, whether we are speaking of a rethinking of Muslim law with respect to recent initiatives to provide *fatwa* guidance to European Muslims (Rohe 2007, 137–165; Caeiro 2010) or the manner in which inter-*maddhab* surfing occurs in cyberspace (Yilmaz 2005b; Ali 2010). Part of the reason may lie in the rather reluctant manner in which Islamic jurisprudence has historically acknowledged custom (Libson 1997). As Roy (2010, 29) puts it: "In Islam, the existence of the secular is illustrated by the autonomy of politics and of customary law, even if legal scholars tend to deny or restrict this autonomy which they are forced nevertheless to accept . . ."[45] However, in addition to this limited theoretical recognition of custom within Islam, there is also the, often implicit, assumption in Western contexts that Muslim law is governed by texts, the doctrines they contain, and the beliefs based on them, all of which are assumed to found practices. As many Muslims are also no doubt tempted to theorize, therefore, practices are (or should be) a reflection of (religious) belief and do not stand on their own ground. The Western approach, shaped and honed by Christian anthropology, endorses and pushes this attitude further by encouraging the identification and elimination of practices *implicitly* considered pagan from within a Muslim culture.[46] On a wider canvass, while this case can also be seen as benchmarking the struggle among Muslims in Western societies, which extends to the legal sphere, about working out the ethics of being a Muslim (Ramadan 1999, 2008), we can underline the fact that in this struggle, elevating the doctrinal elements of Islam tends to have the effect of suffocating an understanding of other legal elements.

Concluding remarks

The evidence discussed here, primarily in relation to the English case, bears out the merits of assessing the realm of unofficial law as introduced by diasporic minorities in Europe with reference to the pervasive cognitive influence of the Western Christian heritage. Secularization has entailed the spreading of Christian theological concepts and attitudes into the common sense of European (and North American) societies and legal orders. Within Western legal systems, non-Western cultures are resultantly viewed through a secularized form of the older distinction based on true and false religion and the secular. The identification of false, 'pagan' practices is therefore now done implicitly, before they are admitted as acceptable to the realm of secular Western law. The case of Muslim law in England demonstrates that this dynamic provokes an internal reconfiguration of legal bricks under the gaze of Western culture and law. This results in the suffocation or marginalization of custom, which is regarded as something that should be specifically cleansed of idolatry. Meanwhile, doctrinal elements come to the fore and claim a space that they may not otherwise have had. These combined processes have been referred to here as 'shariatization,' an exacerbation of the inherent priority given within Islamic law theory to doctrine. The processes described in this article therefore point to the nature of religions in their legal aspects and what occurs to the structuring of legal experience when two religious cultures meet. That there is a situation of legal pluralism seems like a trivial observation in this context. Rather more important to understanding is the kind of restructuring of legal experience that is introduced such that practice is increasingly justified by doctrine, even as doctrines come under criticism from the dominant legal order. More work certainly needs to be done to study under what conditions and in what directions such restructuring and distortion occurs.

Acknowledgements

The research leading to this article was performed within the framework of the RELIGARE project. This project received funding from the European Commission Seventh Framework Programme (FP7/2007–2013) under grant agreement number 244635. The views expressed during the execution of the RELIGARE project, in whatever form and or by whatever medium, are the sole responsibility of the author. The European Union is not liable for any use that may be made of the information contained therein.

Notes

1. Among the rising number of publications on 'Islamophobia,' see Runnymede Trust (1997), Gottschalk and Greenberg (2008), Allen (2010), and Sayyid and Vakil (2010).
2. I make no claim that the shortcomings in Asad's account, evident after a reading of Balagangadhara's work, are unique. However, I highlight Asad's work because it was referred to me by several interlocutors, including one of the referees of this article, who held it up as "one of the best contributions to this topic." Frustratingly, in an otherwise important account, Roy (in particular, 2007) refers to neither Asad nor Balagangadhara.
3. Specifically, Roy cites Friedrich Schleiermacher, Dietrich Bonheoffer, and Harvey Cox.
4. *R (on the application of the National Secular Society and another) v. Bideford Town Council* [2012] EWHC 175 (Admin), where a local authority was found to have been acting *ultra vires* when prayers were said as an integral part of the formal meetings of the council.
5. Inter alia, *Lillian Ladele and Gary McFarlane v the United Kingdom*, application nos. 51671/10 and 36516/10, judgment of 15 January 2013.
6. *Case of Lautsi and Others v. Italy*, application no. 30814/06, judgment of 18 March 2011.
7. Dr Williams thereby opened a series of lectures on 'Islam and English Law' mounted by the Temple Church and the School of Oriental and African Studies, University of London.
8. On interfaith respect supported by the Church of England, see Modood (2012, 138–139), who also notes that "local and national consultations with Muslim groups have continued to grow and probably now exceed consultations with any Christian body and certainly any minority group. Inevitably, this has caused occasional friction between Christians and Muslims" (138–139).
9. In a good-natured response to his critics, the Archbishop subsequently gave an explanation before the General Synod of the Church, paraphrasing Ronald Knox with the opening remarks: "The prevailing attitude . . . was one of heavy disagreement with a number of things which the [speaker] had not said!" See for transcript and video, Presidential Address to the Opening of General Synod, 11 February 2008, http://www.archbishopofcanterbury.org/articles.php/1326/presidential-address-to-the-opening-of-general-synod-february-2008 (accessed July 24, 2012).
10. Roy (2010, 157–158) interestingly links these responses to a discussion of 'inculturation,' about which there are also hard and soft positions within the churches, the more hard-line views arguing against the approach because of its invitation to paganism.
11. The group's website www.onelawforall.org.uk provides more information and the criticisms made by the group can also be read in their report, One Law for All (2010). Interestingly, the group's name reflects a secularized version of the biblical injunction in Leviticus 24:22 (twenty-first-century King James' version): "Ye shall have one manner of law, as well for the stranger as for one of your own country; for I am the LORD your God."
12. In earlier drafts of this article, I had used the terminology of 'nonstate law' but have replaced it with the term 'unofficial' as used by Chiba (1986, 6): as "that legal system not officially sanctioned by any legitimate authority, but sanctioned in practice by the general consensus of a certain circle of people, whether within or beyond the bounds of a country." The reason for this change is that the notion of 'state law,' and therefore 'nonstate law,' seems rather more culture specific, and see also note 19 herein.
13. It is also important to note that according to Balagangadhara (1994), maximally, the Semitic religions are what religions are, and Asian cultures do not have religion.
14. For a brief description of Christian positions on 'culture' and, in particular, pagan culture, see McGrath (2011, 115–118). He notes at page 115: "A study of church history strongly suggests that the Christian church is engaged in a perennial struggle to clarify its relationship with culture." For a sustained discussion of the contemporary tensions experienced within religions because of culture, see Roy (2010).
15. See Balagangadhara (1994, 31–53) on the debate in Rome among Christians, Jews, and pagans on the necessity, insisted upon by Christians, of providing justification for ancestral practices. This was an early demonstration of the way in which Christianity had begun to frame practices as expressing or embodying the beliefs that human beings entertain and how paganism became an expression of a set of false or corrupt beliefs. This rehearsal was then re-enacted against Catholics by Protestants, who charged the former with idolatry. The argument continues today.
16. See, specifically, Berman (1983, 112–113) on the effect of the Gregorian reforms of the eleventh century: "Faced with an obnoxious custom, the Gregorian reformers would appeal over it to truth, quoting the aphorism of Tertullian and St. Cyprian, Christ said, 'I am the truth.' He

did not say 'I am the custom.'" Further, see especially his account (144–145) of the work of Gratian and his fellow canonists and the authority they assigned to natural law, as found in reason and conscience, over custom. See similarly Brague (2007, 219).

17. This statement is of course a broad-brush characterization of the view of Islam in Western Christian discourse. In the period of the Crusades, when Western Christians were learning more about Islam, Muslims were often referred to as pagans, i.e., the unbaptized (Hamilton 1997). Later, characterizations of Islam changed somewhat. Masuzawa (2005, 59) writes: "Thus four seemingly well-marked categories – Christianity, Judaism, Mohammedanism, idolatry (or heathenism, paganism, or polytheism) – recur in book after book with little variation from at least the seventeenth century up to the first half of the nineteenth century." For a summary of Christian approaches to other religions generally, see McGrath (2011, 435–443).
18. In striking parallels to how Christian theologians thought, medieval Muslim comparativists, reflecting on knowledge of Indian and other traditions, took the view that pagans had 'deviated' from the true religion and practiced idolatry, also placing much emphasis on the distinction between book and nonbook traditions (Lawrence 1976, Latief 2006). See also Alam (2004) on the status of pagans under theories of *shari'a*.
19. Admittedly, the discussion here does not take into account the views of well-studied 'Islamists' like Sayyid Qutb and Mawdudi who saw secularization as a means of Westernization that had to be resisted as an enemy of Islam (Waardenburg 2003, 251–254). Also, we should take note of the observation by Schmitt (1985 [1922]), articulated in the first quarter of the twentieth century: "All significant concepts of the modern theory of the state are secularized theological concepts not only because of their historical development – in which they were transferred from theology to the theory of the state, whereby, for example, the omnipotent God became the omnipotent lawgiver – but also because of their systematic structure, the recognition of which is necessary for a sociological consideration of these concepts." From this perspective, it would seem impossible for devout Muslims to accept the idea of the secular state, as they could not accept the secularized vision of sovereignty that is so widely accepted in the West.
20. See the case, *Bhatti v. Bhatti* [2009] EWHC 3506 (Ch) for a reported instance of the Ahmadiyya dispute resolution mechanism, which has a transnational dimension linking Pakistan and the United Kingdom. Ahmadiyyas are regarded by other Muslims groups as being outside the fold of Islam and being an Ahmadiyya is unlawful in many Muslim-dominated countries.
21. *Jivraj v Hashwani* [2011] UKSC 40 is a case involving the Ismaili Conciliation and Arbitration Boards, which also have a transnational dimension. The case of Masuma Jariwala discussed in the House of Commons, 10 June 2009, cols. 255WH-261WH, concerned the Shia Dawoodi Bohra community where a former husband apparently withheld the pronouncement of *talaq* (divorce) for some 14 years after they had been divorced officially, while the leaders of that Bohra community could not do anything about it. The case shows that the general appeal to *shari'a* councils for the issuance of Islamic divorces does not hold in all cases.
22. See, e.g., Katja Gelinsky, 'Deutsche Gerichte wenden die Scharia an,' *Frankfrter Allgemeine*, 29 December 2012, who notes, "The arbitrations of MAT are enforceable in court, unlike the decisions of the informal Sharia councils, which conduct mediations on Islamic marriage contracts or settle family disputes." Translation by this writer. For another case of misreporting, see, Abul Taher, 'Revealed: UK's first official sharia courts,' *The Sunday Times*, September 14, 2008.
23. See *Bhatti v. Bhatti* [2009] EWHC 3506 (Ch) (for Ahmadiyyas) and *Jivraj v Hashwani* [2011] UKSC 40 (for Ismailis).
24. *Al-Midani v. Al-Midani* [1999] C.L.C 904, [1999] 1 Lloyd's Rep. 923 concerning what was described by the judge as the division of the deceased's 'great estate.'
25. In detail, see Korteweg and Selby (2012).
26. http://www.matribunal.com/ (accessed November 10, 2012).
27. See Lord Lester, House of Lords Debates, 30 June 2000, cols. 1246–1247.
28. Ahmad Hajj Thomson, a barrister, is quoted (in Ameli et al 2006, 81) as saying: "In fact the various UK Shari'a Councils are the precursors of what will eventually become Shari'a courts, insh'Allah – but they need to be improved and unified."
29. In nineteenth-century colonial Algeria, French citizenship became linked with giving up claims on Islamic jurisdiction. In other words, claims to live under Islamic personal law and citizenship were regarded as incompatible. On the colonial backdrop in Algeria, see Brett (1988).

30. *Refah Partisi (Welfare Party) and others v Turkey*, application nos. 41340/98, 41342/98, 41343/98 and 41344/98, judgment of 13 February 2003.
31. *Fazilet Partisi and anor v Turkey* [2006] ECtHR 488, application no. 1444/02, 27 April 2006.
32. For the contrasting socio-legal developments in Turkey, Pakistan, and England, see Yilmaz (2005a).
33. See, similarly, Rohe (2007, 90) and Büchler (2011, 27–34).
34. The Archbishop's message for the closer examination of a possible accommodation of *shari'a* in English law was echoed by social anthropologist Christian Giordano at the University of Fribourg, who argued for the official acknowledgment of legal pluralism. See http://www.swissinfo.ch/eng/politics/Theres_no_place_for_Sharia_in_Switzerland.html?cid=7147982 (accessed November 10, 2012).
35. *Radmacher v. Granatino* [2010] UKSC 42.
36. For example, *AAA v ASH* [2009] EWHC 636 (Fam), involving a father's loss of child custody. As with some others, this case also illustrates that men can suffer a gender penalty in official legal contexts and that could also be part of the explanation for the numerical significance of unregistered marriages as a way of de-linking from official English law. For a recent judicial confirmation that Islamic marriages taking place in England without registration are 'nonmarriages,' see *El Gamal v. HRH Sheikh Ahmed Bin Saeed al-Maktoum* [2011] EWHC B27 (Fam).
37. For audio links or the texts of speeches given at one such interesting debate held at the Houses of Parliament on 28 June 2011, see http://www.onelawforall.org.uk/successful-debate-on-sharia-law-in-britain-at-house-of-commons/. See also the debate in the second reading of the Bill, House of Lords Debates, 19 October 2012, cols. 1682–1715, and for the televised version: http://www.parliamentlive.tv/Main/Player.aspx?meetingId=11486&st=12:01:30.
38. *Muneer Awad v. Paul Ziriax, Oklahoma State Board of Elections, et al.* 670 F.3d 1111; 2012 U.S. App. LEXIS 475; see http://journalrecord.com/23rd-and-Lincoln/files/2012/01/Awad10thcir011012.pdf (accessed November 17, 2012).
39. See Elsayed (forthcoming) for a breakdown of the types of enactments in different US jurisdictions that seek to prevent reliance on *shari'a* rules.
40. A report, MacEoin (2009), published by the think-tank Civitas preceded the Bill. It is widely cited in the context of discussions about the Bill. Using questionable methodology, it reported on examples of unacceptable practice from the allegedly 85 or more *sharia* courts in the United Kingdom. The press release accompanying the report states: "sharia courts operating in Britain may be handing down rulings that are inappropriate to this country because they are linked to elements in Islamic law that are seriously out of step with trends in Western legislation that derive from the values of the Enlightenment and are inherent in modern codes of human rights." See http://www.civitas.org.uk/press/prcs91.php (accessed November 17, 2012).
41. See Glenn (2010, 224–225) summarizing such 'reformed' arguments used by Muslims.
42. [2009] EWCA Civ 1205; see also Bowen (2010).
43. Using many examples of cases on dower, Fournier (2010) sees such conversions as forms of distortion by Western law.
44. See further the fascinating evidence produced by Bowen (2010, 430–433) on custom (*urf*) in the context of marriage gifts and *shari'a* council decision-making, again demonstrating the ambiguity toward custom among *ulema* in Britain.
45. Glenn (2010, 212–213) describes custom as 'tolerated' and as not being an independent source of Islamic law.
46. I follow de Roover (2011) here in his suggestion that a secularized counterpart to the mechanism filtering idolatry was developed in the post-Reformation period and *implicitly* applied, as he shows, to reform Hindu law in the colonial period.

References

Alam, Muzaffar. 2004. *The languages of political Islam: India 1200–1800*. Chicago, IL: University of Chicago Press.

Ali, Shaheen S. 2010. Cyberspace as emerging Muslim discursive space? Online *fatawa* on women and gender relations and its impact on Muslim family law norms. *International Journal of Law, Policy and the Family* 24: 338–60.

Allen, Christopher. 2010. *Islamophobia*. Farnham: Ashgate.

Ameli, Saied R., Beena Faridi, Karin Lindahl, and Arzu Merali. 2006. *Law & British Muslims: Domination of the majority or process of balance*? London: Islamic Human Rights Commission.

An-Na'im, Abdullahi. 2008. *Islam and the secular state: Negotiating the future of Shari`a*. Cambridge, MA: Harvard University Press.

Asad, Talal. 1993. *Genealogies of religion: Discipline and reasons of power in Christianity and Islam*. Baltimore, MD: Johns Hopkins University Press.

Asad, Talal. 2003. *Formations of the secular: Christianity, Islam, modernity*. Stanford, CA: Stanford University Press.

Badawi, Zaki. 1995. Muslim justice in a secular state. In *God's law versus state law*, ed. M. King, 73–80. London: Grey Seal.

Balagangadhara, S.N. 1994. '*The heathen in his blindness...' Asia, the West, and the dynamic of religion*. Leiden: E. J. Brill.

Ballard, Roger. 2006. Ethnic diversity and the delivery of justice: The challenge of plurality. In *Migration, diasporas and legal systems in Europe*, ed. P. Shah and W.F. Menski, 29–56. London: Routledge-Cavendish.

Bano, Samia. 2007. Muslim family justice and human rights: The experience of British Muslim women. *Journal of Comparative Law* 2: 38–67.

Berman, Harold J. 1983. *Law and revolution: The formation of the western legal tradition*. Cambridge, MA: Harvard University Press.

Bowen, John R. 2010. How could English courts recognize Shariah? *University of St. Thomas Law Journal* 7: 411–35.

Brague, Remi. 2007. *The law of god: The philosophical history of an idea*. Trans. L.G. Cochrane. Chicago, IL: University of Chicago Press.

Brett, Michael. 1988. Legislating for inequality in Algeria. *Bulletin of the School of Oriental and African Studies* 51, no. 3: 440–61.

Bunting, Annie. 2009. Family law's legal pluralism: Private 'opting-out' in Canada and South Africa. In *Multijuralism: Manifestations, causes, and consequences*, ed. A. Breton, A.D. Ormeaux, K. Pistor and P. Salmon, 77–97. Farnham: Ashgate.

Büchler, Andrea. 2011. *Islamic law in Europe? Legal pluralism and its limits in European family laws*. Farnham: Ashgate.

Caeiro, Alexandre. 2010. The power of European fatwas: The minority fiqh project and the making of an Islamic counterpublic. *International Journal of Middle East Studies* 42: 435–49.

Chiba, Masaji, ed. 1986. *Asian indigenous law in interaction with received law*. London: KPI.

de Roover, Jakob. 2011. Secular law and the realm of false religion. In *After secular law*, ed. W.F. Sullivan, R.A. Yelle, and M. Tausig-Rubbo, 43–61. Stanford: Stanford University Press.

de Roover, Jakob, Sarah Claerhout, and S.N. Balagangadhara 2011. Liberal political theory and the cultural migration of ideas: The case of secularism in India. *Political Theory* 39: 571–99.

Douglas, Gillian, Norman Doe, Sophie Gilliat-Ray, Russell Sandberg, and Asma Khan. 2011. *Social cohesion and civil law: Marriage, divorce and religious courts: Report of a research study funded by the AHRC*. Cardiff: Cardiff Law School. Available at http://www.law.cf.ac.uk/clr/Social%20Cohesion%20and%20Civil%20Law%20Full%20Report.pdf (accessed February 1, 2013).

Elsayed, Muhammad. Forthcoming. Contracting into religious law: Anti-Sharia enactments and the free exercise clause. *George Mason Law Review* 20, no. 3.

Fournier, Pascale. 2010. *Muslim marriage in western courts: Lost in transplantation*. Farnham: Ashgate.

Fulchiron, Hugues. 2010. The French family judge encounters cultural pluralism. In *Cultural diversity and the law: State responses from around the world*, ed. M.C. Foblets, J.F. Gaudreault-DesBiens, and A.D. Renteln, 613–33. Brussels: Bruylant.

Gauchet, Marcel. 1999. *The disenchantment of the world: A political history of religion*. Princeton, NJ: Princeton University Press.

Glenn, H. Patrick. 2010. *Legal traditions of the world*, 4th ed. Oxford: Oxford University Press.

Gottschalk, Peter, and Gabriel Greenburg. 2008. *Islamophobia: Making Muslims the enemy*. Lanham, MD: Rowman and Littlefield.

Hallaq, Wael B. 2009. *Shari'a: Theory, practice, transformations*. Cambridge: Cambridge University Press.

Hamilton, Bernard. 1997. Knowing the enemy: Western understanding of Islam at the time of the Crusades. *Journal of the Royal Asiatic Society* 7: 373–87.

Korteweg, Anna C., and Jennifer A. Selby, eds. 2012. *Debating sharia: Islam, gender politics and family law arbitration*. Toronto: University of Toronto Press.

Latief, Hilman. 2006. Comparative religion in medieval Muslim literature. *American Journal of Islamic Social Sciences* 23: 28–62.

Lawrence, Bruce B. 1976. *Shahrastānī on the Indian religions*. The Hague: Mouton.

Libson, Gideon. 1997. On the development of custom as a source of law in Islamic law. *Islamic Law and Society* 4: 131–55.

Maceoin, Dennis. 2009. *Sharia law or "One Law For All"*? London: Civitas.

Malik, Maleiha. 2012. *Minority legal orders in the UK: Minorities, pluralism and the law*. London: British Academy Policy Centre.

Masuzawa, Tomoko. 2005. *The invention of world religions or, how European universalism was preserved in the language of pluralism*. Chicago, IL: University of Chicago Press.

Mcgrath, Alister. 2011. *Christian theology: An introduction*, 5th ed. Oxford: Wiley-Blackwell.

Menski, Werner. 2006. *Comparative law in a global context, the legal systems of Asia and Africa*, 2nd ed. Cambridge: Cambridge University Press.

Menski, Werner. 2011. Life and law: Advocacy and expert witnessing in the UK. In *Cultural expertise and litigation: Patterns, conflicts, narratives*, ed. L. Holden, 151–71. London: Routledge.

Milbank, John. 2010. The archbishop of Canterbury: The man and the theology behind the Shari'a lecture. In *Shari'a in the West*, ed. R. Ahdar and N. Aroney, 43–57. Oxford: Oxford University Press.

Modood, Tariq. 2012. Is there a crisis of secularism in Western Europe? *Sociology of Religion* 73: 130–49.

Moore, Kathleen M. 2010. *The unfamiliar abode: Islamic law in the United States and Britain*. Oxford: Oxford University Press.

Nielsen, Jorgen S. 1993. *Emerging claims of Muslim populations in matters of family law in Europe*. Birmingham: Centre for the Study of Islam and Christian-Muslim Relations.

One Law For All. 2010. *Sharia law in Britain: A threat to One Law for All and Equal Rights*. London: One Law for All. http://www.onelawforall.org.uk/new-report-sharia-law-in-britain-a-threat-to-one-law-for-all-and-equal-rights/ (accessed January 31, 2013).

Pearl, David, and Werner Menski. 1998. *Muslim family law*. London: Sweet & Maxwell.

Pew Research Centre. 2011. *The future of the global Muslim population: Projections for 2010–2030*. Washington, DC: Pew Forum on Religion and Public Life. http://pewforum.org/uploadedFiles/Topics/Religious_Affiliation/Muslim/FutureGlobalMuslimPopulation-WebPDF-Feb10.pdf (accessed March 14, 2013).

Lord Phillips of Worth Matravers. 2008. Equality before the law. Speech at the East London Muslim Centre, 3 July. Available at http://www.judiciary.gov.uk/Resources/JCO/Documents/Speeches/lcj_equality_before_the_law_030708.pdf (accessed January 31, 2013).

Ramadan, Tariq. 1999. *To be a European Muslim*. Markfield, Leicestershire: The Islamic Foundation.

Ramadan, Tariq. 2008. *Radical reform: Islamic ethics and liberation*. New York: Oxford University Press.

Rohe, Mathias. 2007. *Muslim minorities and the law in Europe: Chances and challenges*. New Delhi: Global Media Publications.

Roy, Olivier. 2007. *Secularism confronts Islam*. Trans. G. Holoch. New York: Columbia University Press.

Roy, Olivier. 2010. *Holy ignorance: When religion and culture part ways*. Trans. R. Schwartz. London: C. Hurst & Co.

Runnymede Trust. 1997. *Islamophobia, its features and dangers*. London: Runnymede Trust.

Sayyid, Bobby S., and Abdul Karim Vakil, eds. 2010. *Thinking through Islamophobia: Global perspectives*. London: C. Hurst & Co.

Schmitt, Carl. 1985. *Political theology: Four chapters on the concept of sovereignty*. Trans. G. Schwab. Cambridge, MA: MIT Press.

Shah, Prakash A. 2009. Transforming to accommodate? Reflections on the *shari'a* debate in Britain. In *Legal practice and cultural diversity*, ed. R. Grillo et al., 73–94. Farnham: Ashgate.

Shah, Prakash A. 2010. Between God and the Sultana? Legal pluralism in the British Muslim diaspora. In *Shari'a as discourse: Legal traditions and the encounter with Europe*, ed. J.S. Nielsen and L. Christoffersen, 117–39. Farnham: Ashgate.

Shah, Prakash A. 2011. When South Asians marry trans-jurisdictionally: Some reflections on immigration cases by an 'expert.' In *Cultural expertise and litigation: Patterns, conflicts, narratives*, ed. L. Holden, 35–52. London: Routledge.
Shah-Kazemi, Sonia. 2001. *Untying the knot, Muslim women, divorce and the Shariah*. London: Nuffield Foundation.
Sullivan, Winnifred F. 2007. *The impossibility of religious freedom*. Princeton, NJ: Princeton University Press.
Taylor, Charles. 2007. *A secular age*. Cambridge, MA: Belknap Press.
Waardenburg, Jacques. 1999. *Muslim perceptions of other religions: A historical survey*. Oxford: Oxford University Press.
Waardenburg, Jacques. 2003. *Muslims and others*. Berlin: Walter de Gruyter.
Williams, Rowan (the Rt. Rev.) 2008. Civil and religious law in England: A religious perspective. Speech given at the Royal Courts of Justice, 7 February. http//www.archbishopofcanterbury.org/1575 (accessed January 31, 2013).
Witte, John Jr. and Joel A. Nichols. 2010. Faith-based family laws in Western democracies? *Fides et Libertas: The Journal of the International Religious Liberty Association* 122—35. http://ssrn.com/abstract=1805304 (accessed January 31, 2013).
Yilmaz, Ihsan. 2005a. *Muslim laws, politics and society in modern nation-states*. Aldershot: Ashgate.
Yilmaz, Ihsan. 2005b. Inter-maddhab surfing, neo-ijitihad, and faith based movements. In *The Islamic school of law: Evolution, devolution and progress*, ed. P. Bearman, R. Peters, and F.E. Vogel, 191–206. Cambridge, MA: Harvard University Press.

The "women's court" in India: an alternative dispute resolution body for women in distress

Sylvia Vatuk

University of Illinois at Chicago, U.S.A.

The 'women's court' (*mahila adalat* or *mahila mandal*) is a fairly recent but increasingly prevalent phenomenon in contemporary India. A particular kind of alternative dispute-resolution forum specifically designed to address women's marital and related family problems, it aims to provide a safe and unthreatening environment wherein women can air their grievances, work out satisfactory settlements with husbands and in-laws, or find ways to escape their difficult situations altogether. It encourages women to resolve domestic disputes informally, rather than by resort to the state's judicatory institutions. Most women's courts are run by women's NGOs, often with financial support from foreign donor agencies or, in some cases, from governmental or semi-governmental agencies such as State Women's Commissions or Legal Aid Societies.

This paper discusses the structure and workings of some of these women's courts, based on two decades of ethnographic observations and interviews in such venues as well as on the work of other scholars who have studied similar bodies more intensively than I. It highlights some of the unique features of these 'courts,' shows why they are the forum of choice for so many poor women, and asks how effective they are in delivering justice to those who come to them for help.

The recent proliferation of what I will here call 'women's courts' in India has received relatively little attention in the literature on 'legal pluralism' or 'alternative dispute resolution (ADR)' in that country. I use the term 'women's court' to refer to a broad and somewhat diverse category of dispute resolution bodies set up specifically to deal with women's marital and family problems, usually by counseling and mediation between the complainant and her husband or other relatives. Their goal is to avoid matrimonial litigation and, if possible, find a way to reconcile the couple and keep the family unit intact. They do this by persuading the parties to agree to some kind of compromise settlement of their differences that usually includes commitments by both parties to change behaviors that have created conflict between them in the past. These bodies go by a variety of names in local languages, such as *mahila* (or *nari*) *adalat* (women's court), *mahila mandal* (women's circle), *mahila panchayat* (women's council), *mahila manch* (women's platform), *nari nyaya samiti* (women's justice committee) and so on. Some are official government bodies, other are run by voluntary organizations under the guidance of – and with some financial support from – government agencies whose responsibility it is to promote the welfare and empowerment of women. Others have no official status at all, but are set up and run independently by women-led non-governmental organizations (NGOs). The latter cover their expenses largely with charitable donations and grants, often from international development agencies that in recent years have devoted a great deal of effort and significant amounts of funding to the promotion of endeavors of this and other kinds for the benefit of poor and troubled women.

Of particular interest to me here are women's courts of a particular type that I will call 'all-woman courts.' These bodies are structurally unique in at least two respects: (1) all of the mediators are female and (2) they ideally come from the same locality, belong to the same class and have a similar social and cultural background to that of the women in the court's client base – they are thus best characterized as 'peer mediators.' The organizations that run all-woman courts reason that an abused woman – or one involved in some other kind of serious domestic dispute – needs a safe and non-threatening space wherein to air her grievances, one in which those who hear her complaint are not only sympathetically inclined, but are of her own sex, share her cultural values and beliefs and are intimately familiar with local customs and traditions that need to be taken into account when devising a solution to her problems.

Leaders of the NGOs and most staff members of the government agencies that sponsor these all-woman courts are typically middle or upper class, college-educated women. But rather than preside over the courts themselves or use trained social workers for the purpose – as most other types of women's courts do – they prefer to recruit and train local women for these roles. They feel that the cultural gap associated with a marked class differential between mediators and the women seeking help creates a barrier to open communication and often leads to 'solutions' that are both inappropriate and unworkable in terms of the realities of their clients' everyday lives.

Scholars who have critically examined the work of these all-woman courts have raised a number of questions about their effectiveness. Do they, in fact, provide remedies for abused and otherwise troubled women that are both more workable and more just than what they would obtain from a formal state-run court, a government-sponsored ADR institution or a non-state caste, community or religious sectarian dispute-settlement body (see Bhatla and Rajan 2003; Magar 2003; Merry 2006; Iyengar 2007; Sekhon 1999; Lemons 2010; Basu 2011; Grover 2011)? While neither scholars nor activists have reached a firm consensus on this issue, there is one recurrent theme in the literature on these bodies. That is, that despite the best intentions of the organizations that sponsor them, women's courts – including those that follow the 'all-woman' model – cannot escape being influenced by 'patriarchal' Indian cultural assumptions about what constitutes appropriate feminine behavior, roles and responsibilities within marriage and within society generally. These assumptions strongly color the kinds of resolutions those who preside over these bodies devise for the complaints that women bring to them, just as they do in other types of dispute-resolution fora.

All-woman courts have at least one significant advantage over their alternatives: they provide relatively congenial spaces within which a poor, minimally educated and unsophisticated woman can feel free to speak openly about the woes that beset her. In these spaces a woman can also feel some confidence that what she says will be understood and interpreted appropriately by those to whom she is relating her story. But the very fact that the woman petitioner and the panel of mediators share a common set of cultural assumptions and beliefs may also mean that she is persuaded to enter into a compromise settlement that entails her agreeing to accept constraints on such things as her freedom of movement and association or her ability to dispose of her own earnings, in exchange for a promise by her husband to begin supporting his family, treat her more kindly, give up his addictions to alcohol or drugs or cease having sexual relations with other women. These accommodations to what is a fundamentally inequitable husband-wife relationship, which the woman is urged to accept in the interests of preserving the marital bond, are not very different from what she would be asked to agree to had she turned for help to one of the other dispute resolution venues that are available to women in her situation.[1]

I will provide here some historical background to and some of the rationales behind the development of all-woman courts and other dispute resolution venues that have been specifically designed to give women relief from domestic violence and other types of marital and family conflicts. I base my remarks largely upon secondary sources – including scholarly articles and books, official reports and evaluations issued by their sponsoring organizations and articles in newspapers and on the internet – and supplement these with some personal observations from women's courts and other women's dispute-resolution bodies that I have attended in different Indian cities over the past twenty-plus years. I made most of these observations in the course of ethnographic and archival fieldwork on various aspects of Muslim Personal Law and its impact on women's well-being that I was conducting in Chennai, Hyderabad, Mumbai and Delhi.[2] Inasmuch as women's courts were not the main focus of that research, it was only in one of my field sites that I regularly attended the weekly meetings of such a body over the course of several months.[3] I was able to make only one or two visits to most of the other venues that I describe here.

Historical background

The development of women's courts in India came about within the context of judicial reform movements in India that date back to the early years after the country gained its independence from Great Britain. As Galanter and Krishnan have argued, the inefficiencies, the over-crowded dockets, the prevalence of corruption and the many other defects of India's courts had created in the public mind a widespread distrust of and lack of confidence in the judicial system:

> For large sectors of society and large areas of conduct, civil courts afford no remedies or protection. When pressure builds to provide usable remedies for a particular sort of grievance, the solution, understandably, is not to undertake the Sisyphean task of reforming the lower courts, it is to by-pass them (2003: 203).

One way of accomplishing this was by setting up new types of dispute resolution bodies as alternatives or supplements to the state-sponsored judiciary. The Government of India began setting up specialized tribunals to hear particular kinds of cases and encouraging the arbitration of disputes by means of mechanisms provided for in the colonial-era Arbitration Act of 1940. It also attempted to revive – or to reinvent – supposedly indigenous methods of dispute resolution. Thus in the late 1950s a system of judicial councils or *nyaya panchayats* was introduced; although it was claimed that these councils were modeled upon existing rural community or caste *panchayats*, they differed from the latter in a number of ways. Most importantly, their members were democratically elected rather than drawn from a self-selected group of influential local elders. Furthermore, they were to administer the law of the land, rather than to enforce local custom. But this attempt to devise an alternative route to justice at the village level ultimately proved to be unworkable and by 1970 the institution had become 'moribund' (Meschievitz and Galanter 1982).

Soon thereafter legal reformers began advocating the establishment of a different kind of alternative dispute resolution system, the so-called 'people's court' (*lok adalat*). These courts were to be presided over by appointed mediators.[4] They were envisioned as venues that would be more accessible as well as more effective than the official courts, especially insofar as the needs of the disadvantaged were concerned. They would also help to relieve the courts of overcrowding by taking on disputes that were better suited to arbitration or negotiation than to litigation.[5] Many millions of such cases have been 'settled,' or 'compromised' by *lok adalats* since the first one began operating in 1982.[6] While acknowledging that they offer some procedural advantages over the regular courts, critics have cast doubt upon the extent to which these bodies actually deliver 'justice' to the weaker party, inasmuch as he (or she) usually ends up being forced, in exchange for a cheaper and speedier resolution of his case, to accept a much less advantageous award than he would otherwise have been entitled to under the law (Galanter and Krishnan 2003, 114–116). This observation is illustrative of Nader's contention – with reference to the larger, worldwide movement for what she calls 'trading justice for harmony' in order to 'get the "garbage cases" out of the [regular, overcrowded] courts,' (1992, 468) – that an almost inevitable consequence of diverting disputes between unequals to ADR bodies for mediation is that the powerful will prevail (see also Nader 2002).

In the late 1970s and early 1980s feminists also began to actively press for judicial reform. This was a time when issues of violence against women, including (but not limited to) domestic violence, were arousing increasing public concern. Women activists employed a variety of methods to raise public awareness of these issues and sought ways of lessening its prevalence, punishing its perpetrators and providing succor to its victims (Katzenstein 1989). One of their key approaches was to press for the enactment of laws that would criminalize particular forms of violence against women. In this they had a number of successes.

Thus in 1983 Section 376 of the Indian Penal Code (IPC) was amended so as to increase the penalties for rape and better protect the privacy of victims (Dhagamwar 1992, 237–287; Agnes 1998, 84–102). A new Section 498A of the Criminal Procedure Code (CrPC) was enacted in the same year that made 'dowry harassment' – or severe and continuous cruelty inflicted on a woman for any other reason – by her husband or in-laws a crime. Over time, the number of cases filed under this section has continuously risen, though conviction rates remain low (Dave and Solanki 2000). Women's organizations that had supported passage of the law soon began to raise serious doubts about its effectiveness, particularly since it only indirectly addressed the problem of domestic violence *per se*. Some feminists began to question whether a criminal law was the most suitable mechanism for dealing with this complex phenomenon. As a result of their efforts, a new law – the Protection of Women from Domestic Violence Act (PWDVA) – was finally enacted in 2005 and came into effect in October 2006. It provides a comprehensive set of *civil* remedies for victims of domestic abuse.

This act too has been something of a disappointment to many. There have been numerous problems of implementation, some of which are a consequence of the central government's failure to allocate any funds for its enforcement. Some state governments have provided at least partial funding for the purpose but most have not. And there has been a widespread failure to hire the 'protection officers' who, under the terms of the act, are supposed to receive complaints of domestic violence and personally assist the victims throughout the legal process. Instead, state governments have simply assigned those tasks to existing officials, without relieving them of any of their other duties (Jhamb 2011).

The act also provides for local women's NGOs to be assigned as 'service providers' to assist the protection officers in, for example, ensuring the safety of women who have filed under the act while still living in their matrimonial homes. But in many locations no such arrangements have been made (Ghosh and Choudhuri 2011, 328). Furthermore, some recent High Court and Supreme Court judgments have reinterpreted and thereby weakened important provisions of the act,[7] making it more likely – in the view of at least one critic – that lower court decisions will be affected by judges' personal gender biases (Badarinath 2011). Numerous other factors – for example, the fact that the police rarely inform battered women who report a crime under S498A of the IPC that they can get additional relief under the PWDVA – contribute to limiting the extent to which those for whom the act was intended are actually able to benefit from it in practice (Lawyers Collective 2012).[8]

In the 1980s, also due to the efforts of the women's movement, additional legislation was enacted to target gender violence. A new Section 304-B was introduced into the IPC in 1984, in response to rising public outrage over media reports of so-called 'dowry deaths' – the killing of young wives, often by burning in supposed 'kitchen accidents,' in retaliation for their inability or unwillingness to extract from their parents gifts of cash or expensive consumer goods.[9] The same year also saw passage of the first of two amendments to a 1961 law that prohibited giving and receiving cash or other valuables as a consideration for a marriage (Dowry Prohibition Act 1961). The 1984 amendment defined the offences more clearly and enhanced the penalties for their violation; a second amendment in 1986 further strengthened the act. Yet there is little evidence of a decline in the dowry custom: indeed dowry amounts have continued to escalate, grooms' families are increasingly placing exorbitant 'demands' on the parents of prospective brides, and the practice has spread to castes and religious communities wherein it was formerly unknown (see India, Parliament 1982, Rao 1993, AIDWA 2003, Basu 2005).[10]

Feminist legal activists also argued for improving through legislation the way that the justice system operated, especially insofar as the needs of poor women were concerned. They pressed, therefore, for reforms in the area of judicial access and procedure. They were instrumental in pushing for enactment of the 1987 Legal Aid Services Authorities Act (LSAA), under which poor litigants are to be provided free legal services,[11] and the Family Courts Act of 1984 (FCA), which provided for the establishment of special courts to handle matrimonial causes – suits for divorce, restitution of conjugal rights, child custody, maintenance, and the like. These kinds of cases were formerly tried in the regular courts, along with other kinds of civil suits, and still are so handled in places where family courts do not exist.

The family courts were designed to be more informal procedurally and therefore more accessible and less intimidating to the poor and uneducated and to women in particular. Lawyers, legalistic jargon and strict rules of procedure and standards of evidence would be dispensed with: clients would be allowed to plead their cases directly to the judge in ordinary language. The customary adversarial relationship between petitioner and respondent would be replaced by an emphasis on conciliation. It was also hoped that in these special courts matrimonial cases could be disposed of more expeditiously than was possible in the overburdened civil courts, where lengthy delays are endemic.

The FCA provides for state governments to set up family courts in all cities of over a million inhabitants and also in smaller cities in response to local needs. It took several years to be implemented in most states, however, and even today the network of such courts is not dense enough to meet the needs of the entire population. By 2009 – 25 years after the act's passage – there were, reportedly, only 153 such courts in the entire country (Jamwal 2009).[12] By then, most states had at least begun to implement the law but a few had still not done so. Even in the capitol city of Delhi, with a population of over 16 million, the first family court was not inaugurated until May of that year. Since then two or three more have been set up in other parts of the city (Express News Service 2010; TNN 2011).

Women's low rate of resort to the courts

All of these new 'women-friendly' laws notwithstanding, it is still the case that the vast majority of women victims of domestic abuse and other kinds of marital discord do not turn – and never even consider turning – to the state for succor. And, if they do so, it is usually only after they have been unable to reach a solution to their problems by other means. As Holden reports from her research in rural Madhya Pradesh,

> official law is the very last resort for family disputes. . .even at the level of the official law court the litigants are often involved in forum shopping strategies aimed at unofficial and out-of court arrangements' (2008, 106).

My own findings from ethnographic research among women of a range of social classes in Chennai and Hyderabad – carried out in the family courts of both cities and in the court of the magistrate who handles cases involving crimes against women in Hyderabad[13] – are consistent with Holden's observations (Vatuk 2001; 2003).

Typically, a woman who finds herself in a violent or otherwise unhappy marriage begins by trying to get the elders of her husband's family to take heed of her complaints (unless, of course, they are the ones responsible for her distress!). Very reluctantly she may eventually make her natal family aware of the difficulties she is facing. But more often than not their response is to urge her to adjust to the situation by being more obedient to the wishes of her husband and in-laws, so that they will have no reason to abuse her. If things do not improve, her male elders may decide to approach her in-laws to try to reach a solution. Members of the two families' wider kinship networks may be consulted for advice or a respected and influential man from the caste or from the village or urban neighborhood where they live may be asked to mediate. If these informal efforts prove unsuccessful, she or her family may take her complaint to a local non-state dispute resolution body, such as a council of elders from her caste, community or religious sect.

There are many reasons why women facing marital problems rarely turn to the state for relief – or do so only after vainly trying other remedies. One obvious reason is financial: the almost obligatory bribes extracted by the police for registering an F.I.R.,[14] the series of fees that are imposed at each stage of the court proceedings, the under-the-table payments to court personnel to ensure that the paperwork moves along in a timely manner and the heavy cost of hiring an advocate to represent one in court. For the very poor, help is sometimes available through official legal aid societies, but demand for such services is high and all who need them cannot be accommodated (Mukherjee 1998). Furthermore, these agencies offer only meager compensation to advocates who take their clients and it is therefore difficult to attract the best-trained or the most experienced – barring the occasional exceptionally socially conscious and public-spirited legal practitioner. Another factor contributing to women's low rate of resort to the courts is that legal cases tend to drag out interminably. Even in the family courts, suits for divorce, restitution of conjugal rights or maintenance – the types of cases most commonly dealt with there – can take months and sometimes even years to be resolved.

In any case, in India it is considered shameful for anyone, especially a woman, to take a family dispute to court. Conflicts between close relatives are considered very private matters that should be kept strictly within the family, not broadcast to outsiders. A woman who airs her complaints before complete strangers and asks a judge to pronounce a judgment against her husband or one of her nearest kin demonstrates a willful disregard for family solidarity and breaches all accepted norms of feminine deportment.

Finally, women share their society's widespread skepticism concerning the inability of the lower courts to deliver justice. Corruption is widely believed to be so rife within the judiciary that whoever has greater financial resources and can wield the most influence over court personnel will win out. As a male, low-caste Rajasthani villager once explained to Erin Moore, 'With money you can buy any result you want; if you put the skull of a man whom you have killed into the palm of your hand and lay five or ten thousand rupees on top of that, you will be set free' (1993, 530–531).

But women have a particular reason to doubt that they will receive justice if they go to court: almost all judges are male and overwhelmingly share the patriarchal values of the wider society, often holding the women who come before them to idealized, high standards of feminine behavior. Scholars who have examined High and Supreme Court decisions have shown that judges often by-pass the legal rights of women who, in their perception, have deviated from such standards. Even when prefaced by words of 'sympathy for the "fair sex,"' judgments 'tend to be conditional on women's conformity to expected standards of feminine propriety' (Uberoi 1996, 321). Although I cannot cite concrete evidence that the same attitudes prevail among lower-court judges, there is little reason to expect them to be very different. My own research in the Chennai Family Court confirms that there is, at the very least, a marked paternalistic tendency in the way women are dealt with at this level of the judicial system. I have observed that every effort is made, whether by the court-appointed 'counselors' or by the judges themselves, to persuade female litigants to 'reconcile' with their husbands. They do so because – or so they argue – they believe that it is better for a woman to continue living in a marital relationship – even one in which she is badly treated – than to live on her own as a single woman, with all of the economic and social hardships that such a status entails (Vatuk 2001).

Treatment of women by 'traditional' non-state dispute-resolution bodies

A similarly patriarchal attitude prevails – and is probably both more pronounced and more widespread – in the non-state dispute-settlement forums to which women or their families most often turn for help before – or instead of – taking their complaints of domestic violence or other marital difficulties to the police or to a court of law. I refer, for example, to such bodies as the so-called '*shari'at* courts' (*dar-ul qazat* – see Hussain 2006; Lemons 2010) and mosque committees (*jama'at*) that regularly settle Muslim marital disputes and the caste or community councils (*panchayats*) that convene to settle disputes among those of all religions in rural areas (see Hayden 1999; Moore 1993, 1998) and often also in lower-income city neighborhoods where migrants from rural areas congregate (Solanki 2011).

These bodies are characterized by many observers as particularly insensitive to women's needs (Chowdhry 2007; Moore 1993, 1998).[15] They rarely have any female members and some do not even admit female complainants to their own case hearings but insist that they be represented by a male relative. Even if a woman is allowed to narrate in person her version of events, her testimony is frequently ignored or its veracity questioned.[16] In Bates' words,

> [a]lthough the groups' composition and the level at which they operated are different, the exclusion of women is common to these institutions. Women had little to say either in framing the rules. . .or concerning the process by which [they] were enforced. . .disputes that involved women were settled by male authorities and male-made rules (2010, 71).

Bates is in fact referring here to the situation that prevailed in rural areas during the pre-British period but her description of the makeup and mode of functioning of such local dispute resolution fora is equally valid today.

The practices of village exogamy and patrilocal post-marital residence mean that most married women – especially in northern India – are living in their husband's home village and therefore have no nearby natal relatives on whom to call for help or support in times of need. Their husbands, on the other hand, have the great advantage of living among their own close relatives and others they have known since birth, all of whom are naturally predisposed to side with them in case of any marital dispute, rather than with their 'stranger' wives.

Furthermore, the men who preside over such councils understandably tend to share their society's assumptions about the proper roles of spouses in a marriage: namely, male dominance and female subservience. A woman seeking to leave a difficult marriage is therefore likely to find that those to whom she has brought her complaint are so firmly committed to this paradigm and to the notion of marriage as an indissoluble bond (or one that only the husband has the prerogative of breaking), that they take for granted the wife's obligation to uncomplainingly cohabit with and cater to the needs of her husband, however badly he treats her. Even those (mostly low-caste, nomadic, or 'tribal') communities that attach little stigma to divorce and have a recognized procedure for releasing a woman from an unwanted marriage, typically require her (or her lover or her natal family) to compensate her husband – financially or in some other way – for leaving him (e.g., see Holden 2008, Hayden 1999).

Although none of these informal dispute-resolution bodies have state-backed authority to enforce their decisions or to ensure that the settlements that they broker between disputing parties are adhered to, their members are almost invariably drawn from among the most powerful and wealthy men of the caste, community or religious congregation, who are in a position to exert considerable social pressure, issue threats and even employ physical violence to impose their will upon the parties.

Media critiques of *panchayats* and *shari'at* courts

In recent years there has been a plethora of negative media reports detailing alleged abuses by such bodies as so-called *shari'at* courts and caste or clan (*khap*[17]) *panchayats*, especially in rural areas of such northern Indian states as Haryana, Punjab, Uttar Pradesh and Rajasthan. Reports appear regularly in the news of the harassment of women, Dalits (formerly called 'untouchables') and members of other marginal groups by conservative-minded, all-male *panchayats* (run by members of upper-caste landowning families and their supporters), for alleged offenses against local custom. Anti-woman *fatwas* issued by Muslim religious authorities or *shari'at* courts in various parts of the country have also been widely publicized, creating considerable public outrage (Metcalf 2006). Such male-run councils act as moral police, issuing edicts that, for example, sanction young women for wearing tight clothing, bar them from shopping in the market and require them to cover their faces when they go out in public. In some places young people have been banned from using mobile phones (see, for example Srivastava 2012; Rai 2012). The most egregious incidents involve the harassment of couples who have dared to marry by personal choice rather than waiting for their elders to arrange matches for them (Chowdhry 1998, 2007; Kahol 2012).[18] Rapes and so-called 'honor killings' of one or both parties to such marriages – particularly common where the spouses are of different castes or religions or the union is a quasi-incestuous one between members of the same clan or residents of the same village – have allegedly occurred with increasing frequency in recent years and there have been many calls for the government to intervene and put a halt to the activities of these bodies (see Karat 2004; India, Ministry of Panchayati Raj 2006; Special Correspondent 2006; Reddy 2010; Sangwan 2010; Yardley 2011; Wikipedia n.d.). Little in the way of concrete measures to weaken their power and influence has been undertaken, however, and in some cases political party leaders and government officials have even issued statements suggesting at least indirect support of their activities (Headlines Today Bureau 2012; Siddiqui 2012).

Alternative dispute settlement venues designed specifically for women

It is not surprising, therefore, that feminist activists would be critical, not only of the state's formal judicial system, but of these kinds of 'customary' quasi-courts as well, for failing to deliver justice to women whose husbands and/or in-laws[19] have subjected them to abuse. Therefore in the late 1980s, as a result of urging from women's organizations, various government agencies began setting up alternative dispute resolution bodies to specifically address women's needs. Though funded by the government, they were not designed as official arms of the judicial system but rather as a means of settling marital and other family disputes by mutual agreement between the parties to obviate the need for litigation.

One of the first experiments along these lines involved setting up special women's 'cells' in police stations. Female police officers or social workers would be assigned to deal with women's complaints of dowry harassment, domestic violence, abandonment, rape, incest and so on. In 2006 I visited on several occasions a so-called Women's Counseling Centre, attached to the office of the Police Commissioner in a Muslim-dominated neighborhood of Hyderabad's Old City. The volunteer counselor was a young Muslim woman advocate with a diploma in marriage and family counseling who held office hours for women supplicants every evening. Most of those whom she counseled had been referred to her by the police station, which they had approached to complain of domestic abuse. The Commissioner told me that the policy he followed was to encourage women to delay filing formal charges against their husbands and/or other family members until they had first tried, with the counselor's help, to work out a mutually agreeable settlement with those who had been mistreating them.

The counselor had been assigned a small two-room office just inside the outer gate of the police station compound. Women referred to her by the police would first come to her for a private hearing. After this she would summon the husband (or other relatives) to come to her office the following week. The wife and sometimes other relatives – hers and his – often attended these sessions, in which the counselor would question the man about his wife's charges and ask what he was willing to do to improve their relationship. On these occasions the discussions among those present often became heated. The counselor's goal – not always attainable, she admitted – was to reach a compromise, whereby each party agreed to change certain of their behaviors so that a reconciliation could be achieved and the marriage preserved.

All-woman police stations

In many of the larger cities, free-standing 'women's police stations,' entirely staffed by female police officers, also began to come came into existence during this period. These stations sometimes employed – or recruited as volunteers – professionally trained social workers or psychologists to counsel women clients. In other cases, female police officers performed counseling duties themselves (see Poonacha and Pandey 2000, 568–569).

Counseling services run by trained social workers in the employ of the of the Tamil Nadu State Social Welfare Department were available in all three of the All-Women Police Stations operating in Chennai in 1998–99. Like the counselor whose sessions I later observed in Hyderabad, one of those whom I interviewed in Chennai in 1998 told me that her goal was:

> to reunite the couple. . .Otherwise the women have no way to support themselves. They are economically dependent and their parents usually aren't in a position to take on that responsibility, especially if they have children.

According to this counselor, once she had gotten the parties to agree on a future course of action that would defuse the hostility that had developed between them, she would follow up their progress by having them return to her office each month to talk about what had been happening in their marriage since she saw them last. If they were still having problems, she would advise them further on how to improve their relationship.

Women's *lok adalats*

Women's *lok adalats* – structured along the same lines as other specialized *lok adalats* discussed above – have also been set up under the auspices of various state governments during the past 30 years. One of these began operating in Hyderabad in 2001, under the joint sponsorship of the Andhra Pradesh Women's Commission and the A. P. Legal Services Authority. At that time it had two judges – a retired (female) lawyer/public prosecutor and a retired (male) social worker – who met once a month to hear cases referred to them by those parent agencies. Most of the women who came before them were seeking a divorce or a maintenance order (under S125 of the CrPC) or had filed charges of dowry harassment or cruelty against their husbands under S498A of the IPC. Again, like the women's police station counselors whom I cited above, the woman judge of this *lok adalat* explained that their goal was to 'reconcile' couples. In order for their case to be heard by this *lok adalat,* both husband and wife had to agree to submit to arbitration. They would appear on the same day to present their respective versions of the case, which, if it was especially intractable, might take several sessions to be resolved. Once the panel had rendered a decision there was no avenue of appeal. Should either party be dissatisfied or fail to abide by the judgment, they would have to go back and fight their case from the beginning in a regular court.

A different kind of forum, but one with the similarly optimistic agenda of ensuring the preservation of families, was the weekly *madar sangam* (literally 'women's association' but called in English 'Centre for Women'), run by the Tamil Nadu State Legal Aid Authority.[20] As mentioned above, I attended these gatherings on a fairly regular basis for several months in 1998–99. Hearings were convened every Saturday afternoon in a large, run-down government warehouse building in downtown Chennai. The (male) Secretary of the Authority, a retired (female) social worker, a retired (male) executive with Burmah Shell and a young woman alcohol addiction counselor constituted the mediation panel. They sat at a long table on a raised platform before a largely female crowd. There were not enough chairs to accommodate everyone – almost half of the supplicants with their accompanying relatives had to stand at the back or await their turn in the yard outside.

Almost all of the cases involved marital problems of one kind or another. On one of my visits, for example, the first complainant was a second wife, married to the widower of her deceased sister whose children had been, from the outset, hostile to their new stepmother. The situation had caused conflict between her and her husband and she had recently left him to return to her parents' home. At the hearing she was allowed to tell her story first and then her husband's father was given the opportunity to speak. He introduced himself as a former professor and, unlike everyone else in the room, made a point of addressing the panel in English, rather than in Tamil, the local language. The Secretary asked him a few questions and then suggested that the children talk privately to the social worker, so that she could determine why they so disliked their stepmother and whether it might be possible to find a way to bring the family together.

However, he said, in the meantime the complainant's husband should be paying her a monthly maintenance stipend. His father replied that the husband had been maintaining his wife all along but the wife's brother broke in to sharply contradict him. At this, the *wife's* father stood up and asked – also in English – to be allowed 'to vent my feelings!' But he was told that nothing positive could come of permitting him to do that now: he would have to wait until the next meeting. After some discussion among the members of the panel and between them and the husband's father it was finally agreed that the following week the latter would bring Rs. 1500 for his daughter-in-law to the Legal Aid office. Another meeting was scheduled for a month hence. In the interim the social worker would meet individually with each of the concerned parties and try to come up with a possible solution to their problems.

On another occasion a small, thin woman, came up to the podium to explain that she had been married for only a year to a drunkard who regularly beat her up. But before she had a chance to elaborate upon her story, her husband – a large, heavy man – stood up to interrupt and refute her version of events, shouting and shaking his finger threateningly. He was given the floor and proceeded to present his case. His wife listened for a while, then interrupted him and began crying. Soon both were excited and angry, talking at once. She kept addressing herself to the woman social worker, calling her by the English title, 'Madam,' and appealing to her for understanding. The latter listened sympathetically for a while but then became impatient and started scolding the young woman to 'stop crying and just say what you want to say!' Eventually the Secretary suggested that they postpone the discussion for the following week.

These encounters and others that I observed revealed interesting class and gender disparities and disjunctions, both among the counselors serving on the panel and between them and the women and men who had come to have their disputes resolved. There was a noticeable element of hierarchy in the relationships among the panelists themselves. Not only the female social worker but also the male former business executive allowed the Secretary of the Legal Aid Authority to dominate the questioning and take the lead in proposing solutions. The young addiction counselor said very little except when a question was put to her directly about a man who drank excessively or was addicted to drugs. The older woman social worker also tended to defer to her male colleagues, except when responding to a direct appeal from a woman complainant.

During discussions about the marital problems of the women who had come to the *sangam* for help, the two male panelists directed their questions mainly to the husbands and other males in the assembled group and often gave them more time than they gave the women to expand upon their versions of what was going on in the marriage. Male clients likewise addressed themselves mainly to the Secretary and the other man on the panel, while women consistently directed their remarks to the senior woman, addressing her, even when speaking in Tamil, with the honorific English title of 'Madam'. Her manner was usually sympathetic and reassuring but she became quite irritated and often spoke sharply to women who were becoming – in her view – overly emotional or failed to make their points clearly and in an organized fashion.

Furthermore, when speaking to individual supplicants, the counselors consistently used the familiar Tamil forms of pronouns and verbs, such as are customarily employed when speaking to social inferiors, such as servants, workmen or vendors. On the other hand, those who had come seeking help used the more polite and respectful grammatical forms when addressing the panel members. Of course, when, as in the first case, a client was clearly of a social class similar to that of the counselors and was therefore speaking in English, this linguistic issue did not arise.

Many political parties, both on the left and on the right, also run women's counseling or advice sessions, usually under the auspices of their 'women's wing'. Scholars who have observed the activities of the Mahila Aghadi, the women's branch of the right-wing Shiv Sena party in Mumbai and elsewhere in the state of Maharashtra have mentioned their performing such services for women victims of domestic violence in their local neighborhoods, though they are also known to use public threats and shaming and even physical attacks to discourage men from continuing their abusive behavior (see, for example, Sen 2007; Bedi 2009, 2010). The All-India Democratic Women's Association (AIDWA), affiliated with the Communist Party of India (Marxist) does not engage in methods of this kind. In its New Delhi office it holds weekly mediation sessions for troubled women and their families every Saturday morning. I was present there one day in 2011 when two mediators spent the better part of three hours dealing with the marital problems of two Muslim and one Hindu couple. Both mediators are middle-class, university-educated Muslim women, but they also involved in each case a less well-educated, lower or lower middle-class member of the party's 'women's committee' (*mahila samiti*) from the complainant's own neighborhood. The latter did not take very active roles in the process, however, only occasionally offering some additional information or making a tentative suggestion about what might be done to resolve the issue at hand. Here cases were dealt with, not in a large, almost public, forum, as in the Chennai *madar sangam,* but separately, in private sessions held inside the small AIDWA office. Those who arrived while an earlier case was being discussed had to wait outdoors in the building's front yard until it was finished.

The cases were similar to those that I observed being mediated in Chennai. A woman who had been married for only a few months had left her husband because, she claimed, he was addicted to alcohol and had been mistreating her. She was adamant about wanting a divorce, so most of the discussion revolved around arrangements for the return of the goods her family had given as dowry when they married and an appropriate cash amount to be paid to her as a divorce settlement. The second case was a dispute over child custody between an elderly couple and the widow of their recently-deceased son, who had already moved back into her natal home and intended to remain there: again, much of the discussion centered around monetary issues.

This was not the first time that the AIDWA leaders had met with these families; they had already established a relationship of trust with the complainants and, to some extent, with their opponents as well. They asked questions and listened attentively to what each had to say, then offered concrete suggestions about how they might resolve their differences. They urged each party to make compromises, financial and otherwise, in order to reach a mutually agreeable settlement. They spoke kindly and sympathetically to the each of the complainants, but didn't hesitate to say so when they felt that one of them was being unreasonable or had behaved badly. Perhaps not surprisingly, they seemed somewhat less patient with the erring husbands than with the women who had sought their help.

Unlike the counselors whom I observed in Hyderabad and Chennai, the AIDWA mediators – on this particular occasion, at least – made no serious attempt to persuade the complainants to return to their marital homes, nor did they, in our interviews, suggest that their principal goal was to reconcile couples or preserve marriages. Instead, their efforts were mainly devoted to ensuring that the women had the resources to manage living outside of the bonds of matrimony, if that is what they chose to do. They tried to make sure that the women had a place to live and had at least some funds with which to support themselves (and their children, if any), at least for the immediate future. For example, they suggested to the young childless woman that she finish a training course that she had begun before her marriage and then find a job. When her younger, unmarried brother – who had accompanied her to the mediation session – blurted out that he had no intention of allowing her to work outside of the home, both mediators indignantly berated him for his retrograde views. One remarked somewhat sarcastically that he would probably change his opinion once he married, since his future wife might not be so willing to have him support his divorced sister indefinitely on his own meager earnings!

All-woman peer-led courts

None of the alternative dispute resolution systems that I have described are entirely satisfactory from the perspective of many feminist activists, who feel increasingly strongly that all-female dispute-resolution bodies provide a better model than any of these for resolving women's marital problems. In their view, the class – and in some cases also the gender – differences between the mediators and the women they serve that are present in almost all of these venues, both hamper open communication and make it likely that middle-class, patriarchal values will be imposed upon the poor women who form the bulk of their clientele. For these reasons they advocate the use of all-woman courts led by peer-mediators.

All-woman, peer-led courts are designed primarily to serve the poor, though they welcome all comers and are even approached occasionally by well-off, middle-class complainants. They are in most cases overseen by one of the many NGOs active in India today that devote themselves to women's welfare and empowerment, but many of them are government aided or even set up and directly run by a government agency. Their leaders tend to be well-educated women from middle or upper class and caste backgrounds but local women of the same general class, geographical, linguistic and cultural background as their client base are usually recruited to serve as mediators. The latter may be only minimally educated, if at all, but undergo a period of feminist conscious-raising, are given instruction in the particular NGO's philosophy of dispute settlement, and acquire a basic knowledge of the relevant legislation before taking up their responsibilities.

The rationale for using such women as mediators is based on the conviction that in order for a distressed woman to air her grievances adequately she should be provided a setting in which she can accuse and even confront face-to-face those who have harmed her, without being hampered by feelings of inferiority, embarrassment, fear and powerlessness. She should be able to describe and explain her problems in her own words to women like herself who are intimately familiar with the social and cultural context of her life, who share her own assumptions about right and wrong behavior, who understand – not simply intellectually but through personal experience – what she is going through.

Mediators who are in these respects the woman's own peers are in a much better position than an educated middle class man or woman, however well-trained and well-meaning, to help her reach a solution that is both appropriate within the local social and cultural context and also workable – whether it takes the form of a mutually satisfactory compromise settlement or a suggestion about how to escape the situation altogether and begin life anew.

All-woman courts typically meet on a regular basis, on a fixed day and time every week, at a convenient location within the neighborhood that they serve. They are usually run as group, rather than one-on-one, sessions. While one 'case' is being discussed and dealt with, others who are waiting to be called upon are sitting in the same room, listening to and even on occasion participating in the often lively debates that ensue. In those that I have attended, as in those described by other scholars, the peer-mediators model their procedures broadly upon those followed in civil courts, keeping a register in which cases are numbered and dated, along with a separate file for each case, in which is noted down whatever advice was given to the client in previous meetings, the details of any decisions made or agreements or settlements reached, and reports on later follow-up visits to the client's home. Since most NGOs charge a small fee for hearing a case, the amounts paid are also recorded in each supplicant's file (see Merry 2006, Lemons 2010, Grover 2011).

When a woman comes in to complain against a husband (or other relative), she is asked for the latter's address and other contact information. An 'official' letter is then sent – or nowadays a call made to his mobile phone – summoning him to appear in a week or two to present his side of the story and discuss what might be done to improve the situation. After several sessions, if all goes well, the couple is assisted in drafting an agreement to which both parties – and other family members present – affix their signatures or thumbprints. If the mediators cannot 'reconcile' the pair by such means, they may try to find another solution, perhaps accompanying the woman to the police station to register a complaint or to a civil court to file suit for divorce or maintenance.

If possible, they will find a sympathetic women lawyer who is willing to offer her services *pro bono*. Regrettably, however, female advocates are few and far between even in large cities and not all of them choose – or can afford – to waive their fees for an indigent client. In small towns and rural areas female advocates are even less abundant. For this and other reasons – some of which I have reviewed above – if an all-woman court is unable to find a satisfactory solution to a poor client's problems, the option of turning to the state for relief may not be easily available to her.

Hundreds, perhaps thousands, of all-woman courts are in operation today in villages and urban areas all over India. Interestingly, they are modeled not on any formal state judicial body, but rather on such 'traditional' male-led dispute-resolution fora as the village, tribal, clan or caste *panchayats* mentioned above. One all-woman court that has attracted considerable media attention is the 'women's *jama'at*' – explicitly modeled upon local male-run mosque committees (*jama'at*) – which was set up in 2003 by Daud Sharifa Khanam, founder of the STEPS Women's Development Organization in Pudukottai, Tamil Nadu. It caters mainly, though not exclusively, to Muslim women. When battered women from the locality began coming to the women's community center that she had set up in 1991, Sharifa Khanam recognized the need for a way of resolving women's marital problems that was more female-centered and woman-friendly than the exclusively male *jama'ats* ('mosque committees') to which such disputes were normally referred (Venkat 2008). Another similar body that has been mentioned several times in the press but about whose actual operation little is known, is the *mahila adalat* first convened in 2005 by the newly inaugurated All-India Muslim Women's Personal Law Board in

Lucknow. At its first session it reportedly received 166 women's complaints about unilateral divorce, dowry harassment and other marital problems.[21]

In 2005 I had an opportunity to observe the proceedings of a similar body, a *mahila shakti mandal* ('women's power circle') sponsored by the NGO Women's Research and Action Group (WRAG) in Mumbai.[22] It operates under the aegis of an umbrella organization called Hukook-e-Niswan Mahila Sanghatana ('Women's Federation for Women's Rights') that now includes 25 such 'circles.'[23] The one I visited met every Saturday in a room on an upper floor of a somewhat flimsy wooden structure built along the concrete wall that abuts the tracks leading into the busy Bandra Railway Station. When I arrived I found about 15 women of various ages and two or three young men sitting on the floor in a rough circle. I was introduced to the mediators, a group of five or six middle-aged women sitting together on one side of the circle, a bound register book and a stack of file folders piled up beside them.

A wide variety of cases was scheduled to be heard that day, not all of them matrimonial in nature. For example, a young Muslim woman had come to complain that her mother-in-law would not permit her to continue studying at the girls' *madrasa* (Qur'anic school) that she had been attending before her marriage. The mother-in-law was asked to explain her reasoning. Even before she had finished speaking, some of those who were waiting their turn to be heard began interjecting their own views on the matter. Soon everyone in the room was talking at once. The mediators had difficulty trying to quiet the crowd, but once they had done so they began fervently urging the older woman to reconsider her opposition to her daughter-in-law's wish to continue her education. They told her that not only the young woman herself, but any future children she might have, would benefit if she were educated. They assured her that part-time school attendance would not prevent her son's wife from fulfilling her household responsibilities. They were unable to convince the older woman to change her mind but asked her to think it over and come back again later in the month to discuss the matter further.

Another complainant, a young woman clothed in a black *burqa,* complete with face covering (*niqab*), was accompanied by her mother and carried a small infant in her arms. She explained that she had been married less than two years ago to a widower 20 years older than she. He was unemployed and continually harassed her for more dowry. Furthermore, her mother-in-law made her do all of the housework. So she had left her in-law's house and gone home to her mother. She wept throughout her recital, which made it difficult, even for the mediators, to understand very well what had happened or what she wanted to do about it. The *mandal* leaders consoled her while encouraging her to tell them more: 'Speak up! Let it all out! Don't hold it in or you'll get sick!' They finally suggested that she come back the following week, by which time they would have been able to contact her husband and mother-in-law and call them in to discuss – and hopefully begin working on resolving – the situation.

Action India's *mahila panchayats*

Another NGO sponsor of all-woman courts that is heavily dependent upon overseas funding is the Delhi-based Action India (AI) (Sekhon 1999, 39). begun as a purely voluntary welfare project in some of the 'resettlement colonies' that had been set up during the then Prime Minister Indira Gandhi's 'Emergency' (1975–77) to accommodate hundreds of thousands of squatters removed from the public lands that they had long occupied in different parts of the city. In 1979 some of AI's women members, influenced by India's growing women's movement, began to organize women at the community level. These educated, middle-class women saw themselves 'not as leaders, but facilitators' for the formation of autonomous women's groups, called *sabla mahila sanghs* ('associations of empowered women'), that would work for women's welfare and empowerment within their own neighborhoods (Sekhon 1999, 28–29). By the 1990s complaints of domestic abuse were regularly being brought by local women to the attention of the neighborhood women's associations. In response the AI decided in 1992 to launch a program to focus upon issues of women and the law, a centerpiece of which would be the establishment of all-woman conflict-resolution bodies, called *mahila panchayats* ('women's councils'). Today AI directly runs a number of such *panchayats* in the same localities and is also linked to a network of 84 all-woman courts run by other Delhi NGOs, whose members they train in their own methods of dispute settlement with funding from the Delhi Commission for Women, a municipal government agency (Sekhon 1999; Action India 2009; Magar 2003; Lemons 2010, 58–88; Grover 2011, 153–202).

According to AI's website, a total of 6756 cases were dealt with by the *panchayats* in this network between September 2004 and November 2009, of which 5720 are said to have been 'solved.' Unfortunately, these figures are not accompanied by any explanation of what criteria are used to determine which cases had a successful outcome. I interpret the term 'solved' to mean that the mediators drafted and had the parties sign settlement agreements. Whether all of these couples were permanently reconciled and are living happily ever after is another matter. These *nari adalats* and some all-woman courts run by other women's organizations do try to regularly follow up their clients for a period of time through monthly home visits. But, for obvious reasons, they cannot continue to do this indefinitely for every couple. If, after a few months, they have detected no new signs of difficulty, they may interpret this to mean that their interventions have succeeded.

Nevertheless, as AI claims on its website, there are some other positive impacts of the program: women victims of domestic violence have been 'empowered,' have begun to realize that they are not alone in their suffering, have learned how to articulate their problems without feeling guilt or a sense of personal failure, have improved their decision-making abilities and have developed higher levels of self-esteem and self-confidence (Action India 2009).

Two of AI's *mahila panchayats,* one located in a predominantly Hindu locality (Grover 2011) and the other in a Muslim neighborhood (Lemons 2010), have recently been studied by ethnographers. Grover finds that the great majority of women who come to the *panchayats* she studied have what she calls (using the Hindi expression) '*karcha-pani'* complaints: that is, husbands who are not providing financially for their wives and children, either because they are not working, are using their earnings for other purposes, are living with other women or have deserted their families altogether. Another very common set of complaints revolve around unfounded accusations by the husband that his wife is having sexual relations with other men. Domestic violence is a recurring issue that represents a constant in the lives of most of the women (2011, 174–176; cf. Magar 2003: 514–516). But despite the growing number of *mahila panchayats* that have been set up in the city in recent years, there has been no

> significant elimination of domestic violence in low-income localities or...a fundamental shift in attitudes. The mahila panchayats concept is a salient addition to the array of non-legal institutions that are attempting ...to eliminate violence in the conjugal home...but given their limited resources they cannot by themselves bring about rapid change (Grover 2011, 185).

Another problem that Grover sees is that, in the compromise settlements they broker, these courts 'validate the male breadwinner ideology' in which the woman's role is that of dependent housewife. These settlements 'reinforce the understanding that women should subscribe to hierarchical gender roles' (185). Here Grover draws upon Kandiyoti's notion of the 'patriarchal bargain,' according to which women in male-dominated societies, rather than actively resisting patriarchy, respond to the constraints it imposes by trying to maximize their options within it (1988).

Lemons' analysis of the outcomes of sessions she observed in another of AI's all-woman courts raises similar issues. She confesses being

> haunted by the observation that in spite of producing more democratic woman-centered spaces of adjudication, the *mahila panchayats* reinscribe certain gendered norms that they explicitly claim to combat. . .[since] mediations are settled through expressions of the existing gendered hierarchies in which disputants are mired (2010, 59).

She points out that many of the domestic violence victims end up being persuaded by the *panchayats* mediators to return to their marital homes, after agreeing 'to behave properly, and not to pick fights,' 'to do a better job of maintaining peace in the household' and, as in one case, to apologize for her role in the dispute 'as profusely as her husband.' This emphasis on compromise 'seems to undermine the aim of greater equality between men and women that Action India. . .explicitly espouse[s]' (Lemons 2010, 87–88).

Both ethnographers have thus noted that in a substantial majority of cases the solutions proposed by mediators and the resulting settlements agreed to by disputing spouses have the wife return to her abusive or financially neglectful husband, on the basis of *his* promise to treat her more kindly and *her* promise to submit to his demands for greater obedience and more limits to her mobility. So, for example, the negotiated settlement document in a typical case described by Grover has the complainant (who originally came to the women's court determined to leave her abusive husband) promising not to leave the house without informing her husband or his mother and not to visit her parental home (*pihar*) 'too frequently' – this was one of the original bones of contention between the couple. In return, he promises that in the future he will not beat her any more and will stop accusing her of engaging in illicit sexual liaisons (2011, 167). Lemons cites a similar agreement, in which the man promises not to cause his wife any more 'sadness' (an apparent allusion to her complaints of beatings and accusations that she is unchaste). She, in turn, promises not to argue with him or his parents and to do whatever is 'correct' or 'proper' while living in their house (2010, 87). Thus, as Lemons puts it, while the *mahila panchayats* do provide 'more democratic, woman-centered spaces of adjudication, [they also] reinscribe certain gendered norms that they explicitly claim to combat' (2010, 59).

Nari adalats sponsored by Mahila Samakhya

A somewhat similar but much larger network of all-woman courts (variously called *nari adalat, mahila manch* or *nyaya samiti* ['justice committee']) operates with state government support in a number of Indian states. It dates back to the mid-1990s, when it was set up in certain districts of Gujarat, Karnataka and Uttar Pradesh as an NGO/government partnership, an outgrowth of a 'women's confederation' (Mahila Samakhya [MS]) that was established in 1989 by the Ministry of Human Resource Development, Government of India.[24] MS began by setting up village women's groups (*mahila sangh*) and training them to work for their own empowerment. Later, having become aware of the seriousness and widespread prevalence of the problem of domestic violence in the rural areas in which it was working, it initiated a program of all-woman courts (Iyengar 2007, 8; see also Bhatla and Rajan 2003; Merry 2006; Mahila Samakhya Karnataka 2012; Basu 2011). These courts meet on fixed dates in a central location – often in a government building – to which women from surrounding villages come with their marital and family grievances. The vast majority of supplicants have experienced domestic abuse associated with such issues as dowry demands, the wife's failure to bear sons, suspicions of her infidelity, the husband's involvement with other women, his addiction to alcohol or drugs, etc.[25]

After a complainant's application is filed with the *adalat,* the other party or parties are contacted and summoned to appear at a later date. Only when both sides are present do the negotiations begin. The organization believes strongly in the importance of community support for successful resolution of marital disputes, so arbitration is always carried out in 'an open and public forum' and local women's groups participate in the process, 'collecting all basic facts, generating opinion in favour of the victim. . .and monitoring the [*nari adalat's*] decision' afterwards (Bhatla and Rajan 2003, 1660). Much of their ability to enforce their decisions against violators of women's rights rests – just as it does for traditional male-run *panchayats* – on the social pressure that lay participants in the process can exert upon them. They believe that using the public square to shame the perpetrator and put him under public scrutiny produces in him a strong motivation to change his behavior (Iyengar 2007, 19).

Yet, in the most thorough and useful of the several available evaluations of these *nari adalats*, Iyengar echoes concerns similar to those expressed by Grover and Lemons. She points out that '*Their priority is to find a solution. . .within the ambit of social justice rather than applying more generic principles of judicial procedure or human rights . . .*' [italics in original] and asks whether, given that

> they retain their emphasis on ascertaining the rights of women *within* the framework of marriage, . . .the *Nari Adalats'* attempt to mirror the values and attitudes of those for whom they adjudicate has led to [their way of administrating] justice becoming a subversion of human rights (2007, 9–10).

These courts use knowledge of local practices, customs and social networks to gather evidence and negotiate agreements, generate social opinion against the offender and sometimes use threats to involve the legal system as a means to intimidate him. However, the fact that maintaining the home and family to which the complainant belongs remains 'critical to their core understanding of gender justice' (2007, 10) clearly constrains them in terms of the kinds of remedies they feel able to offer to the abused women who come before them.

Conclusions

The foregoing discussion of Indian women's courts – and all-woman courts in particular – raises a number of questions, the first of which is whether it is really appropriate to discuss these bodies within the conceptual framework of 'legal pluralism'? The institution is clearly – at least in its origin – a 'non-state' one. But what is its 'jurisdiction,' beyond that which it claims for itself over the generality of troubled and abused women? It is the state's judicial system that has overarching legal jurisdiction over most of the issues that impel such women to approach all-woman courts. But because the official courts are difficult to access and unsatisfactory in both methods and outcomes – from the perspective of the majority of their potential clients – all-woman courts are often a preferred venue, at least in the initial stages of a distressed woman's search for a resolution of her marital problems.

The concept of legal pluralism is generally agreed to refer to a system wherein the state commands different bodies of law for different categories of persons in the population (cf. Merry 1988). India has such a system in the sphere of family law, where citizens of each of the major religious groups is governed by a distinct code of family law and long-standing 'customary laws' that may conflict with these are also recognized by the state under certain conditions. But the norms that guide the decisions or the settlements brokered by all-woman courts are not officially recognized by the state on the same basis as the foregoing. To comprehend the place of these norms and values within the concept, Griffiths' (1986) distinction between the 'weak' and the 'strong' varieties of legal pluralism is useful. He uses the latter term to describe the 'empirical state of affairs' in most societies, where many legal orders coexist but *do not* belong to a single legal 'system' and as such do not come under the direct purview of the state and are not recognized by it as having equal legal validity. A similar idea, very pertinent to understanding the place of all-woman courts with respect to the notion of legal pluralism, has been offered by Vanderlinden, who speaks of societies being characterized by 'pluralistic normative orderings,' where individuals are 'embedded within social networks and individually shopping in these many normative fora' (Dupret 2007, citing Vanderlinden 1989).

Women's courts are clearly a type of 'alternative dispute resolution' forum, though, unlike official tribunals set up by the government under the Arbitration Act, their 'decisions' are not officially recognized by the state-sponsored judicial system nor does the authority of the state stand behind them. Although they frequently employ a quasi-judicial rhetoric when referring to their aims and modes of operation and are often observed to replicate judicial procedure and methods of record-keeping at their hearings, their role vis-a-vis the state is peripheral at best and their goals overlap only partially with those of the formal justice delivery system, as represented by the police and the courts. This is true even in the case of women's courts – such as those run by MS – that began as joint state/NGO efforts and continue to be state-sponsored (or at least partially so), receiving government funds and operating under the aegis of official state agencies.

A very important difference between these bodies and the state courts is that in most cases the aim of the former is not to see that the women who come to them for help get the 'rights' to which they are entitled under human rights principles or even under Indian law. Their avowed purpose is to defuse the hostility that has developed between the parties to a dispute – usually a married couple – and to find a compromise solution that will allow them to continue to live together in relative peace. They provide an alternative way – which they consider a better way – of *mediating* marital disputes, outside of the formal legal system, offering women what they term 'social justice,' rather than the 'legal justice' dispensed by state courts. Of course, they recognize that the women who come to them, including those whom they have persuaded to enter into a compromise settlement, are not thereby precluded from going to a civil court or filing a formal charge of cruelty with the police at some later date, particularly if the agreement worked out by the peer mediators turns out to be unworkable or unsustainable in the long run.

Although even the sponsors of all-woman courts sometimes speak of their process as involving the 'arbitration' of disputes, the word is actually a misnomer in this context. As that term is usually understood, it refers to a process in which the parties commit themselves to being bound by the decision of the presiding 'judge' or 'arbitrator.' But the women who come before a women's court make no such commitment. What they are offered is the opportunity to enter into a voluntary written agreement or contract with the party or parties that they allege are persecuting them. If one or both of the parties fail to live up to their promises to change their behavior, there is nothing that the peer mediators can do, beyond suggesting that they all come back to discuss it further or advising and helping the woman to file a criminal charge against her husband or a suit for divorce or maintenance in a court of law.

Iyengar, in relation to her own study of the Gujarati *nari adalats* that I have mentioned above, addresses the question of the relationship between these bodies and the law of the state. Are they simply a 'supplementary' forum for pre-litigation conciliation and settlement or a 'complementary' system that has a different, culturally more appropriate and, at the same time, equally 'just' way of getting women their rights (2007, 27)? Most of the 70 *nari adalat* leaders who were asked this question by her research team chose the latter formulation. They see themselves as operating a system of justice delivery that is *parallel* to that of the state as well as superior to it in terms of outcomes. They are neither intended nor were they designed simply to relieve the courts and police of their workload by settling cases ahead of time so that they need not proceed to the litigation stage, as were the various tribunals set up by the Indian government in the context of the movement for ADR in the years after Independence.

The other key set of questions that has concerned scholars who have examined the actual practices of women's courts in different parts of India has to do with how successful they are in achieving their aims and living up to their feminist convictions. In contrast to what a woman experiences when she stands before a courtroom judge, faces a panel of male caste elders, or even when she narrates her problems to a professionally trained female social worker, one who tells her sorry tale in the setting of an all-woman court knows at least that her listeners can really understand and empathize with her situation, if only because they themselves are women from backgrounds similar to her own, who have perhaps personally experienced similar situations in the past or have at least seen them play out before in the lives of their own relatives or neighbors. Such a woman also knows that when these mediators try to come up with suggestions for ameliorating her situation, they will take into consideration the particularities of her personal circumstances and propose solutions that are appropriate within the context of a shared set of cultural norms and assumptions about how a woman's life is supposed to be lived.

Thus one cannot deny that all-woman courts provide certain benefits to women who have little access to any other form of recourse when their married life becomes intolerable. They offer, at the very least, a congenial space, not available anywhere else – in either the formal court system or the traditional male-run community councils – where women can speak out freely and without shame about their suffering and can hear what measures others think could be taken to relieve it. But one cannot equate the solutions that these courts offer with the kind of justice that the law is designed – at least in an ideal world – to dispense. But, of course, much hinges here upon what one means by 'justice'. Clearly there is a great disjuncture between the Indian judiciary, the international human rights movement and the advocates of all-woman courts on this point.

As I have indicated, when asked what their immediate goals are, the women who run these organizations invariably say that they aim to 'reconcile' couples, that they try to 'mend homes rather than break them' (cf. Grover 2011, 169). Of course, this goal is also shared by the personnel of women's police stations and legal aid society women's centers. Even family courts are required by law to operate according to this principle (see footnote 1). In her critical discussion of the emphasis on mediation in Kolkata Family Court proceedings, Basu points out the many pitfalls for women that result from this policy of striving to 'reconcile' disputing couples. Too often, the patriarchal values that lie at the root of the women's problems are validated by the agreements they are encouraged to sign and they are sent back into the marriages they were trying to escape from, with only a superficial and unenforceable promise of some slight improvement in the conditions they had come to court to complain of (Basu 2012: 479–488; see also Vatuk 2001). Thus, given their commitment to this goal of keeping marriages intact, we may ask to what extent woman-only courts are able to live up in practice to the feminist principles of the NGOs that are responsible for having set them up in the first place and that, in most cases, continue to run them?

Most of these NGOs' wider aim is to bring about gender equality in society at large, to eliminate the dominant 'patriarchal' norms and values that keep women in a subordinate position and prevent them from full access to the rights to which they are entitled under the Constitution and the laws of the land. One of the principal motivating factors for those who originally conceived of the notion of an all-female dispute settlement forum was their belief that both the organs of the state that are charged with punishing crimes and dispensing justice, as well as such non-state dispute resolution bodies as caste and community councils, are so enmeshed in the existing 'patriarchal' system of values and assumptions about proper gender roles in marriage and the family that they are unable (or unwilling) to mete out true justice to the women who come before them. But are these NGO-sponsored all-woman courts, despite their lofty goals, similarly unable to extricate themselves from the assumptions of the culture within which they live and are they, as a result, unwittingly reproducing the same structures that in theory they aim to destroy?

The difficulty is, that returning home to an abusive husband who has promised to mend his ways may indeed be a woman's only realistic option, in a society where an unattached woman is not only viewed with suspicion and risks sexual harassment or worse but typically has no ready means of supporting herself or even securing more than a temporary roof over her head. Separation or divorce is, furthermore, not necessarily what every woman wants. Nor, even from an outsider's perspective is it always the optimum solution for an economically vulnerable woman who finds herself trapped in a violent marriage. This was what a volunteer social worker with the Madras Family Court responded when I asked him why women who had come to file for divorce or maintenance were consistently being urged to 'reunite', despite the violence, emotional and physical, that the counselors knew they had suffered at their husbands' hands: '[If she divorces,] where will she go? What will she do?' (Vatuk 2001).

The unfortunate reality is that women in this situation don't have many viable alternatives. If they leave their husbands, how will they support themselves – and their children, if any? Their natal relatives are not necessarily prepared to keep them for the long term. To live on their own apart from relatives is socially disapproved and risky and, if they have young children, makes it difficult to leave home every day to go out to work. But most have few or no work skills in any case and, even for those who do, employment opportunities are few and far between.

So, rather than the all-woman court insisting on a radical solution to such a woman's problems, one can argue that it makes sense for mediators to try to at least ameliorate her situation by talking to both parties and make them realize that they have a real stake in keeping their marriage together. In this way they may be able to get the husband to step up to the plate in terms of his financial responsibilities and to convince the wife that she will be better off if, rather than leave her marital home, she 'adjusts' to the situation by conforming as best she can to the ideal model of a submissive housewife, in the hope that her husband will live up to his promise to begin playing his proper role as well.

However, with no state-backed authority to enforce – or even to formally recognize – the agreements they broker, the only way that all-women courts can ensure that the terms of their settlements are complied with is to develop a reputation for fairness and even-handed treatment of both men and women and to rely upon social pressure and persuasion to ensure that their decisions are complied with, just as the male-led clan, caste and village panchayats upon which they model themselves have been doing for centuries. Their success in this regard is likely to be uneven, though unfortunately we have no empirical evidence available as to the extent to which the settlements they devise result in lasting marital reconciliations. A longitudinal investigation, in which one followed a series of individual cases over several years' duration would be required before one could even begin to answer this question.

One of the most positive features of the all-woman court's approach – as its advocates see it – is that peer mediators are able to suggest solutions based on the realities of the women's lives, taking into account the social and cultural context in which they live. Yet, as I have noted above, some of those who have observed the functioning of these bodies first hand have suggested that the women who preside over these courts, despite their generally lower-class origins, often embrace – or gradually *come* to embrace – the middle-class ideology of monogamous, arranged marriage – which is very much the same ideology that guides the decision-making of most male-run caste *panchayats* and the state courts as well. Even though it diverges markedly from the realities of most women's daily lives in this stratum of society, in this way of thinking, the man is the breadwinner/provider and the woman the obedient, stay-at-home housewife. It is clear that too strong a commitment to this kind of traditional ideal, in which a woman's only proper place is within a monogamous marriage, can hinder mediators from finding ways to help a victim of domestic violence escape permanently from an intolerably conflictual marital relationship, get herself on a sound economic footing and start her life anew.

But before reaching a negative assessment of the work of all-woman courts, one must acknowledge that the problems of domestic violence and marital conflict that all-woman courts are attempting to remedy on a case-to-case basis are intricately related to the widely prevailing male bias and resulting gender discrimination that characterizes India's society and culture as a whole. These factors are both related to and exacerbated by the fact that, despite laws to the contrary, women rarely avail themselves – for a variety of reasons – of the property rights to which they are entitled under the law (see Basu 1999). Furthermore, even if they do own property or earn an income from their own labor, they are rarely in a position to fully control their disposal. In addition, a high proportion of Indian women, especially those who live in rural areas, are illiterate; among the rest, the average level of educational attainment remains low. These and other detriments contribute to women's lack of self-confidence in dealing with the world outside of their homes and to their reluctance to step out of the bounds of society's rules for feminine comportment. There are many institutions and organizations – both governmental and non-governmental, and including a plethora of international agencies – that have been devoting themselves for decades to the larger issue of how to banish all kinds of gender inequities within Indian society. That is exactly what AI and MS and other NGOs that sponsor these all-woman courts have been doing from the outset and have continued to do, especially by organizing poor women in local rural and urban communities to work for their own empowerment. But progress, though moving forward in the right direction, is slow.

Tackling these larger social problems is not within the power – nor is it within the mandate of – the kinds of women's courts that I have discussed her. Those who run these courts of course recognize the existence of wider social problems but must restrict themselves to their more immediate task of trying to better the lives of the individual women who come before them with concrete problems. Of necessity, they work, as best they can, within the constraints impored by the larger dominating patriarchal milieu in which they themselves, like their clients, are living every day. In terms of this more modest agenda, they appear to be having some, though admittedly a very mixed, degree of success.

Notes

1. It should be noted that, even if such a woman files suit for divorce or maintenance in a family court, she will be under pressure to compromise her differences with her husband, rather than allow her case to proceed to a judgment. The Family Courts Act 1984 (in Chapter IV9(1)) explicitly instructs these courts to encourage the parties to a dispute to arrive at a settlement, thus obviating the need to present their case to the judge for a decision. For this purpose, litigants must undergo a series of compulsory counseling sessions conducted by social workers (whether professionally trained or not) appointed to the court. Judges also try to mediate between spouses who have been unable to agree even after counseling appear before them to have their cases adjudicated.
2. Publications resulting from this research include Vatuk 2001, 2003 and 2013. My research was funded by a variety of sources, including a Fulbright-Hays Faculty Research Fellowship, Senior Fellowships from the American Institute of Indian Studies and travel grants and research leaves from the University of Illinois at Chicago. I am grateful to these agencies and institutions for their generous support.
3. This was in Chennai, in the winter of 1999.
4. Typically, it is retired judges and other legal professionals and social workers who are most often chosen to serve as mediators in these courts.
5. Today these bodies handle a wide variety of cases, among which automobile accidents and minor criminal offenses are especially prominent. Special 'women's *lok adalats'* (see below) deal mainly with domestic disputes. Inasmuch as the *lok adalats* cater mainly to the poor, '[m]any proponents see them not as a species of court reform but as a species of legal aid, one particularly suited to the poor, the oppressed, and women' (Galanter and Krishnan 2003:109).
6. See Moog 1991 for a first-hand description of the structure and *modus operandi* of such a body, observed by the author in a north Indian town in the late 1980s.
7. In particular, those defining 'the matrimonial home' and 'relationships in the nature of marriage.'
8. The latter lengthy report of an evaluation of the act's effectiveness over time – in India generally and in three states (Delhi, Maharashtra and Rajasthan) in particular – identifies and describes in more detail numerous factors that affect the implementation of the law and recommends a number of improvements.
9. Official statistics on dowry deaths from the early years after passage of this law are difficult to come by but the National Crime Records Bureau of the Government of India provides data showing that, at least since the late 1990s, the incidence of both arrests and convictions under S340-B has been consistently rising. The average number of such deaths reported each year has grown from 6699 in 1999 to 8383 in 2009 (India, Ministry of Home Affairs 2009). The most recent figures indicate that this upward trend has continued, with 8618 women allegedly dying in such incidents in 2011, the latest year for which figures are available (India, Ministry of Home Affairs 2011).
10. See also several articles on the dowry phenomenon in India today in Bradley, et al., 2009.
11. The act, however, did not become operational until 1998.
12. I have not been able to locate more recent all-India figures.
13. This court is commonly known as the Mahila [Women's] Court. Its presiding magistrate also hears cases filed under the Muslim Women (Protection of Rights on Divorce) Act, 1986.
14. A 'first information report,' the first step in initiating a criminal case.
15. But see Holden 2008 and Solanki 2011 for more nuanced views.
16. I found this to be the policy of two mosque committees whose leaders I interviewed at length on several occasions in Chennai in 1999. In one *shari'at* court that I visited in a district town

in Tamil Nadu women complainants were allowed to attend the hearing of their case but were seated in an alcove on one side of the room, behind a heavy curtain. From there they could listen to their male relatives discuss with the *qazi*, their husbands and his male relatives the contentious issues they were seeking to resolve. They could answer questions put directly to them by the *qazi* but could not make spontaneous oral interventions of their own. Even during my interview with him I was directed by the *qazi* to sit within this curtained space. On the other hand, in other *shari'at* courts that I visited (in Chennai, Hyderabad and Delhi), women complainants were admitted to the main hearing room (in one case, on an open verandah) and were able to present their cases directly to the *qazi*, within the hearing of everyone else seated there awaiting their turn.

17. See Pradhan 1966.
18. For a recent example of such an incident, see Rai 2012.
19. In a surprisingly high percentage of cases of domestic violence that are brought to the courts – 40%, according to some studies – the husband's mother and/or other *female* family members allegedly participated in the abuse (Gangoli and Rew 2011, 421, citing Dave and Solanki 2000 and Panchanadeswaran and Koverola 2005).
20. In 1998 the Authority was running 45 such centers in different parts of the state (Raja 1998, 11). It had been officially established in November of 1997, under the Legal Services Authorities Act of 1987, but for the prior two decades many of its functions were already being performed by a predecessor Legal Aid and Advice Board, a registered voluntary society funded by the state of Tamil Nadu (Raja 1998, 1–3). According to the Authority's own figures, 5602 women (from all parts of Tamil Nadu) submitted applications for legal aid between November 1, 1997 and October 31, 1998, the first year of its operation. Over a third of these women (1510) were involved in a matrimonial dispute of some kind. An unknown number were referred for pre-litigation mediation to one of the Authority's *madar sangams* (The Tamil Nadu State Legal Services Authority 1998, 8).
21. The Hindu 2005. See also Vatuk 2013, 350.
22. WRAG was founded in the wake of the communal violence that shook Mumbai in 1992; it concerns itself with a variety of issues affecting Muslim women. Over the years it has received funding from such institutional sources as the Global Fund for Women, Oxfam India, the Consulate General of Germany and a family foundation of the prominent Indian industrialist, J.D.R. Tata, as well as from other philanthropic organizations and individual donors (Women's Research and Action Group n.d.).
23. See Hukook-e-Niswan n.d. In 2009, according to their website, the federation 'reached and helped 200 women facing domestic violence, destitution and discrimination at the hands of Muslim law.' This is a very small number (an average of only eight per *mandal* per year), especially considering that the one *mandal* I visited claimed to deal with approximately 100 'cases' per year and on the day that I observed its proceedings discussed the problems of at least six different women (I had to leave while the session was still in progress). Therefore I assume that the federation's figure of 200 women 'helped' is either a misprint or refers only to those women whose problems the groups were able to 'resolve' by working out a settlement or other informal arrangement to improve their situation or by successfully guiding them through some kind of legal process.
24. MS now operates in a total of ten states, not all of which include the *nari adalat* component in their programs (Jandhyala n.d.).
25. According to one evaluation of the programs in Gujarat, 89% of the cases heard by *nari adalats* fall into one of these categories (Iyengar 2007, 10).

References

Action India. 2009. "Mahila Panchayat Program." Available at: <http://actionindiaworld.org/pages/programs-campaigns/women-law-and-social-change-mahila-panchayat-program.php> last accessed on September 15, 2011.

AIDWA. 2003. *Expanding Dimensions of Dowry*. New Delhi: All India Democratic Women's Association.

Agnes, Flavia. 1998. "Violence Against Women: Review of Recent Enactments." In *In the Name of Justice: Women and Law in Society*, edited by Swapna Mukhopadhyay, 81–116. Delhi: Manohar Publishers.

Badarinath, Pooja. 2011. "The Challenge of Subjectivity Within Courts: Interpreting the Domestic Violence Act." *Economic and Political Weekly* 46 (12): 15–19.

Basu, Malika. 2011. "Solution Exchange for the Gender Community Consolidated Reply: Nyaya Samitis for Dispensing Gender Justice – Experiences, Advice." Available at <ftp://ftp.solutionexchange.net.in/public/gen/cr/cr-se-gen-20071001.pdf> last downloaded on July 10, 2011.

Basu, Srimati. 2012. "Judges of Normality: Mediating Marriage in the Family Courts of Kolkata, India." *Signs* 37 (2): 469–492.

Basu, Srimati. 2005. "The Politics of Giving: Dowry and Inheritance as Feminist Issues." In *Dowry and Inheritance*, edited by Srimati Basu, i–liv. New Delhi: Women Unlimited.

Basu, Srimati. 1999. *She Comes to Take her Rights*. Albany: State University of New York Press.

Bates, Karine. 2010. "The Indian Legal System: A Unique Combination of Traditions, Practices And Modern Values." In *Communication, Culture and Confrontation*, edited by Bernard Bel, Vibodh Parthasarathi and Jan Brouwer, 69–98. New Delhi: Sage Publications India Pvt. Ltd.

Bedi, Tarini. 2010. "The (Im?) Possibilities of a Situated Feminist Subject in Shiv Sena: Shiv Sainiks, Governance, and Adjustment in Maharashtra, India.' In *Histories of Intimacy and Situated Ethnography*, edited by Karen Isaksen Leonard, Gayatri Reddy and Ann Grodzins Gold, 21–82. New Delhi: Manohar Publishers.

Bedi, Tarini. 2009. "Shiv Sena Women and the Gendered Politics of Performance in Maharashtra, India." Unpublished Ph.D. Dissertation, Department of Anthropology, University of Illinois at Chicago.

Bhatla, Nandita and Anuradha Rajan. 2003. "Private Concerns in Public Discourse: Women-Initiated Community Responses to Domestic Violence." *Economic and Political Weekly* 38: 1658–1664.

Bradley, Tamsin, Emma Tomalin and Mangala Subramaniam, eds. 2009. *Dowry: Bridging the Gap Between Theory and Practice*. London: Zed Books.

Chowdhry, Prem. 2007. *Contentious Marriages, Eloping Couples: Gender, Caste and Patriarchy in Northern India*. Delhi: Oxford University Press.

Chowdhry, Prem. 1998. "Enforcing Cultural Codes: Gender and Violence in Northern India." In *A Question of Silence? The Sexual Economies of Modern* India, edited by Mary E. John and Janaki Nair, 332–367. Delhi: Kali for Women.

Dave, Anjali and Gopika Solanki. 2000. "Special Cell for Women and Children: A Research Study on Domestic Violence." In *Domestic Violence in India: A Summary Report of Four Records Studies*, 25–32. Washington, D.C.: International Center for Research on Women.

Dhagamwar, Vasudha. 1992. *Law, Power and Justice: The Protection of Personal Rights in the Indian Penal Code*. New Delhi: Sage Publications.

Dowry Prohibition Act. 1961. Available at: <http://wcd.nic.in/dowryprohibitionact.htm> last downloaded on February 4, 2013.

Dupret, Baudouin. 2007. "Legal Pluralism, Plurality of Laws, and Legal Practices: Theories, Critiques, and Praxiological Re-Specification." *European Journal of Legal Studies* 1 (1). Available at <http://www.ejls.eu/1/14UK.pdf> last downloaded on February 4, 2013.

Express News Service. 2010. "Second Family Court Opens in Rohini." *Indian Express*. Available at: <http://www.indianexpress.com/news/second-family-court-opens-in-rohini/578348> last accessed on July 22, 2011.

Galanter, Marc and Jayanth K. Krishnan. 2003. "Debased Informalism: Lok Adalats and Legal Rights in Modern India." In *Beyond Common Knowledge: Empirical Approaches to the Rule of Law*, edited by Erik G. Jensen and Thomas C. Heller, 96–141. Stanford: Stanford University Press.

Gangoli, Geetanjali and Martin Rew. 2011. "Mothers-in-law Against Daughters-in-Law: Domestic Violence and Legal Discourses Around Mother-in-Law Violence Against Daughters-in-Law in India." *Women's Studies International Forum* 34: 420–429.

Griffiths, John. 1986. "What is Legal Pluralism?" *Journal of Legal Pluralism and Unofficial Law* 24: 1–40.

Grover, Shalini. 2011. *Marriage, Love, Caste and Kinship Support: Lived Experiences of the Urban Poor in India*. New Delhi: Social Science Press.

Ghosh, Biswajit and Tanima Choudhuri. 2011. "Legal Protection Against Domestic Violence in India: Scope and Limitations." *Journal of Family Violence* 26: 219–330.

Hayden, Robert M. 1999. *Disputes and Arguments Amongst Nomads: A Caste Council in India*. New Delhi: Oxford University Press.

Headlines Today Bureau. 2012. "No Country for Women? UP Minister Azam Khan Backs Khap Leaders for Taliban-Like Diktat." Available at: <http://indiatoday.intoday.in/story/up-minister-azam-khan-khaps-love-marriages/1/208023.html> last accessed on October 1, 2012.

Holden, Livia. 2008. *Hindu Divorce: A Legal Anthropology*. Aldershot: Ashgate Publishing Ltd.

Hukook-E-Niswan. n.d. <http://hukook-e-niswanmahilasanghatana.blogspot.com> last accessed on October 1, 2012.

Hussain, Sabiha. 2006. "Shariat Courts and Women's Rights in India." Available at: <http://www.cwds.ac.in/OCPaper/ShariatCourts-Sabiha-ocpaper.pdf> last downloaded on July 22, 2011.

India, Ministry Of Home Affairs. 2009. *Crime in India*. Available at: <http://ncrb.nic.in/CII-2009-NEW/Statistics2009.pdf> last downloaded on September 1, 2011.

India, Ministry Of Home Affairs. 2011. *Crime in India*. Available at: <http://ncrb.gov.in/CD-CII2011/cii-2011/Chapter%205.pdf> last downloaded on September 1, 2012.

India, Ministry Of Panchayati Raj. 2006. *State of the Panchayats, A Mid-Term Review and Appraisal, 22 November 2006*. New Delhi: Government of India.

India, Parliament. 1982. *Report: Joint Committee of the Houses to Examine the Question of the Working of the Dowry Prohibition Act 1961*. New Delhi: Lok Sabha Secretariat.

Iyengar, Sushma. 2007. *A Study of Nari Adalats (Women's Courts) and Caste Panchayats in Gujarat*. Bangkok: United Nations Development Programme. Available at: <http://regionalcentrebangkok.undp.or.th/practices/governance/a2j/docs/CaseStudy-05-India-NariAdalat.pdf> last downloaded on July 22, 2011.

Jamwal, Namita Singh. 2009. "Have Family Courts Lived Up to Expectations?" *Mainstream* 47 (12). Available at: <http://mainstreamweekly.net/article1205.html> last accessed on January 6, 2011.

Jandhyala, Kameshwari. n.d. "Empowering Education: The Mahila Samakhya Experience." Available at: <www.portal.unesco.org/.../ea8dc35fd1a0a150c7f436b3ba0380afEmpowering+Education.+The+Mahila+Samakhya+Experience.doc> last accessed on October 5, 2012.

Jhamb, Bhumika. 2011. "The Missing Link in the Domestic Violence Act." *Economic and Political Weekly* 46 (33): 45–50.

Kahol, Vikas. 2012. "Khap Panchayat Orders Family to Disinherit Couple or Face Social Boycott." *India Today*. Available at: <http://indiatoday.intoday.in/story/khap-panchayat-family-disinherit-couple-social-boycott/1/222893.html> last accessed on October 5, 2012.

Kandiyoti, Deniz. 1988. "Bargaining With Patriarchy." *Gender & Society* 2 (3): 274–290.

Karat, Brinda. 2004. "India: Price of Honour – Caste Panchayats as Instruments of Terror." *Times of India*. Available at: <http://www.sacw.net/article1048.html> last accessed on September 10, 2011.

Katzenstein, Mary F. 1989. "Organizing Against Violence: Strategies of the Indian Women's Movement." *Pacific Affairs* 62: 53–71.

Lawyers Collective. 2012. *Staying Alive: 5th Monitoring & Evaluation 2012 on the Protection of Women from Domestic Violence Act, 2005*. Available at: <http://www.lawyerscollective.org/files/Staying%20Alive%205th%20M&E.pdf> last downloaded on September 13, 2012.

Lemons, Katherine. 2010. 'At the Margins of Law: Adjudicating Muslim Families in Contemporary Delhi.' Ph. D. Dissertation, Berkeley: University of California.

Magar, Veronica. 2003. "Empowerment Approaches to Gender-Based Violence: Women's Courts in Delhi Slums." *Women's Studies International Forum* 26: 509–523.

Mahila Samakhya Karnataka. 2012. "Gateway to Justice." Available at: <http://www.mahilasamakhyakarnataka.org/publications.html> last accessed on October 6, 2012.

Merry, Sally E. 2006. "Transnational Human Rights and Local Activism: Mapping the Middle." *American Anthropologist* 108: 38–51.

Merry, Sally E. 1988. "Legal Pluralism." *Law and Society Review* 22 (5): 869–896.

Meschievitz, Catherine S. and Marc Galanter. 1982. "In Search of *Nyaya Panchayats*: The Politics of a Moribund Institution." In *The Politics of Informal Justice: Comparative* Studies, edited by Richard Abel, 47–77. New York: Academic Press.

Metcalf, Barbara D. 2006, "Imrana: Rape, Islam, and Law in India." *Islamic Studies* 45: 389–412.

Moog, Robert S. 1991. "Conflict and Compromise: The Politics of *Lok Adalats* in Varanasi District." *Law and Society Review* 25: 545–569.

Moore, Erin P. 1998. *Gender, Law, and Resistance in India*. Tucson: University of Arizona Press.

Moore, Erin P. 1993. "Gender, Power, and Legal Pluralism: Rajasthan, India." *American Ethnologist* 20: 522–542.

Mukherjee, Roma. 1998. *Women, Law and Free Legal Aid in India*. New Delhi: Deep and Deep Publications.

Nader, Laura. 2002. *The Life of the Law: Anthropological Projects*. Berkeley: University of California Press.

Nader, Laura. 1992. "From Legal Process to Mind Processing." *Family Court Review* 30 (4): 468–473.

Panchanadeswaran, Subhadra and Catherine Koverola. 2005. "The Voices of Battered Women in India." *Violence Against Women* 11: 738–758.

Poonacha, Veena and Divya Pandey. 2000. "Responses to Domestic Violence: Government and Non-Government Action in Karnataka and Gujarat." *Economic and Political Weekly* 35 (3): 566–574.

Pradhan, Mahesh C. 1966. *The Political System of the Jats of Northern India*. London: Oxford University Press.

Rai, Rajat. 2012. "UP Panchayat Bans Love Marriages, Bans Women From Using Mobile Phones." *India Today*. Available at: <http://indiatoday.intoday.in/story/up-panchayat-bans-love-marriages-bars-women-from-using-mobile-phones/1/207792.html> last accessed on July 14, 2012.

Raja, M. 1998. *Legal Aid Programme in Tamil Nadu*. Unpublished Report, Tamil Nadu State Legal Services Authority.

Rao, Vijayendra. 1993. "Dowry Inflation in Rural India: A Statistical Investigation." *Population Studies* 47: 283–293.

Reddy, Sheela. 2010. "Khaps Have to Reform." *Outlook India*. Available at: <http://www.outlookindia.com/article.aspx?266072> last accessed on August 1, 2012.

Sangwan, Jagmati. 2010. "Caste Panchayats Defying the Law of Land." Available at: <http://southasia.oneworld.net/fromthegrassroots/caste-panchayats-defying-the-law-of-land> last accessed on September 15, 2011.

Sekhon, Joti. 1999. "Grassroots Social Organization and Empowerment in India: The Case of Action India Women's Program." In *Democratization and Women's Grassroots Movements*, edited by Jill M. Bystydzienski and Joti Sekhon, 25–48. Bloomington Indiana University Press.

Sen, Atreyee. 2007. *Shiv Sena Women: Violence and Communalism in a Bombay Slum*. Bloomington: Indiana University Press.

Siddiqui, Pervez I. 2012. "Rashtriya Lok Dal Supports Diktat of Baghpat Khap Panchayat." *Times of India*. Available at: <http://articles.timesofindia.indiatimes.com/2012-07-15/india/32684790_1_khap-panchayat-panchayat-orders-panchayat-members> last accessed on July 15, 2012.

Solanki, Gopika. 2011. *Adjudication in Religious Family Laws: Cultural Accommodation, Legal Pluralism, and Gender Equality in India*. Cambridge: Cambridge University Press.

Special Correspondent. 2006. "Caste Panchayats "Illegitimate," says Panchayati Raj Ministry." *The Hindu*. Available at: <http://www.hindu.com/2006/11/26/stories/2006112602221000.htm> last accessed on September 10, 2011.

Srivastava, Piyush. 2012. "Panchayat Imposes Fine on Listening to Music on Mobile in Ghatampur Village." *India Today*. Available at: <http://indiatoday.intoday.in/story/panchayat-imposes-fine-on-listening-to-music-on-mobile-in-ghatampur-village/1/217834.html> last accessed on October 5, 2012.

Tamil Nadu State Legal Services Authority. 1998. *Analysis for October 1998*. Unpublished Statistics.

The Hindu. 2005. "Muslim Women Board Registers 166 Cases." February 27. Available at: <http://www.hindu.com/2005/02/27/stories/2005022702101100.htm> last accessed on April 25, 2006.

TNN. 2011. "New family court at Saket." *Times of India*. Available at: <http://articles.timesofindia.indiatimes.com/2011-06-01/delhi/29607540_1_saket-court-family-courts-act-matrimonial-disputes> last accessed on July 22, 2011.

Uberoi, Patricia. 1996. "When is a Marriage Not a Marriage? Sex, Sacrament and Contract in Hindu Marriage." In *Social Reform, Sexuality and the State*, edited by Patricia Uberoi, 319–346. New Delhi: Sage Publications.

Vanderlinden, Jacques. 1989. "Return to Legal Pluralism, Twenty Years Later." *Journal of Legal Pluralism and Unofficial Law*, 27 (1): 149–157.

Vatuk, Sylvia. 2013. "Islamic Feminism in India: Indian Muslim Women Activists and the Reform of Muslim Personal Law." In *Islamic Reform in South Asia*, edited by Filippo Osella and Caroline Osella, 346–382. Cambridge: Cambridge University Press.

Vatuk, Sylvia. 2003. "Moving the Courts: Muslim Women and Personal Law." In *The Diversity of Muslim Women's Lives in India*, edited by Zoya Hasan and Ritu Menon, 18–58. New Brunswick: Rutgers University Press.

Vatuk, Sylvia. 2001. "'Where will she go? What will she do?' Paternalism Toward Women in the Administration of Muslim Personal Law in Contemporary India." In *Religion and Personal Law in Secular India: A Call to Judgment*, edited by Gerald J. Larson, 226–238. Bloomington: Indiana University Press.

Venkat, Vidya. 2008. "An Act of Faith." *The Hindu*. Available at: <http://www.flonnet.com/fl2508/stories/20080425250811300.htm> last accessed on September 25, 2010.

Wikipedia. n.d. "Manoj Babli Honour Killing Case". Available at: <http://en.wikipedia.org/wiki/Manoj-Babli_honour_killing_case> last accessed on October 6, 2011.

Women's Research and Action Group. n.d. <www.wrag.org> last accessed on October 1, 2012.

Yardley, Jim. 2011. "Unelected Councils in India Run Villages with Stern Hand." *New York Times*. Available at: <http://www.nytimes.com/2011/06/05/world/asia/05india.html?pagewanted=all> last accessed on September 15, 2011.

Daughters' inheritance, legal pluralism, and governance in Pakistan

Livia Holden[a] and Azam Chaudhary[b]

[a]*Department of Anthropology, Lahore University of Management Sciences, LUMS, Lahore;*
[b]*National Institute of Pakistan Studies, Quaid-i-Azam University, Islamabad*

This paper explores social actors' arguments regarding daughters' inheritance, their use in court, and the implications of legal pluralism on governance in Pakistan. It scrutinizes the notion of custom, non-state law, and positive law as crucial dynamics that shed light on the ways social actors make sense of power and governance. In Foucauldian terms, this paper deals with the formation of statements – their temporalization and their becoming but in particular sheds light on the potential logics of the perpetuation of gender discrimination in inheritance laws. This paper suggests that the everyday arguments that play a role in the elaboration of the story told to the courts and received by the judge have the role of *actants*. Within the framework of proceedings it is possible to isolate the micro-units on which the legal discourse is elaborated either for state- or non-state jurisdiction, or for both of them, not necessarily seen as antagonistic places, and not necessarily seen within a framework of justice and injustice. This paper concludes that notwithstanding polarized discourses on centralized and decentralized governance, everyday practices of law in Pakistan tend rather to perpetuate non-state law together with positive law as continuous and concomitant interlegalities in and beyond the state instead of exclusive and conflicting sources of legitimacy.

Introduction

Empowerment of women through improved legal consciousness has gained a prominent role in the programmes of social activists aiming at gender equality in South Asia. Family law has been amended so as to increasingly favour women, at least formally, and codified personal laws recognize women's inheritance rights even if this is in conflict with custom. The *Muslim Personal Law (Shariat) Application Act*, 1937 and successively the *Muslim Personal Law (Shariat) Application Act*, 1961 of the former West Pakistan provided for limited inheritance rights for Muslim women (contrary to the customs that instead would disinherit women): as a general principle daughters have a right to half the share of their brothers or 2/3 if there are no brother/s with further differences depending on the configuration of the family and depending on the sect. The Constitution of 1973 broadly speaking also protects women's inheritance and the *Prevention of Anti-Women Practices (Criminal Law Amendment) Act*, 2011 specifically prohibits women's disinheritance with section 498 A and 498 C, reported hereafter for the convenience of the readers:

> *498A. Prohibition of depriving woman from inheriting properly.* Whoever by deceitful or, illegal means deprives any woman from inheriting any movable or immovable

property at the time of opening of succession shall be punished with imprisonment for either description for a term which may extend to ten years but not be less than *five years* or with a fine of one million rupees or both.

498C. Prohibition of marriage with the Holy Quran. Whoever compels or arranges or facilitates the marriage of a woman with the Holy Quran shall be punished with imprisonment of either description, which may extend to seven years which shall not be less than three years and shall be liable to fine of *five hundred thousand rupees.*

Explanation - Oath by a woman on Holy Quran to remain unmarried for the rest of her life or, not to claim her share of inheritance shall be deemed to be marriage with the Holy Quran.

As this paper shows, Muslim women in Pakistan not only can count now on the support of socio-legal activists but their inheritance claims in court are often granted credibility at their onset. As our paper also suggest, the number and the rate of success of women initiated suits in the Muslim contexts may be underrated (see Rosen unpublished draft). Nevertheless, it is also a fact that women seem to prefer relinquishing their inheritance rights by signing away their shares to their brothers. Feminist and socio-legal scholarships have abundantly highlighted the link between gender inequalities and the access and control of property. The feminist standpoint is therefore a point of depart here for a complementary approach that investigates the production of the locally significant social practices in relation to gender. While we do not refute the evident gender imbalance of inheritance practices in Pakistan, we adopt a skeptical approach to investigate the arguments of women's disinheritance as well as the circumstances and temporalization in which women can successfully claim their share. Our paper draws on qualitative case studies collected both out of court and in court in Punjab and on a published case law in Gilgit Baltistan. Thus, this paper offers a range of situations chosen by the authors as representative, even if not exhaustively, of the variety encountered in the long-term fieldwork carried out by the authors. Terms and conditions of daughters' inheritance-claims as outlined in the three different settings will throw light into the relationship between law and custom and their use in court in two different settings of governance: the Punjab, which is considered to be the main decision-making source in Pakistan, and Gilgit Baltistan, which is to date still a contested territory to many extents.

Methodological remarks

The material and the analysis offered hereafter are the outcome of a collaboration between two anthropologists whose research interests and fieldwork have developed along similar lines for what concerns the favour for qualitative methods, the attention to non-state jurisdiction, and the pragmatic approach to data-analysis. One author was born in Pakistan and has long-term experience of fieldwork and academia in Germany. The other was born in Italy and has long-term experience of fieldwork and academia in South Asia. Such an essentialist positioning is proposed here to acknowledge the potential social perceptions of our collaboration. Although we are not always on the same page, on the basis of the comparison of our data we have found several points of agreement that we will signal by talking in first person plural.

Similarly to some of our respective works, we privilege here the data collected in the field through direct observation and interviews. However we also pursue a multidisciplinary dialogue between law and anthropology by including the analysis of published and non-published case law. This is not done without a careful consideration of the different settings and modalities of data collection. The published case law is interpreted in the light of the analysis elaborated in the field, and the data collected through interviews with the judiciary is acting as a link between the fieldwork out of court in the everyday life and the specialized setting of law courts and legal technicalities.

Because of our emphasis on the social actors' arguments, we will propose hereafter the case studies first of all and will progressively include our analysis without however overindulging in theoretic definitions. Although presented here in the format of case studies the following may be better understood as polyphonic narratives in the sense of accounts of facts that meet the approval of the involved social actors. For this reason the points of analysis that stem directly from the social actors' narratives will not be removed from the accounts. Eventually as our conclusion will show even though these cases are not absolutely commensurable the interest of their comparison lies in their similarities in spite of the difference of their settings.

Misalpur (Punjab)

Three case studies collected in Misalpur (Punjab) have been selected for this paper. These case studies have been followed over the last 20 years by Azam, thanks to his very close point of observation and participation in the context described here.[1] They should not be understood as absolutely representative of female inheritance cases in the Punjab and not even in Misalpur. Nevertheless they are chosen as discursive illustration of the modalities and potential of women's inheritance claims. Similarly to most qualitative case studies focusing on the temporal construction of arguments, these case studies exceed the narrow focus on women's inheritance to involve the interests of entire families. As such they will be particularly useful in highlighting the social implications of the relinquishment of inheritance rights by women in Pakistan.

Case study 1: Mavara, Khadija, and Mandan

Mavara is the only sister of five brothers. Her father has a small landholding of one and a half acres. She is married to Shafiq, the son of her maternal uncle. She is the third child

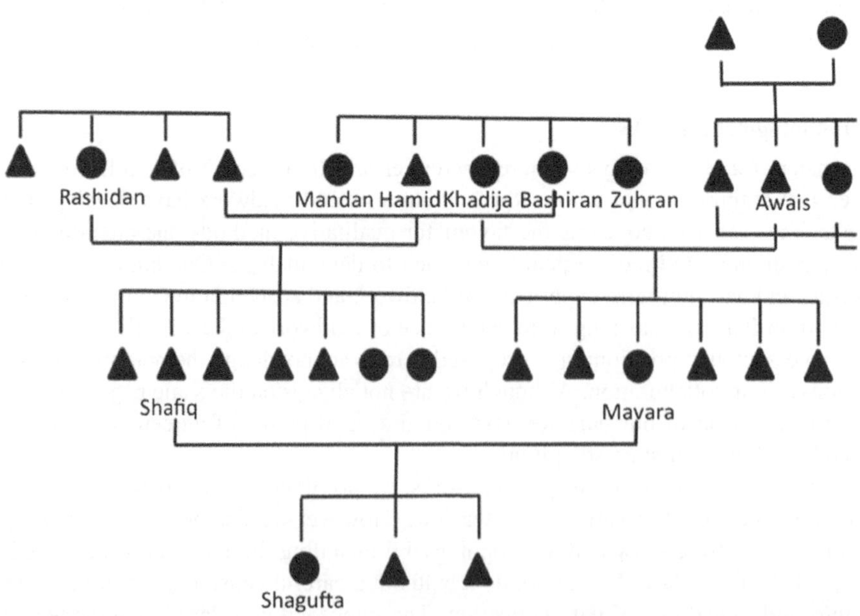

but was the first one to be married – as it is common for women to be married earlier than her male siblings. Her brothers received a good education, secured higher positions at different, mostly government institutions, and now they run their own business in Islamabad. Mavara did not receive any education. When Shagufta, the eldest daughter of Mavara, reached school age, she went to Islamabad to attend school and lived with her maternal uncle's family. Later on, Mavara's brothers established a business for Shafiq. Mavara joined her husband in Islamabad and started to live close to her brothers. Mavara is, however, not considered to be a part of the joint family system of her brothers, which does not mean that she is deprived of her family's support. On the contrary, Mavara's brothers, besides supporting the establishment of their brother-in-law's business, also help their sister in the daily affairs of life including the education of her children (two sons and one daughter) and her business. Mavara gets her gifts, collectively known as *dian* (daughter's gifts) in the Punjab, on all occasions including: yearly *Eids* (one called *Eid-ul-Fitar* celebrated at the end of Ramadan, the Muslim fasting month, and the second *Eid-ul-Azha*, the Muslim slaughter festival); occasional family ceremonies like marriages, circumcisions, birth of male children, etc. She quarrels with her brothers if the gifts she receives do not meet her expectations. She may even temporarily refuse to receive *dian* if she finds that it is not enough. Yet she would vehemently refuse any proposal to claim her share of family patrimony.

Khadija, Mavara's mother, has one brother and three sisters. Khadija's mother, Barkat Bibi, migrated at the time of partition of India in 1947 from Indian Punjab to the Pakistani Punjab and chose to settle in the village of her brother because Allah Bakhsh, Barkat Bibi's husband, was seriously ill and later on died during that same year. Khadija was married to a second paternal cousin, Awais. Khadija, who is considered to be an intelligent and resourceful woman, has great aspirations for her children. She has succeeded in getting higher education for her children and she also helped her paternal family in every possible way. Among other things she has managed to help her mother to organize the marriages of her two younger sisters and the second marriage of her only brother after he divorced his first wife. Khadija also helped her mother and brother, Hamid, to pay-off the loans that they have acquired to arrange all these marriages. Later on, she has also helped, to arrange the marriages of Hamid's four sons and two daughters. Eventually the second son of Hamid, Shafiq was married to Mavara, Khadija's daughter.

Disputes arose between Hamid and Khadija as a result of conflicts between the children of Hamid. Hamid wrote off three of his five sons from the inheritance to which Shafiq too has right to a share. Hamid transferred most of the landed property to his other two sons. The sons who were excluded called a village *panchayat* (council of village elders and respectable persons) that however failed to end the differences between Hamid and his sons. Khadija fell herself into disagreement with her brother and disgusted by his deeds she declared her intentions to claim her share of the patrimony. Hamid responded with a counter-claim for the share of Mavara who was also his daughter-in-law. Hamid laughed at the idea that Mavara and Khadija may even consider claiming a share. Eventually Khadija did not go to court nor called the *panchayat* to make the claim.

Mandan, Khadija's elder sister, had instead secured her share in the agricultural land of her deceased father through the intervention of the court. She was married to Ali Ahmed her cousin on her mother's side, who was living next door. Mandan was the eldest out of four sisters and one brother. Bashiran, the third one, and now the only living sister, recently expressed her desire to get her share, but Hamid made a counter-claim here too for Rashidan, his wife, who is the sister of Bashiran's husband. Zuhran, the youngest sister of Khadija, had developed conflicts both with Khadija and Hamid on matters relating to the marriage of her children. Zuhran has four sons and two daughters. The only daughter of Khadija was engaged to the eldest son of Zuhran and Zuhran's two sons were engaged to Hamid's two daughters. Zuhran, however, got seriously ill and her husband lost his job in Saudi Arabia. Due to the deteriorating economic conditions of Zuhran, both Khadija and Hamid broke off the engagements. Zuhran and her husband both died and their children never mentioned the inheritance claims of their mother. The brothers of Rashidan sold their land and gave their sister her share in cash. Eventually the conflicts between Hamid and his sons were resolved and he decided to divide his land among his sons. He purchased the share of Bashiran and gave a cash share to the sons and daughter of Khadija who died last year. The share of Zuhran, which could be claimed by her six children, remains unresolved.

Case study 2: Awais Bibi nicknamed Shado

Shado is the sister of Awais, the husband of Khadija in the case study 1. When Shado's brothers gathered to divide their agricultural land there was a sour exchange among them. The cause of the quarrel was not only their sister's claim, but also the question of who shall get which piece of agricultural land, what portion of the house and which animal. As for the share of Shado, the sole sister, one brother, Ali, insisted on giving her the due share of land. The other brothers, most of them farmers, did not agree. Shado had not demanded her share until then and had never raised the issue with her brothers. However, she would not have refused to inherit either.

Her brothers, except Ali, explained that they felt ashamed because in their entire *shrika* (close patrilineage) no other woman had ever claimed her property. Shado, on her part, explained that she wanted her share because she was angry with her brothers especially the eldest two who refused to accept her daughters in marriage for their sons. Arshad, the only son of Niaz, her eldest brother, was married to his cousin on his mother's side. This was actually the fourth marriage between these two families – two brothers of Awais were married there, his sister Shado's first marriage and the marriage of Arshad: they had all married the children of their maternal uncle. Similarly, Khadija, the wife of Awais, also did not agree to a marriage between one of her sons (she had five sons) and one of Shado's daughters. Khadija, on her part, was angry for being 'ill

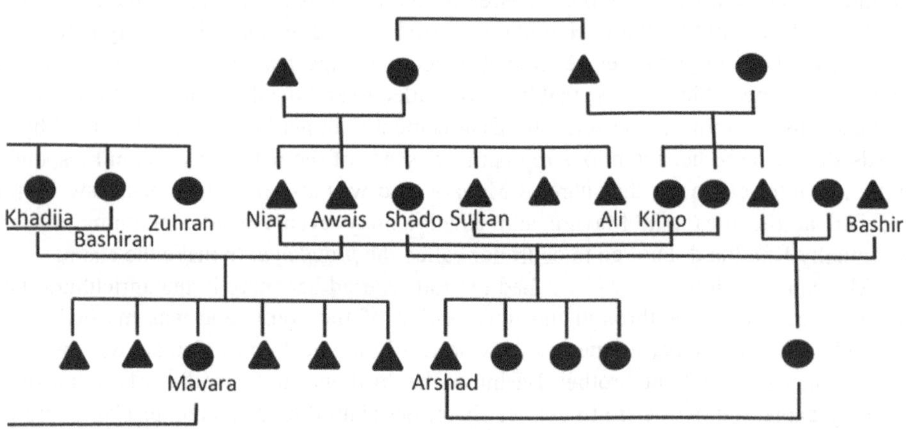

treated' by Shado as sister-in-law during the early years of Khadija's marriage. Shado was also angry that her brothers have not been generous in giving *dian* (gifts of daughter) for the marriage of her children. The brothers claimed that they had married her off twice and both times with full dowry and had given full *nankishak* (special marriage gifts given to the sister's children) at the marriage of her children. Her brother, Ali, was the only one to argue that Shado's share was her legal, Islamic right.

There is no wide support in the family for female inheritance. Two of Shado's brothers had married the daughters of their maternal uncle and these daughters never claimed their share of inheritance, which was taken by their brothers. Their husbands have also never asked them to do so. Ali, similarly, left it to his wife to decide and she did not claim her share. His father-in-law is still alive but has sold all his agricultural land and has instead bought a house in Islamabad. This house has been registered in the name of only one of his four sons. He has disinherited the other three sons because of family disagreements. Kimo, the wife of Niaz, the eldest brother of Shado, and Kimo's only daughter in-law are both against the idea of the women's share of inheritance. Kimo's three daughters and Niaz, all of them married with grown up children, do not want to claim their shares from Arshad, their only brother. Arshad, who is a clerk in a government office in Islamabad, on the contrary, is of the view that it is his father's property and he can do as he pleases. He is not very convinced either of the idea of daughters' inheritance' share. Sultan, another brother of Shado, has no daughters and only one son named Munir. Fatima, the wife of Sultan, died long ago. Sultan does not want his wife's share and his daughter-in-law, Kulsum, also does not want to claim her share. Actually one brother and one sister of Kulsum are living with them, which makes even more insignificant Kulsum's potential claim.

When Bashir, the husband of Shado, who lives in a distant village, came to collect the rent of his wife's newly claimed land nobody welcomed him in the family of his in-laws. The brothers of Shado, their children and wives especially, taunted him. They abused him for being greedy and claiming the share of his wife all the more in that he does not want to give his daughters their share. They further taunted him by assuming that he must be actually praying for the early death of his daughter-in-law's father so that he can soon collect the rent of her share too. Quite interestingly Shado and her husband Bashir are also against giving their own three daughters their inheritance.

Case study 3: Shahnaz

Shahnaz's husband, Aslam, is a *beupari* (Urdu middleman between farmer and consumer). He buys animals and agricultural products from farmers and sells them in the city. They live as a joint family with Aslam's elder brother, Arsalan, and parents. Arsalan who has lost one leg in an accident many years ago helps his father in farming. They have a very small landholding barely enough to grow some wheat for their own consumption and some fodder for one or two water buffalos that they keep for milk. The three sisters of Aslam are already married. Aslam leaves every morning after breakfast on his bicycle to travel to nearby villages or the city of Faisalabad for business. Sometimes, he will earn something but very often he will come home with little success. Aslam hands over whatever he earns to his father, Karim, who as the head of the house controls all the resources. The food is cooked and eaten together and Sultana, the mother, distributes the portions. The family has not much money and from whatever they earn they also try to save something.

Shahnaz and her husband quarrel almost daily. She wants money to buy shoes, clothes and books for her children. Aslam does not even tell her how much he earns – "It is not

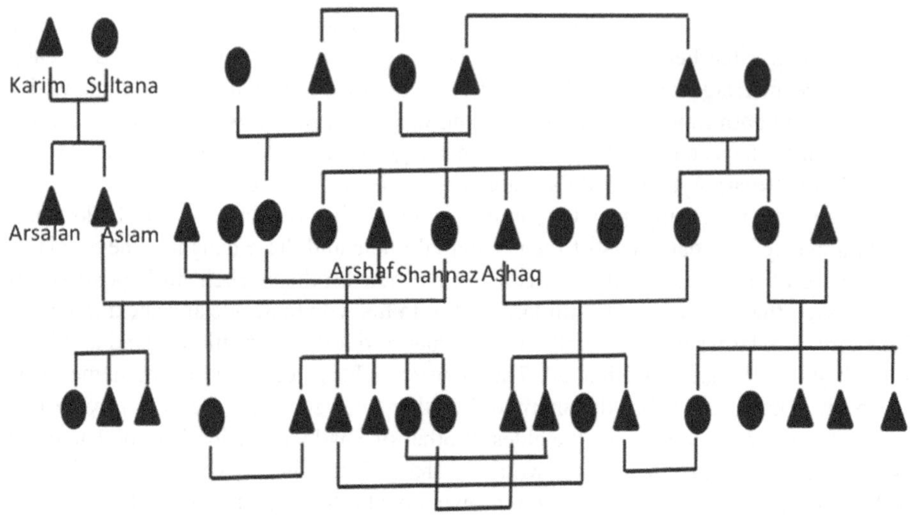

your concern" – he tells her. She has a very heavy daily workload which includes going to the *haveli* (farm house) early in the morning where she milks the buffalos, gives them fodder, cleans the stalls, etc. Afterwards having cleaned the house she cooks for everybody and washes the clothes. After all this work she does not get even small pocket money. She was beaten by her husband's elder brother, Arsala, and by her father-in-law on several occasions for demanding money and a separate house for her. She complained to Aslam but he flatly told her that he cannot prevent his father and elder brother from beating her especially when she demands a separate house or money. In the five years of her married life, she has left her husband's house seven times after fighting with her in-laws. Every time, the elders and relatives belonging to the two families gathered and made peace between them. In the meantime, she had three children. Her two brothers and father send her some money every month for the school fees of her children and for their clothes and books. All this is by no means unusual in the village. The daughters of the village in the early years of their marriage have these conflicts, which are known as "*lar ke aie*" or "*gharaun kad diti*" (Urdu literally means "came having quarrelled" or "was thrown out of the house").

Shahnaz's *maike* (Urdu maternal home) consists of two brothers and four sisters. Ashraf, the eldest brother, is married to the paternal uncle's daughter. Ashaq, the younger brother, is married to the maternal uncle's daughter. Three sisters of Shahnaz are also married within the close family. Shahnaz is the only sibling who is married outside the "*sharika*" (Urdu close patrilineage). Two brothers of Shahnaz and her father on several occasions considered getting a divorce for her. They know that it will be very difficult to find a new husband for their divorced daughter especially as she already has three children. All these years they hoped the situation would change for the better. Her brothers once made plans to beat Arsalan and Aslam but this came to nothing as beating the husband of one's sister reflects to their own disgrace.

Shahnaz fell seriously ill – it was thought she had a cancer – and was not taken much care of at the house of her in-laws. Ashraf, her elder brother, brought her back to her parental family along with all three children. Her brothers took her to the hospital and proper diagnostic tests were performed. She was diagnosed with tuberculosis. She stayed with her brothers until she recovered. The brothers bought clothes for her and her children and gave her money for the medicine. Shahnaz and her other three sisters have written off their claim of property in favour of their brothers.

Ashaq, the younger brother, has three sons and one daughter and Ashraf has three sons and two daughters. Two sons of Ashaq are married with Ashraf's two daughters and one son of Ashraf is married to the only daughter of Ashaq. One son of Ashaq is married outside of the close family because (as Ashraf told) there was no girl in the close family. One of the two remaining sons of Ashraf is married to the mother's sister's daughter. The last is still unmarried. The agriculture land and the commercial property owned by the two brothers have already been transferred to the names of the sons. The two brothers are of the view that daughters and sisters should not get any share because they anyway come to the brothers if they have any difficulty. Their share is safe with the brothers but not if it is transferred in their names because then the husbands take it over like the dowry. Shahnaz is still young and insecure in the family of her in-laws. This will most probably change after the death of her father-in-law and mother-in-law.

Temporalization of claims

From a conventional feminist standpoint, the reported case studies can be viewed as merely confirming the ethnographic scholarship signalling that women in Pakistan do not get their share of inheritance (see among others Ali 1997; Alavi 1972; Chaudhary 2010; Haque 2000; Mehdi 2002; Patel 1979). And in fact in the early 1990s in Misalpur only two women out of a population of more than 15,000 inhabitants were reported to have claimed their inheritance. These cases were very well known in the village and referred to as "bad practice". Socio-legal scholarship has detected a wide spectrum of causes for women's disinheritance in South Asia. These causes range from women's illiteracy, scarce legal consciousness, and poor access to justice, to the post-colonial scrutiny of legal transplants and including materialistic analysis of the customs that perpetuate the accumulation of wealth. All these suggested perspectives can apply in the Misalpur case studies as well.

It is generally argued that women fear the police and avoid initiating law suits because of the shame that this would bring not only to themselves but to their family as well (Ali 1997; Haque 2000; Mehdi 2002; Patel 1979). It has also been argued that the cross-cousin marriage system itself is structurally informed by the effort to keep the property inside the family. This analysis is confirmed by the popularity of *watta-satta* (Urdu exchange marriage) according to which brides are exchanged between two families: Bashiran and Rashidan in Mavara's case study, and the marriages between the children of Ashaq and Arshad in Shanaz' case study. The practice of the marriage to the Quran, now forbidden but apparently recurrent in the absence of a suitable groom, seems to also confirm the same widespread anxiety for keeping the property from being transferred outside the family (Mehdi 2002). Marriage to the Quran has been considered to have been envisioned "to deny women their rights of inheritance and out of fear of property being passed on to outsiders through the daughters or sisters [i.e. their spouses or children]" (Al-Shafey 2007, http://www.asharq-e.com/news.asp?section=3&id=9656). Similarly Khan (2009, http://www.albaspectrum.com/Articles1/Women/00994.html) writes:

> However primitive it may sound – however primitive it is – it is very easy for a Sindhi to declare his sister, daughter or wife as shameful, and thus opt to kill her . . . when ever there is a monetary, land, property related or other petty dispute, many unscrupulous persons use their sisters, wives, mothers or even daughters as a tool to have upper hand in settlement of the dispute. . . .It is also a common practice in Sindh to marry one's daughter to inanimate and holy

> objects, like the Quran, or even a tree, for example [. . .] The main purpose behind this inhuman act is to avoid the transfer of land property out of family hands at the time of marriage of their daughter or sister.

While the quest for gender equality by the above scholarship is only laudable we argue that further scrutiny of the relationship between custom and religion will throw light on the reasons for the perpetuation of women's disinheritance in spite of legislative amendments. First of all it would be misleading to assume that the origin of these customs is necessarily a religious one. In fact similar customs, as various forms of *karewa* (Hindi levirate) and the marriage to a tree due to the absence of a suitable husband (also used to allow a subsequent marriage that would be otherwise inauspicious if it were a first marriage), are well known for being practiced among Hindus in India and inherently implying some kind of iniquitous control over women and property rights. Custom, as we see here, is often overlapping but also exceeding the personal laws recognized by the state. It is important to point out the danger of the essentialized interpretations that sometimes are found in the official legal contexts as well as in certain scholarship that too easily equate customs with personal laws (see also Introduction, Parashar, Shah, and Menski in this special issue). If we look at the modalities of women's inheritance claims – their temporalization and their becoming – it becomes clear that there are other factors underlying the apparently non-sense choice of forfeiting one's own share.

In fact the principal blind spot of the current socio-legal framework are the reasons why in spite of the rapidly changing infrastructure and improving social awareness of gender inequality, women in South Asia still avoid claiming their inheritance shares. When looking at the circumstances of Khadija's claim we see that her interest in the share materializes at a specific time. After the death of her father, Khadija was by far better off than her natal family because her in-laws were rich and treated her well. Her own concern was instead to support her mother and to help her marrying off her sisters. She had no interest in challenging the authority of her own brother from whom she was getting everyday support that constituted respect and social stability. The situation however changed after Khadija's brother disinherited some of his own children thereby impacting also on the well-being of Khadija's daughter who had been married to her brother's son. This had caused the utter discontent of Khadija. Hence her inheritance claim which however she might have very well never fully finalized if she were still alive because the threat of exercising this right amounts also to power that might be more useful in embryo.

Our case studies suggest that inheritance claims are more easily initiated by women who have secured their position in their husbands' family. This happens after women have children, especially sons as in the case of Rashidan, or where they have played a role in the financial and social stability or even mobility of the family as in the case of Khadija. Khadija's case furthermore shows that tensions with the woman's brother or brothers, here due to divergences in the choice of the children's marriage, can trigger women's initiated inheritance claims. Court sanctioned rights on the other hand, as in Shado's case study, may indeed be linked with urbanization and formal education, but are likely to be met with the overwhelming resistance within the village social context.

Eventually our analysis as refuting the sweeping generalizations that equate custom with personal laws against women's rights may appear, at first sight, to support nativist perspectives that diametrically oppose conventional feminism by arguing for the intrinsic logics of women's disinheritance in South Asia. However we suggest the unproductivity of the polarization between tradition and modernity because this fails to explain the *de facto* co-existence of inheritance and disinheritance claims. These claims are better understood if we take into account the circumstances of their materialization and eventually their strategic role in terms of power and agency. The picture will acquire more details if we have a closer look at how inheritance claims are managed in the setting of official law in Pakistan. Our hypothesis is that a better understanding of the use of customs and of the arguments upholding it in court, may lead to an integrated perspective overcoming the polarization between nativist and modernist approaches.

Punjab – District and session court Kasur

The following is a case that Livia has collected with the collaboration of one of the women judges who have participated on the *Lady Judges of Pakistan* project, during which she has filmed legal proceedings in Pakistan between 2009 and 2012. This case, as one of the 25 pending cases on women's inheritance at the time of Livia's fieldwork, was chosen for this paper because it appears to be representative of the management of these claims at the level of state courts. Again here, we will focus on the micro-units of the legal discourse of the social actors, which play a role in the legal outcome. The use of notion of actant (Greimas 1974, 1976) as later developed by Latour (1987, 1988) with the Actor Network Theory is suggested here as being the directional concretion of forces in a given text or discourse. Hence actant hereafter will be the micro-units of the legal discourse that will be significant in terms of legal outcome.

Nimrah Begum

Nimrah Begum's father died in 1961 after transferring 61 kanals of land (1 kanal = 1/8 acre) to his daughter. For some reasons Nimrah Begum did not think of making use of that land before 1991. Furthermore, knowing that the land had been transferred in her name during the lifetime of her father she did not bother checking whether her property rights had been registered continuously in her name at the land revenue office. In 1991, after her children were all married, she thought to claim the land that in the meanwhile had been used by her brother under what she had considered to be a temporary arrangement. When she made her claim, however, her brother responded that she could not claim back what he had been gifted many years earlier! Nimrah Begum filed a suit against her brother to recover the property and a decree was passed in her favour in 1997. Her brother appealed twice before the High Court but twice it was decided in favour of Nimrah Begum with a last decree passed in 2005.

Remarkably, Nimrah Begum's right was never doubted by any judge and her suit had been successful from the very beginning. However, in 2011, the suit was still pending because of being stuck at the level of execution. The closer examination of Nimarah Begum's very bulky file revealed that a fake donation had been produced at the land revenue office to transfer the property in the name of the brother. According to the judge who was handling the case this kind of fraud have been nothing but widespread for a long time. However, the judge maintained that such fraud would now be more difficult due to the implementation of the computerized identity cards by NADRA (National Database and Registration Authority).

Although this is not the place to digress on the reliability of NADRA, it should be appropriate to note that fieldwork data show that for the time being it is highly unlikely that NADRA may fully substitute the more traditional system of *lumberdar*, which is *de facto* still operative and very much needed in many rural and sub-urban areas in Pakistan. The role of the *lumberdar* dates back to the British rule in the South Asian sub-continent. The *lumberdar* had the task of collecting the taxes from the landowners and was chosen among the most influent local landowners. As a result he was also given power to settle justice and keeping law and order at the local level. The *lumberdar* had also an important role of supervision, record keeping, and acted as trustworthy witness for court disputes. Similarly to other non-state jurisdictions such as *panchayat* and *jirga* in the Indian sub-continent *lumberdars* continue to play a role in the settlement of justice at the local level and they are still called in court as witnesses and trustworthy persons who are informed of what happens in their areas.

In Nimrah Begum's case, in fact, one might argue, as the judge did, that had the revenue office required ID cards, the brother in question would not have been in the position to change the property deed with the simple declaration of another woman posing as his sister. However it could also be argued out that it was instead the failure to acknowledge the *lumberdar* system of registration that facilitated the vacuum in which to easily concretize the fraud.

From a general perspective, Nimrah Begum's case confirms the widely reported empathy of Pakistani law and the judiciary for women's inheritance. Shaheen Sardar Ali (1997, 220), reputed women's right activist and member of the NGO Shirkat Ghar notes that "from 1947 to date we find that whenever a woman has approached the superior courts for protection of her right to inherit, she has met with a very positive response". Mehdi (2002) likewise reports the very positive attitude of the judges towards the women approaching courts to demand their share in the family's patrimony. Mehdi (2002, 38) in particular quotes many cases at length but one in particular is interesting for our paper as it mentions another recurrent argument used for thwarting women's shares:

> the brothers in question claimed that they had spent one million rupees on the two marriages of their sister, ten thousands rupees for the settlement of a murder resulting from her divorce and this on top of the traditional gifts due to sisters.

The judges refused to accept dowry, protection and maintenance as replacement of her right in inheritance and said that "if beyond the bare necessity [the father] does anything concerning the daughter, it has to be treated as gift and not something which would have to be returned by daughter by compensating the father in the tangible property" (PLJ, SC 1990: 155 as quoted in Mehdi 2002, 40). Mehdi (2002, 37) further reports that even in cases of relinquishment deeds, such as it happened for Nimrah Begum, in which women give up their property rights in favour of the male members of their family, judges tend to believe the women who challenge those deeds in court.

Nimrah Begum shows something more: that even in spite of the high level of success of women's inheritance claims, as a matter of fact women are still likely to remain deprived of their rights because of lack of execution. This has been constant in the legal proceedings observed during the past three years in Pakistan, especially concerning maintenance and inheritance at the level of family courts (see Holden and Holden 2013). At the level of the sources of law and their dynamics, Nimrah Begum's case highlights furthermore how custom, Muslim personal law, and state law are not necessarily autonomous fields and instead depend on one another, the overarching factor lying at the level of the praxis in the specific modalities through which women's claims are successful in court (see also Holden 2012).

Hence, we argue, legal pluralism is not a static construct that can be constraint within the boundaries of the state because it includes the finite variety of sources that are observable in the everyday praxis. Law in the everyday praxis is not only linked to the amendable mechanisms of the state recognition and interpretation by the judiciary, but is entrenched within people's intersubjectivities, defined as the shared representations and stereotypes that impact how social actors (judges and practitioners included) make sense of facts and develop arguments in the legal process.[2]

Finally we propose hereafter a case decided by the Chief Court (equivalent of the High Court) of Gilgit Baltistan, a contested territory in the North of Pakistan nestled between Pakistan and India-controlled Kashmir, Afghanistan, and China.

Female inheritance in Hunza: Bibi Sitara

This published case law is of particular interest here because it involves a lengthy disquisition on the sources of law and the role and features of inheritance customs as well as a detailed consideration of the value and use of academic sources in a court of law. Thanks to this case we will be able to compare the data collected in Punjab with the situation in Gilgit Baltistan. Significantly enough, Punjab is referred to down as "down country" in Gilgit Baltistan, sometimes resentfully so for being the hub of governance in Pakistan, whereas Gilgit Baltistan in spite of belonging to Pakistan has still an uncertain status.

Bibi Sitara and her sisters and brother are grandchildren of the late Sangi Khan, resident of Hunza who died leaving four daughters and no sons. Amanullah Khan is the nephew of late Sangi Khan who took possession of Sangi Khan's land after his death. The living daughters of Sangi Khan together with their grandchildren and the grandchildren of the late Sangi Khan, among them Bibi Sitara, initiated a suit against Amanullah Khan claiming themselves heirs of Sangi Khan under the Islamic Law of Inheritance. To this however Amanullah Khan resisted by claiming to be the sole heir of Sangi Khan "under the custom prevailing in Hunza State, whereby daughters are 'deprived' [sic] of their inheritance in favour of their collaterals in consanguinity" (Bibi Sitara 2010, 1237). Amanullah's argument was accepted by the Civil Judge but Bibi Sitara challenged his decision before the District Court in first appeal. Amanullah Khan's arguments were once again accepted and the first appeal was dismissed too. However Bibi Sitara appealed again before the Chief Court against the concurrent findings of both the lower courts. The counsels of both parties submitted their arguments and evidence before the Chief Court: two precedents decided by the Judicial Commissioner, apex judicial authority in Hunza until 1974. Both precedents, in spite of partially conflicting one another, were in favour of women's disinheritance and therefore disregarding Muslim personal law that instead provides women's right to a share. Interestingly, among the submitted evidence figured also three academic publications, one of which was ethnographic: *Tribes of the Hindoo Koosh* by John Biddulph, Indus Publications Karachi Edn, (1977), *Between Oxus and Indus* by R.C.F. Schomberg, London (1935), and *Materialien Zur Ethnographie von Dardistan* (Pakistan) by DLR Lorimer, Austria (1979). But even more interestingly, the Bench, after hearing the parties at length, engaged in a historical survey deemed necessary to their subsequent considerations regarding the applicable law. It was said (1237):

> This Bench heard both the learned counsel for the parties at length, they assisted the Court with the force of above cited cases in support of their divergent pleas but we deem it proper to draw a historical sketch of Hunza State, "[A]s it was ruled by Mirs (Rajas) of Hunza who were having exclusive powers of law making, judiciary and administration within the State. The Mirs of Hunza and Nagar enjoyed the above powers even after accepting the sovereignty of Pakistan. The peoples of both the states were administered, adjudged under the traditions

> and customs framed by the Mirs and regular laws were not extended even by the Government of Pakistan until the Rajgi System was dissolved by the regime of late Zulfiqar Ali Batho in the year 1974 and then regular laws were extended to both the states including the Islamic law of inheritance". The above historical account makes acquainted ones mind to understand the legal System of the Hunza State [. . .].

After the said historical overview the Bench started to consider the precedent by the Judicial Commissioner recognizing the authority of the above-mentioned texts. And the decision report his words (p.1238):

> What is the custom in a certain area is always a question of fact. It was denied to the petitioner in the order under review mainly on the ground that the witnesses were not unanimous and some of the witnesses had also accepted Shariah as a rule of practice in the area. This is challenged vehemently in the present petition that the custom, as alleged by the petitioner, was so strongly prevalent in the area that the flimsy evidence in the case could not operate to negate or refute the same. That there are text books of admitted worth and authenticity which prove the custom, and which in spite of best efforts could not be made available at the previous occasions. The text or treatises relied upon in this behalf were the authentic works of the British and German writers who extensively visited the Northern Areas and minutely studied the origin, habits and customs of the tribes of this area. It is unfortunate that no such publication by any locals/Pakistanis are so written and available.

It is worth noting here that not very differently from the context of transnational litigation and asylum proceedings in which Euro-American and Australian courts grapple with law and legal systems that are largely unknown to them, the issue here is the source and evidence of custom. The danger in using academic works as evidence lies in the confusion between the descriptive and prescriptive aspects of custom as practice observed or otherwise studied by the authors (see also Holden 2008, 3–17). Descriptive features of customs are overrated and as a consequence cultural aspects that are relevant in the specific social setting from which they originate are essentialized and frozen in misleading representations of *jus cogens*. The opposite proceeding is not very helpful either as it leads to the blind exclusion of any source other than positive law, which brings at least in the short term, the complete annihilation of those claims that constitute a threat to societal intersubjectivities such as daughter's disinheritance (see the lack of execution of the forever pending cases notwithstanding women favourable decisions).[3] If instead attention is drawn to the modalities of the translation of the academic discourse in court as object likely to be treated as an evidence or to produce evidence, and to become actant in the legal proceedings, it is possible to highlight the useful distinction between descriptive and prescriptive qualities of the discourse. Whereas socio-legal objects of the academic discourse are apt to produce fair legal outcomes in specific cases but in combination with all the other necessary elements of the legal process, it would be inappropriate to use them alone to legitimize or delegitimize specific practices of law (Holden 2011a, 8, see also Parashar and Menski in this special issue). We will see that the Gilgit Baltistan Bench was partially aware of the above difference but said (p.1238):

> We also have gone through the above treaties and are in consonance with the view taken by the learned Judicial Commissioner that all the above three authors are unanimous on the point that the custom was rule of inheritance under which no female heir of a propositus having any Share in hereditament, if propositus died without male issue and the property was inherited by male collaterals whichever was clearest to the propositus and the custom remained in practice having force of law all over the Rajgi System in the State but with a positive modification by the ruler Mir Muhammad Nazim Khan, who made female heirs entitled to a limited Share not under Islamic Shariah, but under the custom itself, which is one Chuqe out of seven

> Chuqe of land. The learned Judicial Commissioner Mr. Muhammad Nawaz Khan was moved to decide the same point of custom or Islamic Shariah in the Hunza State during Rajgi System, the learned Judicial Commissioner discussed the judgment passed by the learned Mr. Justice Sardar Muhammad Raza in detail and also the text books cited by the learned Justice in his judgment, but has divergently held with the reasons in his own words.

In other words, without challenging the evidence submitted by the counsels regarding the disinheritance customs described by the academic sources, the Bench accepted and elaborated two other arguments: the dynamicity of custom and the authoritative source of law. Not only are customs not immutable but they can be modified by the legislative power that is *de facto* considered as authoritative, in this case the Mir of Hunza. Thus it was concluded (p.1238) that:

> The Mirs in Hunza State had exclusive powers to make laws and to enforce them along with having exclusive administrative powers; as such Mir Muhammad Nazim Khan introduced some amendments into prevailing customary laws and under the amendment, he made the lady members of the families entitled to limited share under the customary law itself and not in recognition of Islamic right of inheritance of female members. So it cannot be termed as change of custom into personal law or discontinuation of custom. The custom once probed in a specific area then it applies to all similar cases and it varies not from case to case in respect of particular families if pleaded categorically in defense [...] The lower Courts have ignored the amendment made to the custom by the then law maker of the State and have deprived the petitioners even from the limited share granted by the custom itself as such, we are inclined to modify both the impugned decrees as such that the petitioners shall be entitled to 1/7th share of the property of propositus under the custom and the suit is decreed to the above extend.

In doing so, the Bench legitimized the woman's inheritance share, thanks to the authoritative source of the Mirs of Hunza. Such an articulated management of custom as interlegalities not only within but also beyond the state is very different from the customary law developed under the British in some areas of the sub-continent, including the actual Pakistan, according to which "as a rule, daughters and their sons, as well as sisters and their sons, were excluded by near male collaterals" (Gilmartin 1988, 48). This was known as the 'agnatic theory' of inheritance based on the legal assumption that the exclusion of daughters in favour of male collaterals, no matter how distant, should always be taken as a basic judicial presumption (Gilmartin 1988, 49). The British argument that daughters were not given a share because of the exogamy could not be more far from the Muslims marriage system of the sub-continent, which instead prefers endogamy as confirmed by our first three case studies.

Eventually the issue is whether colonial and post-colonial state-driven interpretations of customs should act as an obstacle to the consideration of sources of law that are not (exclusively) elaborated within the realm of positive law. As Sousa Santos (1987, 288) says:

> Socio-legal life is constituted by different legal spaces operating simultaneously on different scales and from different interpretive standpoints. So much is this so that in phenomenological terms and as a result of interaction and intersection among legal spaces one cannot properly speak of law and legality but rather of interlaw and interlegality.

From our case studies, it is also clear that inheritance claims are overlapping several legal spaces linked to kinship, financial power, and the marriage arrangements of the children of siblings – this should alert us to the difficulty of executing certain legal decisions that grant inheritance shares to women and perhaps for the unrealistic implementation of a state-only driven social change that excludes any other source of law.

Personal laws and legal pluralism

On the basis of the above data it is not surprising that post-colonial states in the sub-continent, not very differently from the British colonizers, have perpetuated women's disinheritance. On this basis, the attention might be first shifted from the potential danger of legal pluralism to the understanding of the modalities by which the state re-interprets the law – intended in a broader sense as including customs and personal laws – in order to safeguarding patrilineal interests (see also Basu 2005 and Chowdhry 2005, 188). If we look at the practices of law, with an awareness of the ideological framework in which they develop, and in particular at the successful arguments in court, we see not one but a combination of sources of law drawing on state law, codified personal law, and customs. Thus in the case studies reported at the beginning of this paper the claims of Khadija, Mandan, Mavara, and Shado appear closely interwoven with the kinship obligations of the brother–sister relationship. If this latter is faulty and the women are in a strong position vis-à-vis the other family members and only then can the inheritance claim acquire legitimacy in the claimants' intersubjectivities.

In the above framework of intersubjectivities, the daughter's inheritance claim constitutes what Steele (1997) calls a stereotype threat (i.e. a challenge to the shared social assumptions that daughters should not claim their inheritance rights) – hence the difficulty of execution of judgments in favour of women's inheritance. The discourse developed by law courts, even though formally favourable to women, does not possess the authority for a substantial empowerment. It appears in fact misleading to say that Muslim women (and in general South Asian women) do not approach the court to claim their rights. In fact as Lawrence Rosen is pointing out in his forthcoming article, the number of successful litigations initiated by women in the Muslim contexts might be much higher than reported. The massive number of property-related litigation afflicting all kinds of jurisdictions in Pakistan and often concluding in women's favour, however also shows the discrepancies between the formal terms of the litigation and the aims that are in practice pursued by the litigants.

On the basis of the above case studies, we argue that state law (defined as inclusive of codified personal law) is not a self-sustaining system. In fact although significant political considerations can be drawn by the studies that have successfully argued for the independence from religion of the legal domain in South Asia (Pirie 2006), it seems that much more is yet to be discovered when one is ready to accept that everyday litigation is impacted by factors that are not necessarily classifiable as belonging to one domain only (see also Foblets, Renteln, and Gandreault-DesBiens 2010).

As it has been abundantly reported by the socio-legal scholarship focusing on South Asia and social activists alike, state law does not always make sense for the social actors. We have seen on one hand that inheritance claims are preferentially avoided perhaps because of the endogamic marriage system that favours a strong brother–sister relation (see also Jamous 2003). In India, not differently from Pakistan, official justice is better avoided for women's inheritance claims because such cases breed animosity and "destroy harmonious brother-sister relationship which [are] a vital element of the Bohra social structure" (Basu 1995, 38–39). Nevertheless Muslim personal law as recognized by state law in Pakistan, similarly to India, provides for women's right to inheritance. And as Merchant has pointed out for India "[T]here is scope for justice within the constraints of law. With the help of forward thinking lawyers and judges, women could get a fair share". This point is crucial because judicial activism in India and in Pakistan has afforded very significant room for interpretation even beyond the legislator's purpose (Basu 2012; Menski 2001; Holden 2011b). Nevertheless, as this paper has shown, positive law alone is failing in adequately supporting daughter's inheritance claims.

Custom, religion, and governance

Another point that this paper made is the misleading assumption that customs are necessarily linked with religion together with an assumption of exclusion of inter-religious fields (on the notion of religion and secularism see Shah in this special issue). Nelson (2011), however cautious of talking about legal sources outside state law and beyond a strictly pragmatic perspective, shows that customary laws in the area of the Punjab was not always religiously driven and that possibly religious polarization was part of an historic process. Nelson furthermore shows that the shift from customary law to personal law including Shari'ah did very little or nothing at all in order to overcome the agnatic constraints that legitimized women's disinheritance. In the words of the Nelson (2011, 194):

> The point [. . .] did not lie in avoiding the district courts. Nor did it lie in the production of any substantive or enforceable decree (rendered, as quickly as possible, within the terms of post-colonial laws). On the contrary, the point lay in the protracted process of postcolonial litigation itself.

This is confirmed by the case of Nimrah Bibi where once again the obstacle was not the recognition of her inheritance rights but the protracted litigation and the execution of her judgment. Nelson sees in the recurrent pattern of property-related litigation in Punjab the attempt to systematically circumvent the law by all means including the deliberate use of state law as a delay tactic in order to achieve a better outcome out of court. By describing the agencies of both voters and politicians, for accessing and circumventing the resources of the postcolonial state, Nelson also points at the class conflicts between the political power of rural élites and the state but then concludes with the ontological difficulty of an Islamic democracy.

The authors of this paper agree with Nelson's analysis concerning the relative but not exclusive independence of custom and religion. However it is worth noting that many of the processes admirably described by Nelson with precision of details and methodological rigor, as being the features of Islamic contexts, are also common to non-Islamic contexts: namely the delay tactics and the shifting arguments in order to circumvent the law (for an example of delay tactics in the Mediterranean context see Holden, Holden, and Manfredonia 2004). To this regard it is useful to remind the readers of the interesting use of academic texts and analysis of custom by the Gilgit Bench. While refusing the prescriptive meaning that the precedents had given to academic works their analysis and data were used to make sense of the relationship between law and governance that was so important to an authoritative decision in the matter of daughter's inheritance. This contextual reasoning might be the perfect reply to the doubts formulated by Fuller (1994) regarding the usefulness of a narrow notion on legal pluralism as constrained by within state law. In his words (Fuller 1994: 8):

> [I]t is clear not only that 'legal' orders are not all equally legal, but also that legal pluralism is at least partially a relation of dominance, and possible resistance that must be understood as such, and that must be situated within and largely explained by its wider, non-legal context.

Conclusions

The legal pluralism outlined in our case studies as both within and beyond state law in a constant dynamic with governance throws light also on the larger conflicts between judiciary and executive in Pakistan. In fact since the restoration of an independent judiciary in 2009, much of the effort of the judiciary has concentrated on consolidating its own independence which has also generated the fear of an overly independent judiciary lacking democratic legitimacy, and perhaps becoming a self-governing body.

This risk of overstepping the division of powers in governance is acutely evident in our Hunza case study where the judiciary in 2010 takes the liberty to override state law in favour of a custom modified by the Mirs of Hunza who lost their sovereignty in 1974 when the area became part of Pakistan. However, if one looks at the way custom is scrutinized by the Gilgit Bench, it also appears clear that the contextual significance of designating an authoritative law pronounced by an authoritative source without falling into the mere perpetuation of iniquitous principles. Ultimately it is a matter of law and governability intended, as Foucault (1991) so well argued in his works on the genealogy of the modern state, as the ensemble of rationalities that constitute the rule. Foucault's theoretical framework could be very usefully applied to the conflict that has agitated the Pakistani judiciary since the very first steps of this young country whose judiciary is increasingly accused of trespassing the boundaries of a democratic division of powers.

Socio-legal scholarship has pointed out, especially in the domain of Muslim family law, the subtle implications of what has been called South Asian judicial activism (Menski 2001; Pearl and Menski 1998; Serajuddin 2011). At the same time, but interestingly unrelated and to a great extent unnoticed, some anthropological studies have shed light on the specific modalities in which stability and apparent accountability of the legal machinery in Pakistan has been largely supported by the many procedures of out-of-court justice (Chaudhary 1999; Mehdi 2002). Most recently, in India, alternative dispute resolution has been moderately incorporated into the governance agenda (Solanki 2011) with consequent neutralization of those instances of resistance sometimes provided by the *fora* of customary dispute settlement (Basu 2012; Holden 2012). It should also pointed out that with these *fora* of alternative dispute resolution and adjudication with the state's imprimatur (see also Vatuk in this special issue) the caste or community-based *fora* (Hindi/Urdu *jati panchayat* and *biradari panchayat*) have continued to settle justice in many areas of the sub-continent (Holden 2008, 82 note 5; see also Sbriccoli in this special issue).

In Pakistan, while on one hand judicial activism has been a mixed blessing (Lau 1996; Menski 2001) and on the other out-of-court systems such as *jirga* and *panchayat* have been largely tolerated by the state, observers have instead concentrated almost exclusively on the dangers of overstepping boundaries between the judiciary and the executive. It should be pointed out however, that the judiciary has been always part of the process of the modernization and liberal governance that began with the Independence of Pakistan – sometimes also when moderately supporting Islamization and non-state sources of law (Lombardi 2010a; 2010b). From a broader perspective, as Nader and Mattei (2008), and Chomsky (2006) have convincingly argued, one might be short-sighted when subscribing to harmony theories that soothe the majorities while pursuing the programme of a strong state. Recent debates about development and legal pluralism also confirm the need for a closer scrutiny of the state monopoly of law (Woodman 2012).

In fact, socio-legal scholarship might not yet have fully realized the reasons why this judiciary-executive stand-off in Pakistan, and more recently in Egypt, have been the object of a great reaction at the international level – although being comparable to similar confrontations in Southern Europe and Latin America. What are the future prospects in this polarized landscape between the proponents of an exclusive rule of law that is not itself free from criticism and the variety of non-state laws on the ground? As we have seen with the analysis of the discourse developed by social actors in Misalpur, the difficult execution of state personal law favouring women in the Punjab, and the tight-rope reasoning of the Bench in Gilgit Baltistan, the legal pluralism that afford the inclusion of interlegalities within and beyond the state may be of complex management but are also the ones that are likely to bring concrete outcomes in matters of gender equality and social diversity in the current circumstances.

Acknowledgements

Part of the data reported by Holden in this paper has been collected within the project *Lady-Judges of Pakistan*. Thanks to the support of Agence Nationale de la Recherche (Justice and Governance in Contemporary South Asia), Centre National de la Recherche Scientifique, Centre d'Études Himalayennes, Lahore University of Management Sciences, and Syed Babar Ali Foundation. For encouragement, logistic support and interdisciplinary collaboration special thanks go to the Judicial Academy and Supreme Court of Pakistan. Similarly the analysis elaborated in this paper on the stand-off between the judiciary and the executive in Pakistan was initiated by Holden in 2010 during her academic consultancy on federalism and social diversity for the Forum of Federations (see Holden 2010). Special thanks also go to Mrs. Sarwat Mumtaz Civil Judge at the Lahore High Court for her unconditional support and everlasting patience in discussing data and providing useful information for this research.

Notes

1. Parts of case study 3 were used in two of Azam Chaudhary's previous articles: 'The logic in the Traditional Share of the Daughter in Father's Patrimony: A Case Study of the Punjab' In *Journal of Law and Social Research* Vol. 1. No.1, 2009–2010, 27–40; and 'A Woman's Marriage to the Quran: An Anthropological Perspective from Pakistan' In *Anthropos* 106.2011: 411–422.
2. For the notion of subjectivities and intersubjectivities see Goffman 1959 and Garfinkel 1967.
3. For a theory on the stereotypc threat, see Steele 1997.

References

Alavi, Hamza. 1972. "Kinship in West Punjab Villages." *Contributions to Indian Sociology* VI: 1–12.

Ali, Shaheen Sardar. 1997. "A Critical Review of Family Laws in Pakistan: A Women's Perspective." In *Women's Law in Legal Education and Practice in Pakistan*, ed. Mehdi Rubya and Fareeda Shaheed, 198–223. Copenhagen: New Social Science Monograph.

Al-Shafey, M. 2007. "Married to the Quran Asharq Alawsat." http://www.asharq-e.com/news.asp?section=3&id=9656 (accessed February 27, 2013).

Basu, Srimati. 1995. *She Comes to Take Her Rights. Indian Women, Property, and Propriety*. New York: State University of New York Press.

Basu, Srimati. 2012. "Judges of Normality: Mediating Marriage in the Family Courts of Kolkata, India." *Signs* 37 (2): 469–492.

Basu, Srimati, ed. 2005. *Dowry and Inheritance*. New Delhi: Women Unlimited.

Bibi Sitara v. Amanullah, 2010 CLC 1237.

Chaudhary, Azam. 1999. *Justice in Practice: Legal Ethnography of a Pakistani Punjabi Village*. Karachi: Oxford University Press.

Chaudhary, Azam. 2005. "The Mullah As Different - the Mullah As Same, a Local Anthropologist's Reflections on the Lebenswelt of Mullahs in the Pakistani Punjab." *Ethnoscripts; Analysis and Data from the Institute of Ethnology at Hamburg University* 7: 57–84.

Chaudhary, Azam. 2009–2010. "The Logic in the Traditional Share of the Daughter in Father's Patrimony: A Case Study of the Punjab." *Journal of Law and Social Research* 1 (1): 27–40.

Doing nothing successfully I (documentary film). By Holden, Marius, Livia Holden , and Lionello Manfredonia, 2004.

Foblets, Marie-Claire, Dundes Alison Renteln, and Jean François Gaudreault-DesBiens. 2010. *Cultural Diversity and the Law. State Responses From Around the World*. Brussels: Bruylant.

Foucault, Michel. 1991. "Governmentality" (lecture at the Collège de France, Feb 1, 1978), in *The Foucault Effect: Studies in Governmentality*, eds. Graham Burchell, Collin Gordon, and Peter Miller, 87–104. Hemel Hempstead: Harvester Wheatsheaf.

Fuller, Chris 1994. *Legal Anthropology, Legal Pluralism, and Legal Thought*. London: LSE Research Online. http://eprints.lse.ac.uk/538/ (accessed February 27, 2013).

Garfinkel, Harold, 1967, *Studies in Ethnomethodology*. Blackwell: Prentice-Hall.

Gilmartin, David. 1988. *Empire and Islam: Punjab and the Making of Pakistan*. London: University of California Press.

Goffman, Erving. 1959. *The Presentation of Self in Everyday Life*. New York: Doubleday.

Solanki, Gopika. 2011. *Adjudication in Religious Family Laws: Cultural Accommodation, Legal Pluralism, and Gender Equality in India*. Cambridge: Cambridge University Press.

Greimas, Algirdas Julien. 1987. "Actants, Actors and Figures." *On Meaning: Selected Writings in Semiotic Theory*. Trans. Paul Perron and Frank H. Collins., 106–120. Minneapolis: University of Minnesota Press.

Greimas, Algirdas Julien. 1976. *Entretien sur les structures élémentaires de signification*. Bruxelles: Editions Complexes.

Haque, Huma. 2000. "Feminist Islam and Sexist Muslims: A Case Study of Rural Punjab." *Pakistan Journal of Social Sciences* XXIII: 1997.

Holden, Livia. 2008. *Hindu Divorce: A Legal Anthropology*. Aldershot: Ashgate.

Holden, Livia. 2011a. *Cultural Expertise and Litigation: Patterns, Conflicts, Narratives*. London: Routledge.

Holden, Livia. 2011b. Social Diversity and the Judiciary in Pakistan. Paper commissioned for the Conference on Diversity organized in Kathmandu, as part of the activities of the Project "Strengthening federal governance in Pakistan" supported by funding from the Ministry of Foreign Affairs of the Federal Republic of Germany, June 2011. http://www.forumfed.org/libdocs/Pakistan2011/Livia%20Holden_DiversityandtheJudiciaryinPakistan.pdf (accessed March 18, 2013)

Holden, Livia. 2012. "Divorce at the Woman's Initiative in South Asia and in the Diasporas." In *Interpreting divorce law in Islam*, ed. Rubya Mehdi, Werner Menski, and Jorgen S. Nielsen. Copenhagen: DJØF.

Jamous, Raymond. 2003. *Kinship and Rituals Among the Meo of Northern India: Locating Sibling Relationship*. Oxford: Oxford University Press.

Khan, Aftab Hussain. 2009. "Women in Sindh." http://www.albaspectrum.com/Articles1/Women/00994.html (accessed February 27, 2013).

Lady Judges of Pakistan (documentary film). Directed by Livia Holden and Marius Holden, Insights Productions, 2013.

Latour, Bruno. 1987. *Science in Action*. Cambridge, MA: Harward University Press.

Latour, Bruno. 1988. *The Pasteurization of France*. Cambridge, MA: Harward University Press.

Lau, Martin. 1996. "Islam and Judicial Activism: Public interest litigation and environmental protection in Pakistan." In *Human Rights Approaches to Environmental Protection*, ed. Alan E. Boyle and Michal R. Anderson, 285–302. Oxford University Press.

Lombardi, Clark B. 2010a. "Can Islamizing a Legal System Ever Help Promote Liberal Democracy? A View From Pakistan." *7 U. St. Thomas Law Journal* 7 (3): 649–691.

Lombardi, Clark B. 2010b. "Islamism As a Response to Emergency Rule in Pakistan: The Surprising Proposal of Justice A. R. Cornelius." In *Emergency Powers*, eds. Victor Ramraj and Arun Thiruvengadam, 436–465. Cambridge University Press.

Nelson, Matthew J. 2011. *In the Shadow of Shari'ah: Islam, Islamic Law, and Democracy in Pakistan*. London: Hurst.

Mehdi, Rubya. 2002. *Gender and Property Law in Pakistan: Resources and Discourses*. Karachi: Vanguard.

Menski, Werner. 2001. *Modern Indian Family Law*. London: Curzon.

Nader, Laura and Ugo Mattei. 2008. *Plunder: When the Rule of Law is Illegal*. Malden: Blackwell.

Chomsky, Noam. 2006. *Failed States. The Abuse of Power and the Assault on Democracy*. New York: Metropolitan Books.

Patel, Rashida. 1979. *Women and Law in Pakistan: An Exposition of the Socio-legal Status of Women*. Karachi: Faiza Publishers.

Pearl, David and Werner Menski. 1998. *Muslim Family Law*. London: Sweet & Maxwell.

Pirie, Fernanda. 2006. "Legal Autonomy As Political Engagement: The Ladakhi Village in the Wider World." *Law and Society Review* 40, no. 1: 77–103.
Rosen, Lawrence unpublished draft. "Why Women Win in Muslim Family Law Courts?"
Serajuddin, Alamgir Muhammad. 2011. *Muslim Family Law, Secular Courts and Muslim Women of South Asia*. Karachi: Oxford University Press.
Sousa Santos, Boaventurade. 1987. "A Map of Misreading, Toward a Postmodern Conception of Law." *Journal of Law and Society* 14, no. 3: 279–302.
Steele, Claude M. 1997. "A Threat in the Air: How Stereotypes Shape Intellectual Identity and Performance." *American Psychologist* 52, no. 6: 613–29.
Woodman, Gordon R. 2012. "The Development 'Problem' of Legal Pluralism: An Analysis and Steps Toward Solutions." In *Legal Pluralism and Development*, ed. Brian Z. Tamanaha, 129–144. Cambridge, MA: Cambridge University Press.

Harmony ideology revisited: spatial geographies of hegemony and disputing strategies amongst the Santal

Fauzia Shariff

Law Department, London School of Economics and Political Science, London, England

In her book *Harmony Ideology* Laura Nader demonstrates that dispute resolution practices within minority ethnically distinct communities may serve not only a quasi-legal, but also a political, hegemonic, function. National governance structures and relations between the state and non-state entities provide a critical context for understanding dispute resolution practices within such communities. This paper examines how the historical legal and social 'othering' of a tribal minority, the Santal, in India and Bangladesh has created two opposing counter-hegemonic strategies, manifest in the people's dispute resolution practices. The paper begins by exploring the historical backdrop of the Santal's exclusion and subordination in the two countries. The paper then examines disputing strategies to assess how dispute processes act as a mirror reflecting back this exclusion, reforming the nuances of separation as a symbol of defiance. My fieldwork data shows that strategies of disputing are closely linked with the spatial proximity of and perceived locality of oppression. Inward looking strategies that promote harmony and re-enforce minority hegemonies act as strategies of resistance where an oppressor takes the form of a distant and untouchable state or power elite. But where the politics of struggle is local and immediate disputing turns outward and confrontation replaces harmony as a counter-hegemonic strategy.

Introduction[1]

Power in the context of legal discourse has become an important theme of inquiry for legal anthropology.[2] Foucault's theorizing of power as a feature of social relations and governmentality in the 1970s and 80s coincided with a renaissance in legal anthropology of the Malinowskian approach that found law in reciprocal social relationships, and ensured the sub-discipline's survival as it adjusted to the post-colonial climate, turning to a study of law alongside the state. At the same time James Scott's '*Weapons of the Weak*' opened up the possibility of a symbiotic relationship between power, oppression and resistance and introduced a new temporality through his focus on everyday resistance.[3] It was during this period that Laura Nader conducted a field study of the little researched dispute resolution practices amongst the Talean Zapotec mountain village community in Mexico, a study that she revisited in her important work 'Harmony Ideology' in 1990. By the 1990s history had become an essential contextualizer in studies of legal anthropology.[4] Taking her data on disputing amongst the Talean Zapotec as components for experimentation she used this in her book to push legal anthropology into new areas of reflection. She considered how historically external macro-processes (colonialism and the spread of Christian/ Western missions) created a context in which disputing took on not only a legal but also a political importance. She found that the breaking up of the Talea into autonomous village units through history both forced and enabled the Zapotec people to develop internal harmony as a counter-hegemonic tool. Keeping harmony in village affairs, she suggested, became not merely a strategy for keeping disputes 'in' but also keeping the state 'out'. This revelation, brought about by analysing the intersection of law, politics and history, is a rich and dynamic field of interdisciplinary research that I hope to contribute to in this paper drawing on my own research in Asia.[5]

My research also concerns a chthonic people, the Santal, who experienced colonial rule and whose survival has depended on their ability to deepen and strength their cultural identity through village level organization. I look at how the wider historical political framework has created a dual response by the Santal, adapted to the nature of oppression they face. While for the Talea, looking inward to their own harmony and resolving disputes internally was a response to an encroaching superordinate power in the colonial rulers, I found that amongst the Santal looking inwards – containing and strengthening commitments to internal dispute resolution – is a strategy that is more common where the Santal see their oppressors, whether the state or other hegemonic body, as too distant to engage with, their power too great to contest. By contrast where the Santal experience oppression in the more immediate location of day to day relations – that is where the locale of struggle is too close to avoid – their strategy turns outward to open confrontation. While disputing replaces harmony as a goal of resistance, this strategy, while counter-hegemonic, invests less in unity and the politicization of identity.

The paper is based on research carried out between 2002 and 2004 in rural villages in India and Bangladesh amongst an important but neglected *adivasi*[6] people, the Santal. Using a comparative and historical perspective I position current Santal dispute resolution practices in the context of a history of Santal exploitation, compared across these two countries, and in the context of four different villages where I carried out my research. The cross-border and multi-sited nature of my research has allowed me to test out these themes in internally comparative contexts: the contrasting national contexts of India and Bangladesh with their inclusive and assimilationist policies respectively; and the differing situations of Santal living in villages relatively isolated from their hegemonic adversaries, and mixed villages where they live among them.

I begin with a discussion of a Santal case from the Santal Parganas in India recorded in the 1970s by a social anthropologist George Somers (Somers 1977). The case serves as an introduction to Santal law from which I will develop my discussion. In the following sections I introduce the Santal as a people by situating an analysis of their current social and political subordination into the context of the Santal's turbulent historical settlement in the areas where I carried out my research. I demonstrate that while local and national politics intersect, experiences of oppression may create different realities of struggle, some located in the immediate environment of the village, day to day life, others perceived in a less tangible, more invisible and distant oppressor, the state. I then turn to my own fieldwork data to examine how these different contexts have impacted on cultures of dispute resolution.

Santal dispute resolution: 'Rape under the JoJo Tree'

In Somers' account of the 'Rape under the Jo Jo tree' a young girl of the Kisku clan accuses three boys of rape on the night of the annual Sakrat festival. The festival, held on the last day of the month of *Pous*, is a day of excitement. An archery contest is followed by drinking and dancing. The young women form the centre of attention. Joining arms they form a line swaying back and forth in a traditional Santal dance, the men beating drums or piping bamboo flutes around them. As the women drop their arms and turn, the men pass through the line and reform in front of the women. Spontaneous laughter and mischief abound and silent exchanges signal an invitation to meet later or signify an imminent more formal proposal. On this particular occasion festivities continued until midnight and the women and girls retreated together, leaving the young men behind. But one of the girls did not return home.

The next morning the *Jog Manjhi* (Santal village official in charge of adolescents) rushed to the house of the village headman, the *Manjhi*, to report that a young woman had been raped. A meeting of the village council was called and the men of the Santal households came together. The girl's father was the first to speak, shaking with anger as he recounted that his daughter had been taken by force and raped in turn by three boys from the village. Unable to move, she had been found by her friends that morning. The father insisted that the council punish the boys or he would go to the police. His threat was unusual, not only because as 'outsiders' the police would not ordinarily be invited to intervene in village matters, if it could be avoided, but also because rape itself was not considered a serious crime. But there were special circumstances. The girl, despite being well over the usual age of marriage, was unmarried. If the council were not to pronounce rape and hold the boys responsible, the girl's reputation would be seriously tarnished, and her marriage prospects and bride price would be affected. An unmarried girl who has had intercourse consensually may be presumed to be seeking sexual relations with any village boy, which would lower the respect held for her and her family in the village.

The boys each gave statements to the council, one claiming he had not touched the girl, another that she had invited him to follow her into the dark and the third that he had also been invited but had gone home when he realized who it was. The *Jog Manjhi* listened then gave his opinion and the villagers discussed what they had heard. The *Manjhi* then spoke and, without pronouncing innocence or guilt, he called on the three boys to each pay a small fine of five *rupees* to the council (for food or beer to mark the resolution of the case) and another five *rupees* to the father of the girl. Before anyone could respond he gave a firm lecture against allowing women out alone at night and men following women into the dark, suggesting that each party had played a part.

But consensus was not achieved. The father of the third boy, a *Kisku*, was unhappy with the implicit judgement of guilt against his son. He declared that if the council were viewing his son as guilty of rape, they would be declaring him simultaneously in violation of the taboo of clan incest. Both he and the girl were of the *Kisku* clan. His pronouncement was daring. A finding of clan incest would have to be dealt with as a serious crime, the punishment against the boy and his family would be severe. The five *rupee* fine given clearly amounted to a presumption by the council that this was not proven. The *Kisku* father demanded an apology from the girl and her father for a false accusation against his son. An awkward silence followed until the *Kisku* father arose proclaiming his refusal to pay the fine, and ignoring a plea from the girl's father that the council's decision must be obeyed. The *Jog Manjhi* suggested the meeting be closed and resumed in the evening when the neighbours had had an opportunity to think through their situations.

But during the day matters took another turn. The girl's father, furious at the denial of an outcome for his daughter, and possibly the prospect of her being questioned if the council re-convened, walked to the police headquarters and reported the rape, naming all three boys. Four policemen returned with him to the village and arrested the boys, tying their hands with heavy rope to stop them escaping. The boys were taken to the *Manjhi*'s house and in his presence the police demanded 150 *rupees* from the boys' fathers – stating if this was not paid immediately the boys would be taken to jail to await trial. The fathers collected what jewellery and cash they had to pay the fine. The girl's father in fact received very little of the monies – the police took the silver worth 120 *rupees*. The *Manjhi* said not a word nor was he invited to speak. This was now a police matter and outside all of their hands.

While the police intervention and the payment of the fine meant that the matter, in so far as the rape was concerned, had now to be considered closed, relations were uneasy and there was a sense that the matter was unresolved. Both the father of the girl and the *Kisku* boy's father had acted in bad faith. The girl's father had brought police into the village, publicizing to the wider area that the *Manjhi* was incapable of resolving village disputes and facilitating what amounted to a virtual theft of 120 *rupees* as the police enriched themselves in the process. The *Kisku* boy's father's conduct was worse still. He had failed to accept the decision of the council, which meant disrespecting not only the *Manjhi* but also the villagers themselves. More problematic still he had raised the matter of incest, a serious crime that if proven would have to be addressed with a ritual of *Bitlaha* – involving a gathering of armed men from the village and sometimes neighbouring villages, out casting of the family and destruction of their property, smashing pots and defecating in their courtyard.[7] Such a ritual would signal to other Santal villages that this village had had a breach of important Santal norms against incest and would have further implications for harmony in the village. While the actions of the girl's father could perhaps be forgiven, after all the police intervention had meant that the council had not had to re-convene to consider the allegation of incest, the actions of the *Kisku* boy's father could not be so quickly forgiven.

The next time the village came together was a few days later when one of the families arranged a celebration to mark the return of a cousin-brother (a patrilineal parallel cousin) from the tea plantations in Assam. This event was an opportunity for the village to re-assert its authority. Although the *Kisku* boy's father was normally called on to provide locally brewed beer on such occasions, the hosts bought their beer from elsewhere. The wife of the organizer of the celebration then refused to offer the rice beer (*handi*) to the father of the *Kisku* boy. Although they attended the celebration the *Kisku* boy and his father gradually withdrew to the edges of the main circle of festivities. They were ignored for most of the time, but when discussion turned from adventures in Assam to goings on in the village, and the rare event of the village council's unresolved case, their presence was noted. The gathering became a spontaneous trial of the *Kisku* boy's father – without the usual formalities. He was criticized for refusing to obey the decision of the council, making a minor matter turn into a major event, and for bringing up the question of incest. The presence of the police was also mentioned – it signalled to neighbouring villages that their village was unable to manage its own affairs and that they were careless in matters of clan incest. The girl's father at that point stood up and, addressing the *Kisku* man, shouted '*be panta*' – out of line – a charge that would see him more formally excluded from social events until he made proper restitution.

Rather than provoking more discord this pronouncement had the effect of opening up an opportunity for restitution. Santal law, like many customary law traditions, aims not merely or primarily to name and punish, but to complete a circle of action that will return relations to equilibrium. The *Kisku* father responded by making his restitution – he brought from his home two large pots of *handi*. He presented one to the *Manjhi* saying "Take this in the good spirit of our ancestors" and another to the girl's father asking him in receiving it to signal that he was no longer offended. The *Manjhi* asked the *Kisku* father to sit with him and suggested that the *handi* be shared and drunk by the villagers present as a sign of forgiveness. The social drinking and return to good relations signalled a return of *ato sogai*, village oneness.

The case reflects the spirit of Santal law and demonstrates the informality of procedure which facilitates maintenance, not of a universal ideal of justice but of a sensitive balance of harmony and discord. The case illustrates the subtle management of relations, use of silences and gaps of time for reflection and unspoken messages of dissent, the ability to view responsibility for infractions as shared, that are central to Santal dispute resolution. This contrasts starkly with the blunt and violent strategy of the state in the form of the police – the lack of a hearing, the handing down of an ultimatum of 'pay the fine or go to jail', the restraining of the village boys with rope, and finally the taking of valuables (possibly intended for a future wedding or as a valuable asset in times of emergency such as illness) by the police for personal benefit.

In recounting the case Somers suggests that the intervention of the police may have bolstered the *Manjhi*'s authority. He claims that in enforcing his decision, and bringing the boys to his house before they made their demands, the police had recognized the authority of the *Manjhi*. In a sense this is true. There is a subtle level of co-operation in these matters in which the police must respect the structure of hierarchy within these communities and work with and through those structures. But this is a practical necessity more than an indication of underlying respect. Police need support from communities if they are to do their job: crimes need to be reported before the police can intervene and no crime can be punished without an accuser and either an admission of guilt or witnesses willing to corroborate the accuser's story. During my own fieldwork I came across many incidents where villagers withheld information from the police, or dropped a case they had brought, frustrating the police's ability to prosecute.

The *Manjhi*'s silence in the presence of the police in Somers' case study could be read as a powerful hint of the separation between the two. This separation between state and village, the charade of respect and the reality of exploitation and disadvantage are themes I explore in the remainder of this paper. What I found in my own fieldwork was that the pushing away and inviting in of the state was not simply a matter of political control. It was a product of how the Santal framed their relationship with the state and the degree to which their own engagement with the state was capable of producing results. This is better understood in the context of who the Santal are, regionally, nationally, historically, and how they view the state and how the state views them both in the context of national policy and more intimate everyday experiences.

The Santal 'Other': rebels, benefactors, subalterns

Jenkins (1996) writes that identity is formed as part of a dialectic relationship between who we think we are and how others see us. During my studies of the Santal I came across terms such as, 'insurgents', '*junglies*', '*upa jatis*' (sub-caste), some pejorative, which sought to define the Santal not simply by their actions, but their history of alterity, each denoting an aspect of 'othering'. But this is not a straightforward relationship of othering. Through history they have occupied different spaces, once favoured by the British in parts of Bengal, protected under special legislation, yet struggling with marginalization, targeted exploitation and land grabbing in which the state has been either complicit or neglectful. I begin by charting this history and demonstrating the contradictory position of rebels, and benefactors, and ultimately subaltern that they inhabit today.

The violence of settlement: exploitation, rebellion and land loss

There are numerous, conflicting theories on the ethnic and geographic origins of the tribe. Theories used to support denial of their claim to 'indigeneity'[8] in South Asia, suggest possible movement of the people from Burma, Persia, Afghanistan and Chinese Tartary.

Other theories suggest they originated in northern India and travelled through the Punjab then down to a region they now inhabit in India, *Chota Nagpur* (Kochuchira 2000, 23). Whatever their origins, both colonial records and the Santal origin myth[9] suggest a history of forced migration in the face of persecution or attack and searches for new land in response to draught and floods up to the nineteenth century. As a result of their turbulent history they are now a diasporic people settled in India across the states of Bihar, West Bengal, Jharkhand, Orissa and Assam as well as north-west Bangladesh and Nepal. In the regions where I carried out my research, the Santal Parganas and Rajshahi, the Santal had settled as recently as the mid nineteenth and early twentieth century, making them relative newcomers.

The story of the Santal settlement in the Santal Parganas district of Jharkhand state, India, has a mythical quality. In the early 1800s the British hired Santal, famous for their skills as swidden cultivators, to clear forest land for agricultural use as part of the Permanent Settlement for land tax.[10] The success of the early settlers drew unscrupulous money-lenders (*mahajans*) and traders to the area from Bengal and elsewhere, who used false measuring tools to underpay the Santal for their produce and forced unsuspecting families into debt – giving loans in leaner periods and forcing families into bonded labour through unchecked interest rate rises or forging deeds of sale or mortgage and taking land in repayment.[11] Growing resentment led the Santal to attack and steal back wealth from their oppressors. While the acts of the *mahajans* and traders had gone unpunished, police dealt with the Santal's counter-attacks as criminal infractions. The failure of the British to respond to growing discontent led to a violent and bloody uprising, the Santal *Hul*, in 1855 when two Santal brothers, who had been visited by the Santal God (*Thakur*), called for attacks on Bengalis and *mahajans* to take back Santal land. The six month rebellion that ensued was responded to with heavy handed retaliation by the British army and many Santal were convicted and jailed (Sinha 1990). Despite its military triumph, however, the British did recognize the need for tighter legal controls to stop exploitation and the Santal Pargana was established as a separate district under Act XXXVII with special regulations to this end.[12]

The new regime had mixed results and despite legislative attempts to end exploitation the Santal suffered further land alienation and unrest. Various authors suggest the violence of the Santal *Hul,* financial problems and a call by the British for the Santal to clear new land in the Barind tract of Bengal led some Santal to leave the Santal Parganas for Rajshahi (now in Bangladesh).[13] Here the Santal faced new adversaries. Muslims predominated in the region constituting 78% of the population, one of the highest ratios of Muslims to non-Muslims in North Bengal and their domination was not only physical (their sheer numbers) but also economic and political.[14] The politicization and growing importance of Islam in the region set the scene for perpetual religious tensions, where the Santal, as animists and Christians, were considered outsiders. Partition of British India on independence in 1947 into Hindu-dominated India and Muslim-dominated Pakistan saw the region fall into East Pakistan, and Hindus, Santal and other religious minorities, fled the area as Muslims migrated to the new Islamic republic. While some Santal returned after the violence had receded, their lands had been reclaimed by incoming Muslims from Bihar who were appointed by the Pakistani authorities to fill the key jobs left vacant by the outgoing educated Hindus.[15] Legislation[16] allowed lands vacated during this period to be redistributed, but this was misused and land belonging to non-Muslims was forcibly reclaimed with immunity in subsequent periods of upheaval such as the *Nachol* insurrection of 1948,[17] the communal riots in 1950, the indo-Pakistan war of 1965 and the Independence war of Bangladesh in 1971.[18] The result is that despite most Santal and other *adivasis* receiving title deeds for their land during British rule, more than 85% of northwest Bangladesh *adivasis* now are landless (Timm 1991, 17).

Relations with the modern state

The application of political theory to problems facing contemporary multi-ethnic society has lead to a focus on citizenship as the basis for understanding interactions between citizens and between minority communities and the state.[19] This approach considers identity, recognition, representation and resource allocation as key factors in inclusion/exclusion of minority communities. It conceptualizes the state at a local as well as a national level, focusing in particular on the impact of relations between citizens. The state is crucial in directing the local forces and ultimately has an interest in them. But localities simultaneously constitute entities to which things are done by outside forces, and themselves shape external economic and social processes (Cooke 1990, 9–10).

India and Bangladesh represent two divergent contexts in this regard. Since the turmoil of their settlement in the Santal Parganas and Rajshahi, the Santal's integration in India and East Pakistan (now Bangladesh) has been affected by seemingly radically opposed government policies which have shaped divergent local experiences of belonging. While India has nurtured a positive inclusive form of nationalism that celebrates diversity, which seeks to recognize and support tribal difference, albeit while making certain demands, Bangladesh's nationalism has fostered the idea of a unified Bangladeshi identity, which excludes difference and has led to a denial of *adivasi* rights.

In India a history of inclusion dating back to the reign of Asoka, and policies of positive discrimination enshrined in the Constitution,[20] have led to a much more politically organized and better-represented Santal presence. In the aftermath of colonial rule India put in place reservations for Scheduled Tribes in the Legislative Assemblies and government posts, and promoted educational facilities nationally which have improved opportunities for at least some Santal. This has facilitated the growth of a small Santal elite, and the existence of Santal people in public representative bodies and services, locally and regionally. But the state, designating Scheduled Tribes amongst what it termed 'Backward Classes', has also been more interventionist, and positive discrimination has been coupled with policies aimed at social reform. Legal restrictions on home-brewing, use of forest products and witch-hunting, have had the effect of de-legitimizing some acts associated with Santal customs and traditions. For example, the brewing of alcohol plays an important part in Santal village life.[21] Alcohol and dancing are symbols of happy life.[22] Nevertheless the state is, at least on paper, committed to recognizing the rights of its Scheduled Tribal communities.

In contrast to this dual approach of positive discrimination and social reform, *adivasis* in Bangladesh have faced assimilationist policies and mis-recognition as 'ethnic minorities' under the guise of a state policy of national unity. In the aftermath of the violent and bloody war of Independence from the Islamic state of Pakistan, Bangladesh's figurehead, Sheikh Mujib, nurtured an idea of a secular, inclusive Bangladeshi nationalism based on a shared Bengali culture. While this began as a celebration of diversity that explicitly excluded religious distinction, after his assassination in 1975 a creeping Islamization lead to growing intolerance of religious and ethnic minorities (Madan 1998, Maniruzzaman 1983, Lam 2006). The protection of this idea of a unified Bangladeshi national identity has become a façade for hard line denial of *adivasi* rights. In July 2011, in a move to explicitly exclude Bangladesh's tribal peoples from benefits under the *UN Declaration on the Rights of Indigenous Peoples* (Barman and Neo 2012, 58–61), the government announced that all references to '*adivasi*' (literally meaning indigenous) in laws, policies, documents and publications of the government, all textbooks and curriculums would be removed and replaced with '*Khudro Nritattik Jonogosthi*' (ethnic minorities).[23] The term *adivasi* is already excluded from the Constitution, which refers instead to 'tribals' and '*upa jatis*' (sub-caste). This is not to say that there are no policies in favour of minority communities but these are not widespread or operational.[24]

This difference in policy in the two countries has had a surprising effect. In Bangladesh situating the denial of recognition in a wider rhetoric of inclusive national identity, which the Santal fought for during Mujib's struggle for independence, has created a nostalgia for an ideal associated with the state. As a result the Santal are more likely to attribute their problems to poverty and local ethnic conflict rather than government policies. In India, however, the long history of embracing difference and the platform for *adivasi* rights created through the Constitutional provisions on Scheduled Tribes has made the Santal more aware of their separate identity and lent itself to a more militant and political struggle for equality. As a result Santal tend to situate their disadvantage in a more remote and less tangible struggle over resources with power brokers associated with the hegemonic state.

This is particularly so for the Santal of the resource rich state of Jharkhand. Here the colonial struggle against *mahajans* and *zamindars* transformed after colonial rule, when the region was administered under the Indian state of Bihar, into a movement for an independent state.[25] By 1950 the formation of the *Jharkhand Mukti Morcha*, *Bisu Sendra* movement (aiming at the removal of all non-*adivasis* from the Santal Parganas) and the creation of a Jharkhand party saw a more focused political campaign for greater socioeconomic and political rights for *adivasis* and a separate state of Jharkhand.[26] While this dream of a new state was realized in 2000, Jharkhand's position as one of the least developed but most resource rich regions in East India made the new state a breading ground for profiteering. The dominance of patron–client relationships shaping access to both private and public resources in the region has meant the benefits have not reached the rural-dwelling *adivasis*.[27] At the village level control over the most important resource, land, continues to be concentrated in the hands of the few, and landownership and control over land (through mortgages) form the basis not only of economic dependence of villagers, but also their political and status subordination.[28] Despite provision in key legislations such as the *Santal Pargana Tenancy Act* 1949 to protect land ownership by *adivasis*, massive land transfer has taken place through mortgages, leases, illegal encroachment and eviction in which the state has colluded (Batra 1999, 115).

While the Santal in India experience their poverty and disadvantage as a macro- and micro-level struggle for power, in Bangladesh these realities have not been politicized with the same success and are hidden behind a ubiquitous culture of subordination (Anwar 1984, 369): the social reality of disrespect, even humiliation, that characterizes their everyday interactions with local neighbours, landlords, officials and contractors. It is not difficult to find examples of Santal work men refused food in Bengali eateries, while their Bengali work colleagues are served and Santal students refused service in restaurants or tea stalls on campus (Das 1996, 39; Barman and Neo 2012, 44). I heard many complaints from those I stayed with of employers making the Santal sit on the floor and being served on disposable (*sal* leaf) plates not used for Bengalis. This applies to all classes of *adivasis* and not just to the poor (Timm 1991, 16). In Bangladesh their adversaries take the form of neighbours, shop keepers, tea sellers (the Muslim population who surround them), whereas in India the source of their problems has been framed in more political terms: an exploitative class of traders (and now industrialists), *mahajans*, or an unresponsive power broker in the state. This locality of oppression does not only have repercussions for how the Santal have responded to disadvantage but has also affected how the Santal deal with disputes, with trouble, whether amongst their own people or with outsiders. I turn now to consider dispute resolution processes and how these relate to the locality of oppression.

The locality of oppression and the resolution of disputes

During my research I found that the more nationalized and distant the perceived sources of their disadvantage, the more likely the Santal were to look inward in resolving their own disputes. This inward looking process was reflected in dispute resolution practices through a greater tendency to revert to their own political and legal institutions for support. In India a greater tendency to define themselves as *adivasis* mirrored a more political sense of self and a stronger commitment to their own Santal dispute resolution processes. In Bangladesh however, the state was seen as a more benign oppressor. Disadvantage and trouble was attributed to more local adversaries, identity was less politicized and dispute resolution less inward looking. Here people faced their battles often without involving the village and although they had a strong sense of identity they engaged more frequently as individuals with state systems of law as part of their struggles with local elites.

I carried out multi-sited research amongst the Santal between 2002 and 2004 involving several trips to collect primary and secondary data from courts, civil society and research archives as well as a longer fieldtrip to stay in four rural villages.[29] Although my fieldwork in the villages was ethnographic, given that I had to share my time across four villages I collected additional data in the villages where I stayed through interviews and focus groups to triangulate and strengthen my ethnographic findings.[30] In the interviews I talked to villagers about their experiences of disputes: of whom they had turned to and who they expected in the future would help. I asked about disputes with fellow Santal as well as with non-*adivasis* (*dikus*). Statistical analysis, in so far as it is a reflection of what in fact occurs, can be useful where it draws out contrasts in responses across variables.

I found that the Santal in India were more likely to keep disputes with fellow Santal in the village, and to treat disputes with *dikus* as matters for the state. They also placed more emphasis on obeying Santal law – seeing this as more important than obeying state law. Following their own law over state law was closely associated with their sense of identity and unity. Their approach to dispute resolution fitted with a harmony ideology model – internal disputes were contained to keep outsiders out, and respecting Santal law was used as a political identifier. In Bangladesh, however, a wider variety of responses were given. In village disputes, whether with Santals or *dikus,* some said they would voluntarily refer to state officials, some the Santal headman (*Manjhi*) and others admitted to simply taking matters into their own hands. Far from seeing Santal law as most important, one in four were more concerned not to break state law, which they felt could not be negotiated with, and another quarter of those interviewed said obeying both state and Santal law were equally important. They viewed law in a more pragmatic way: they would engage with it if there was no alternative, but they would happily manage their affairs without it if possible.

These responses were consistent regardless of the type of dispute. In land disputes with other Santal in India almost all respondents said they would turn to the *Manjhi* whereas in Bangladesh almost half would go the local state official (Union Parishad, Chairman or state court). In the case of minor theft between Santal again in India almost all respondents would rely on the Santal village structures to administer punishment. In

Bangladesh however half would administer the punishment themselves without involving the village, and only a third said they would report it to the *Manjhi*. This was reversed when matters brought in interaction with an outsider. Where a theft by a *diku* occurred, the Santal in India felt it was a police matter and there was a strong belief that the police would arrest the thief and investigate the crime.[31] In Bangladesh villagers were more pragmatic: more likely to treat it as a village matter and not involve the police – who were considered too remote to help. Some said they would involve the Chairman, but most felt there was no need to involve the police if the village could resolve it. This was not so much a matter of keeping things within the village as having confidence that they could manage such issues themselves. This confidence was part of a tendency to treat disputes as open battles, an outward looking strategy that seemed to have nothing to do with containing disputes or strengthening their own unity.

Despite these differences social unity was considered important in both countries. In interviews in both countries villagers told me that they did consider the Santal unified. In India unity was taken for granted. In Bangladesh most respondents felt it had increased over their lifetime as people had become more educated. In both countries villagers told me that fellow villagers would come to their aid when they were in need. Villagers still met together regularly for Santal festivals, or to discuss village problems. A Santal marriage in the village was also a whole-village affair (I witnessed several during my fieldwork) and contributed towards inter-village unity also: wedding ceremonies involved members of the bride's villages traveling *en masse* to celebrate with the groom's village and provided an opportunity for formalizing inter-village relations.

However, in Bangladesh villagers were more likely to envisage a life outside the tribal community – respondents told me exclusion from the village could mean living alone, outside society, whereas in India villagers felt they would have to relocate to another Santal village otherwise they would have no life. Despite being told in the interviews by individual respondents that they considered the Santal unified, in Bangladesh informal discussions I had during my stay revealed concerns that this was lacking when it was most needed. A Santal activist told me there was not much unity amongst the Santal when it came to voting in elections. Being landless and poor, he said villagers often voted for whoever promised them personal benefits (cash, jobs, relief). A young Santal man in Bangladesh, who was standing for local elections, said "it is a Muslim's country, we need to get people together to be unified to progress."

The quantitative data seemed to suggest that in Bangladesh disputes were responded to with outward engagement, often on an individual basis, whereas a nationalized politics of disadvantage meant Santal in India were more likely to turn inwards for their own disputes. While the quantitative data revealed these stark differences, my ethnographic field notes showed another layer of nuances. At the local level of each individual village day to day experiences of disadvantage created a parallel (though intersecting) layer of relationships. Here again the more localized the politics of struggle, the more outward looking the response; and the more distant the politics of struggle, the more inward looking the response.

Micro-politics of struggle in four villages

As I have said my fieldwork in India and Bangladesh took place in four villages: *Thakurban* and *Dhanban* in Rajshahi, Bangladesh and *Madhura* and *Pahara* in Jharkhand, India.[32] While the Santal in each village maintained the same adherence to social and political micro-structure and cultural rituals, the wider context in which this was played out differed greatly in each. I purposefully chose to stay in one mixed and one Santal dominated village in each country. In a mixed village Santal shared village space and amenities (tubewells, wells and ponds, walkways, schools if available) with other *adivasis* and often also Hindus and Muslims. Although the Santal in these villages would usually occupy a section of the village exclusively, this was not always the case. In Santal dominated villages there was no other dominant non-*adivasi* presence. The nearest Muslim or Hindu household would be at least a mile away in a separate village, with little cause for integration between the two. I found that as well as national context, this context of the local presence of Hindus and Muslims had a dramatic effect on disputing processes. Whereas in the Santal dominated villages the physical distance between the Santal and the perceived source of their oppression made harmony an effective ideology of separation and distinction, and a tool of resistance against the hegemonic elite, in mixed villages where the locale of oppression was immediate and visible in daily relations with neighbours, a more open and outward looking engagement with *dikus* was used, in the form of petitions to the local elite and cyclical disputing with *dikus* as a form of open combat.

As a researcher I found that these villages created contrasting contexts for my own reception as ally-researcher. Being able to integrate myself into the daily struggles in *Dhanban* and *Madhura* gave me more opportunity to prove my ally status, whereas in *Thakurban* and *Pahara* there was less room to renegotiate identity: my identity was transposed onto national divisions (Shariff 2013). In the mixed villages of *Dhanban*, Bangladesh and *Madhura*, India the close proximity of the Santal to non-*adivasi* Hindu and Muslim communities created almost daily opportunities for dispute and disagreement. In the Santal dominated villages identities were more fixed, and struggles more subliminal.

In *Dhanban, Naimatpur thana*, 62 kilometres from *Noagaon* town, the Santal lived alongside non-Santal families in a mixed village. The village had been built on government land in mid twentieth century in an area densely populated with Hindus, Muslims and other *adivasis*. Tensions in the area were high, with news of violent attacks, harassment and theft by non-*adivasi* youth and land-grabbing by Bengalis abounding. Non-Santals clearly dominated locally with bigger houses, some with tiled roofs and sanitation (one house even had a television). Local Muslims dominated the trade and commerce of the area running the eateries and stalls nearby. A Muslim man had built a large house amongst the Santal houses – the Santal *Parganait* (regional headman) who lived in the village confided in me that he had not asked their permission to build there. His presence had caused much tension but he and his wife were tolerated and his daughter played with the other Santal children. During my stay he moved freely in and out of the courtyard of the house of the Santal family where I stayed. Yet he was open in his disdain for the Santal: he told me as we sat together in the *Parganait*'s courtyard one day "the Santal are lazy, and they drink too much, we [meaning Muslims] work hard, setting up trade and shops in the area." I replied that the Santal were more recent migrants to the village and had fewer assets and opportunities for enterprise or work, and asked him how many Bengali Muslims would buy groceries from a Santal store or drink tea in a Santal run eaterie? Another Santal man from the village who was sat with us listening exclaimed "she's right" claiming an overdue point in an unequally matched game. On other occasions I witnessed, and experienced, verbal and sometimes physical threats from neighbouring Muslims, which came without provocation, as though an accepted feature of neighbourly relations. Disdain and aggression were characteristic of the daily encounters between the Santal and Muslims.

Although in India tensions between Santal and non-*adivasis* (Hindus and less frequently Muslims) were less visible, there was an undercurrent of tension, and the Santal were very rights-aware and militant in their self-advocacy. As such any local power-brokers who were seen not to be delivering benefits equitably or to the Santal's advantage were a target for criticism. In *Madhura*, a mixed village situated in *Deoghar* district, a locally dominant (Hindu) family run NGO provided just such a context. The NGO owned much of the land in the area and ran an array of small-scale projects from biomedicine to irrigation and a fee paying school with scholarships. Its position on the doorstep of the village made it a formidable presence. The tall impenetrable wall surrounding the main house, headquarters of the NGO, and grounds where the family lived, and where the key workers ate together and carried out some of their activities, provided a visible and unambiguous message of their separation from the village, physically but also symbolically. The NGO family were educated Hindus and although they were committed to helping the poor – they had given their lives and their own personal resources to the work of the NGO – they treated all castes and tribes as equally vulnerable and made no special provisions in their works for the Santal. They did employ some Santal people from the village: one villager helped in the kitchens, another had worked doing odd jobs. But the clear and visible wealth of the NGO with its brick buildings, running water and sanitation contrasted painfully with the poverty of the neighbouring Santal village.

The land in *Madhura* was typically infertile and lack of irrigation was considered an important challenge for the Santal, many of whom depended on subsistence farming. When I first visited the village I was taken to the one small area of the village where the NGO had set up some irrigation. I was shown to a square of lush green paddy, standing out like a sore thumb against the dry barren land all around – symbolizing the fertile potential of the NGO's touch, should it choose to bestow it, in sharp contrast to the villagers' poverty. That the NGO had the potential to improve the prospects of the villagers but had done so little to assist them was a bone of contention that hung like a heavy shadow over the village throughout my stay. As I had been introduced to the village by the NGO but then chosen to live in the village I was seen as a go-between of sorts and villagers shared openly their frustrations at the NGO's inaction during my stay.

Given these local experiences of grievance, it was perhaps not surprising that villagers in *Dhanban* and *Madhura* treated all non-*adivasi* with animosity. When I asked villagers what the term *diku* meant for them they described *dikus* as quarrelsome cheats, violent, angry and threatening. In *Thakurban* and *Pahara* by contrast they were more likely to use the term more neutrally to mean someone of a different caste or the majority group.[33] Yet despite this, there was an easiness about the way the villagers in *Dhanban* and *Madhura* spoke of interactions with *dikus* and I found in these villages I was more able to negotiate my own identity with the villagers (Shariff 2013). There was a sense that in exchanges with non-Santalis the outcome was not fixed.

This impacted on their approach to dispute resolution. Village responses to disputes and infractions were immediate and outward looking. Interviews in *Madhura* revealed a high propensity for quarrels (within the family or Santal village as well as with *dikus*). People used the state courts, rather than the *Manjhi*, freely to resolve these disputes. In *Dhanban* there were also very few disputes resolved internally: the *Parganait* had not heard a case in five months. Disputes that occurred tended to be with local powerful landowners and were played out in the state courts. Battles over land were ruthless, often involving violence and long arduous court cases lasting many years.

In *Dhanban* stories abounded of Santal attending court on cases brought by *dikus* which did not concern them. A young man I met there, *Bishu*, had his name put down on two occasions as a party to a case which he had no connection with – the first one had involved going to court regularly for a year and the second had lasted 10 years before his name was removed from the list. Recounting one of the cases *Bishu* told me that he had had a dispute with a Muslim some years previous to the case. *Bishu* and others had applied to use an area of government *Khas* land adjacent to the village as a burial site for the villagers. A Muslim landowner who had land that backed onto the *Khas* land claimed the land as his own and a dispute began. *Bishu* won the claim to use the land and he said this had inflamed tensions. A few years later the Muslim man brought a case against another Santal man from a neighbouring village, *Noresh*, claiming rights over land *Noresh* was cultivating. The land in fact belonged to *Noresh*'s grandfather who had left it during the 1940s when he fled to India. He never sold the land and *Noresh*, presuming ownership, had paid tax on the land and worked the land for many years. He had ownership papers. But the Muslim man had claimed ownership for himself and in making his application to the courts had included *Bishu*'s name as a respondent. It took the court over a year to realize that *Bishu* had no connection with the dispute. *Bishu* believed that the man who had brought the case had done so only to antagonize him. He believed that the *dikus* saw him as a threat, and used cases in the courts to weaken him, hoping he might go to jail. These stories formed part of a series of cases and counter-cases. The courts were used as part of an open battle between the Santal and local powerful land-grabbers. This is not to say that the law is used triumphantly or willingly. Cases are 'trouble' – one man told me 'if you want to know how long a month can be, take a case to court'. But the local and negotiated nature of the politics of struggle has turned the Santal to look outward – to be more prepared to battle and engage with the local elite in disputes.

In *Madhura* villagers engaged in outward dispute with local elites using state infrastructure as the basis for their demands. In a neighbouring village a Hindu teacher had been appointed to the government school and the Santal of the area protested against his appointment. They had written to the Block Development Officer (BDO) (local government administrator) asking him to replace the Hindu man with a Santal teacher. Near the end of my stay as I went to collect water from one of the village tubewells I noticed a group of men in intense discussion with a man I had not seen before. He had cycled to the village and I was introduced to him – he was one of the Santal teachers from *Madhura*'s primary school. The group seemed pessimistic about the prospects of the BDO appointing a Santal teacher in the adjacent village – they had heard that the Hindu man had paid money to the BDO to secure his appointment (a teaching position was considered a well-paid and respected job). This meant the BDO may not respond to their letter, but they said if this happened they would go to the Deputy Commissioner and then the Member of the Legislative Assembly. They felt strongly that if there were educated people in the local village they should be given priority. There were three Santal in the village with qualifications to degree level.

Whereas in *Dhanban* and *Madhura* perpetual dispute seemed to be a tool of resistance, in *Thakurban* and *Pahara* harmony seemed to be the preferred strategy. In these villages, while the Santal were still acutely aware of their disadvantage, sources of conflict seemed less immediate and visible. Unlike the mixed villages described above, these were Santal dominated *adivasi* villages clearly separated from Muslim and Hindu neighbours. In *Thakurban* in *Gadagari thana*, 50 km from Rajshahi town, I saw very little of the animosity between the Santal and non-*adivasis* I witnessed on a daily basis in *Dhanban*. Instead the politics of struggle was recounted to me in countless stories of strategic exclusion of the state and its apparatus by the Santal. In *Pahara*, in *Poriya Hat thana* 28 km from *Godda* town tensions between Santal and Hindus were also more omnipresent: not a matter of daily wranglings or open disputes but much more theorized understandings of difference and animosity towards high caste Hindus.

The sense that the root of their oppression was more distant made the Santal more inward looking. Even in disputes with local *dikus*, the Santal turned to their own Santal law to find a solution. While I was staying in *Thakurban* a dispute arose. A local Muslim landowner, *Ahmed*, had seen ducks belonging to one of the villagers trespassing on his land. He had allegedly instructed one of the Santal villagers, a *Kisku* man called *Bolanath*, to remove the ducks and kill them. *Bolanath* was not originally from the village (he had married in *Ghar Jamae* form, moving to live in his wife's village so that the two could inherit property from her father).[34] *Paulus*, who owned the ducks, claimed that *Bolanath* had taken the ducks to a neighbouring village where his brother-in-law lived, and killed and eaten them there. A village council meeting was held to discuss the matter.[35] The dispute was framed as an accusation of theft by *Paulus* against *Bolanath*. *Ahmed* was present, but he stood at the periphery and was given little attention until he was called to speak. When his time came he stated unashamedly that he had instructed *Bolanath* to kill the ducks and had no interest in what *Bolanath* had done with them. He spoke angrily, frustrated that the Santal village council was paying so little attention to his own sense of grievance in the matter. The ducks had encroached on his land and eaten his crops. He addressed the meeting without invitation on this point, complaining that his own losses were not being considered and asking who was going to compensate him for his crops. His question was met with silence. It was a powerful gesture. A sense that *Ahmed*, and his crops, were not a concern to the villagers. He was peripheral to the case, a mere witness in an accusation of theft between two villagers. *Ahmed* sensed this and left the meeting clearly unhappy. It struck me at the time as odd that the council had chosen not to include *Ahmed* more centrally in the dispute. After all he was a wealthy landowner and had played a major role in depriving *Paulus* of his ducks and could be liable for a share in the compensation due to him. But holding *Ahmed* to account for the theft of the ducks would have meant giving him recognition as a person with duties *and* rights. The council's silence, their refusal to hear his claims, conveyed that *Ahmed* was irrelevant, in a sense, not a legal person in the council's eyes.

The council meeting continued after *Ahmed* left with statements taken from *Paulus* and *Bolanath* and other witnesses were called. The pronouncement of the *Manjhi*, reflecting a consensus of those attending, was that *Bolanath* was responsible for the theft. He was asked to pay *Paulus* to replace the ducks. When *Paulus* complained that he should also be compensated for the loss of additional income he anticipated from the ducklings the ducks were nurturing at the time of their disappearance, the *Manjhi* gave a lecture about the responsibility of villagers to keep their livestock from trespassing on others' land – without making any reference to the Muslim landowner. This was clearly meant as a reminder of Santal customs, which prohibit animal trespass, rather than of the duties of Santal to non-Santals. *Bolanath* and *Paulus* accepted the decision and left in silence. In resolving the dispute in this way the council had prioritized re-establishing harmony and good relations between the villagers. They had formulated the dispute as a matter of a minor infraction of Santal customs and the decision sought to re-enforce Santal unity while firmly rejecting the *diku*'s call for recognition. This inward looking strategy had achieved a dual counter-hegemonic outcome of asserting their own power within the Santal village and signalling to the *dikus* their lack of power.

While in this case the *diku* was relatively easily side-lined and the matter contained within the village, in other disputes where this was not possible the council showed the reach of its power beyond its own people. *Sapha*, a Santal elder whom I met in a village adjacent to *Thakurban* recounted to me a criminal case involving his nephew.[36] His village had been visited by a group of men from a neighbouring Muslim village. They had threatened the Santal villagers and demanded goods and money. The villagers protested and some of the younger men argued with the intruders telling them to leave. Eventually they chased the intruders and *Sapha*'s nephew attacked one of them as he tried to escape. The man collapsed and died sometime later. Given that the murder would likely be reported by the deceased man's family *Sapha* and his village decided it was better that they report the incident to the police – better that the police hear the turn of events from the Santal's perspective. They did so and although the police registered the case and investigated, *Sapha*'s nephew escaped prosecution: he fled to India and the case was suspended. *Sapha* explained to me that although the case was now in the hands of the state, their inability to prosecute and the lack of closure this created for the Muslim boy's family had left relations strained between the villages. The Santal villagers decided to settle the matter themselves. They met with men from the deceased's village and decided to give the family of the dead man a small area of land in compensation. Interestingly, while the state had formally been given control over the case there was no real investment on the Santals' part in the state system. They had not attempted to locate Sapha's nephew or bring him back to face prosecution. Reverting to their own internal dispute resolution system to resolve the matter was not so much about pushing the state out, however, but demonstrating the greater power of their own system locally. Harmony, for which they were the brokers, was a powerful tool for asserting their power in the area.

Conclusion

My research in Bangladesh and India provided contrasting settings for a study of the historical impact of politics, and the location of oppression on disputing practices. Through a combination of qualitative and quantitative data I found two simultaneous, opposing disputing strategies used by the Santal. While the national contexts of India and Bangladesh provided one set of data, quantitative in form, which demonstrated a tendency towards inward focused dispute resolution in internal matters where the oppressor was located in a amorphous hegemonic power of the state and ethnic power brokers, and an outward focus where the oppressor was close, visible, qualitative data in the villages provided another reality. This time it was the locally situated nature of the politics of struggle rather than the national context that was critical. A high propensity for quarrels in mixed villages where the politics of struggle was local and negotiated contrasted sharply with the preference for harmony as a tool of exclusion and of hegemony in Santal dominated villages. The pivotal variable in each case was the location of oppression and struggle.

This paper, while limited in its empirical sample, may provide a hint towards possible avenues for further research within the wider theme of interlegality in showing that the way the state approaches its relationship with a minority community, not just on the surface but in terms of real commitment, alters in turn how that minority constructs itself. It suggests a need for more careful study of the context and political purpose behind disputing practices amongst minorities. This need not be limited to studies of chthonic peoples in Asia, but may have wider relevance, for example to debates in the West about legal accommodation of religious minorities. Dispute resolution practices amongst minorities, which are only recently being recognized in the West, may be an important site of hegemonic and counter-hegemonic action. In a sense the data here reveal that how this manifests is unpredictable and not simply a matter for the state to decide. At the local level animosity and proximity of perceived aggressors can prompt resistance through outward looking disputing. Where such open disputing is absent, this may signal that the source of oppression is seen as ubiquitous. An image of harmony may hide a hegemonic mission, through which power-brokers assert their own microcosm of exclusion, reaching even at times beyond their own immediate group. These themes are rarely considered in studies of immigrant communities.

Notes

1. This paper is based on empirical fieldwork in India and Bangladesh that received generous funds from the Ford Foundation, New Delhi, and was part of doctoral research funded by the Economic and Social Research Council and the University of Warwick. I owe much to Prof. Upendra Baxi and Prof. Abdul Paliwala for their intellectual advice and guidance.
2. See most recently Darian-Smith (2012), Benda-Beckmann, et al. (2009), Golder and Fitzpatrick (2009), Griffiths (2009). See also Starr and Collier (1989).
3. See Abu-Lughod (1990) and Mitchell (1990) for a critique of his work.
4. Nader (2002).
5. Nader's later work developed this idea further, again seeing harmony as a mechanism of control, this time by the hegemonic order in the form of the US state and in particular its Alternative Dispute Resolution revolution (Nader 2001 'Harmony coerced is freedom denied' *Chronical* of Higher education, 13 cited in French, Jan Hoffman (2005) 'Personal encounters with the work of Laura Nader' *Law and society review* vol. 39 no. 4 pp. 957–963 p. 960.
6. The term is used throughout South Asia to refer to chthonic or tribal peoples. The term itself means autochthonous, native or indigenous. To see an account of its political relevance for the region where I stayed see Shah 2010: 14–16.
7. See Sachchidananda 1969 and 1955; and Chaudhury 1961.
8. The term indigenous has become an important signifier of rights qualification for peoples seeking special dispensations from the state within an international human rights paradigm, but its suitability in countries such as India with its unique history of conquest and ethnic diversity has been heavily criticized (see for a discussion Shah 2007).
9. See O'Malley 1910, 89; Bodding 1942, 5–13; Risley 1891, 225.
10. Hunter 1868, 152. See also Datta 1940, 2; O'Malley 1910, 61.
11. O'Malley 1910, 46, Kochuchira 2000, 73. See also Mallick 1993, 8 and Biswas 1956.
12. The Santal Paraganas Tenancy Act 1949 reserved this special identity for the region.
13. See Sattar (1983, 71), Ray (1975, 3) and Siddiqui (1972) for different views on this.
14. Islam, brought to the region by invading armies from north India in the thirteenth century, had become the dominant religion in greater Bengal and an important political identity for Bengalis seeking to take power from the middle-class Hindus. See further Madan 1998 and Mohsin 1983.
15. For more see Whitaker 1982; Timm 1991.
16. Esp. The *East Bengal (Emergency) Requisition of Property Amendment Act* 1948.
17. The '*Nachol* Insurrection' 1948–49 was a peasant movement against landlords in Nachol, Rajshahi. The peasants proposed a more equitable system for distribution of the proceeds of their labour, the '*Tabhaga*' system (see brief description in Timm 1991, 21). The landowners resisted the change with support from the police. Many, including Ila Mitra, a Hindu woman who led the movement, were arrested and jailed. Others fled to India.
18. Under the *Vesting of Property and Assets Ordinance* 1972 and other Acts which repeated the terms of Pakistan's *Requisition of Property Act*. See Barkat et al. 1997 and Ali 1998.
19. See Kymlicka and Norman (2000); Gutmann and Taylor (1994).
20. The Constitution makes provision in general terms that Scheduled Tribes should benefit from positive discrimination for their advancement, through reservations in public offices (s. 15 and 16), reservations in the House of People, Legislative Assemblies and Village *Panchayats* (s. 330(1), 332 and 243D) and under the Directive Principles for promotion of educational and economic interests and protection from social injustice and exploitation (s. 46). See Shah (2010, 17) for a summary of the political debates that led to these provisions.
21. Rice-beer, palm wine and *Mahua* spirit are a form of social communication and popularity; they accompany entertainment, are a pre-requisite of hospitality, a prologue to festivities and dancing, a currency used to pay a fine imposed by the village council, a part of spiritual rituals, an obligation at ceremonies associated with initiation and death (Kochar 1966, 18). Not

drinking alcohol is associated with Hindu norms and is considered *diku* (non-*adivasi)* behaviour (Kochar 1964, 28).

22. Rice-beer drinking is justified by the story of their creation: the first Santal couple were ordered by Lita to drink and after this produced the first offspring of the Santal race (Tuck 1976, 222).
23. Indigenous People Issues and Resources: http://indigenousperopleissues.com/index.php?option=com_content&view=article&id=11904 accessed 26 July 2012.
24. A recently signed peace accord has attempted to ease tensions in the *Chakma* dominated eastern region of the Chittagong Hill Tracts (CHT). The main provisions of the CHT Peace Accord of 1997 have been implemented and a separate Ministry of CHT affairs created and the withdrawal of army camps in the region has begun (Barman and Neo 2012, 25). However, tensions there persist. Stories of persecution of religious minorities throughout Bangladesh are commonplace (Barkat et al. 1997, Lam 2006, 117). Reservations exist for five per cent of civil service jobs to be filled by people from minorities but lack of basic education in rural villages means even this small quota is not filled (Human Rights in Bangladesh 1997, 37).
25. For background see Sharan et al. 1999; Devalle 1980.
26. See further Prakash 2001, Ekka 2000, Shah 2010, Basu 1994, Mishra and Paty 2010.
27. See on Prakash (2001, 9) and more generally on patron–client relationships in the region Kabeer 2002. See also Singh 2006.
28. See generally on this theme Wood 1994 and Westergaard 1986.
29. Multi-sited research involves shorter periods of stay across several sites, well suited to research that involves cultural understandings of a diasporic or nomadic people (Falzon 2009).
30. I carried out 12 interviews in Santali in each village, 48 in total, and one focus group with the women at the end of my stay in each location between November 2002 to April 2003.
31. While crime is supposed to be the domain of the state law, clearly there are degrees of crime. Note that if it were a matter of murder, however respondents in both countries said they would report it.
32. These are not the real names of the villages.
33. See Shariff 2013, 11.
34. Under Santal customary law there are 14 different types of marriage, each suited to different circumstances including the marriage of widows and divorcees (*Sangha*), marriage of a girl who has an illegitimate child by a man of the same clan (*Kiring Jamae*), marriage to a married woman or female relative after elopement (*Apangir*), and forcible marriage instigated by a boy or girl (*iptut and nirbolok*). *Ghar Jamae* and *Ghardi Jamae* enable a family without sons who wish to pass on their land to their daughter to bring a house husband into their house. No bride price is paid. See further Bodding 1942, 81.
35. See further Shariff 2008, 31–33.
36. See further Shariff 2008, 19–20.

Bibliography

Abu-Lughod, Lila. 1990. "The romance of resistance: Tracing transformation of power through Bedouin women." *American Ethnologist* 17: 41–55.

Ali, Ahsan. 1998. *Santals of Bangladesh*. Midnapur: Institute of Social Research and Applied Anthropology.

Anwar, Ali. 1984. "The question of tribal identity and integration in Bangladesh", in Mahmud Shah Qureshi (ed.), *Tribal Cultures in Bangladesh*. Rajshahi: Institute of Bangladesh Studies.

Archer, William George. 1984. *Tribal Law and Justice: A Report on the Santal*. New Delhi: Concept Publishing Company (Published under the Authority of the Bihar Government).

Barkat Abdul, Shafiqu Uz Zaman, Asisur Rahman, and Avijit Poddar. 1997. *Political Economy of the Vested Property Act in Rural Bangladesh*. Dhaka: Association for Land Reform and Development.

Barman, Dalem Chandra and Mong sing Neo (eds.) 2012. "Human rights report 2011 on indigenous peoples in Bangladesh, Kapaeeng Foundation." January 2012. Available at http://kapaeeng.org/wp-content/uploads/2012/06/Human-rights-report-2011.pdf Last accessed 26 July 2012.

Basu, Rajasri. 1994. *Santals of West Bengal: Ethnophychology and Political Participation*. Calcutta: Progressive Publishers.

Batra, S. L. 1999. *Study of Land Alienation of Tribals in Dumka and Ranchi Districts of Bihar*. New Delhi: Council for Social Development.

Benda-Beckmann, Franz von, Keebet von Benda-Beckmann and Anne Griffiths (eds.). 2009. *The Power of Law in a Transnational World: Anthropological Enquiries*. Oxford: Berghahn Books.
Biswas, Prophilla C. 1956. *Santals of the Santal Parganas*. Delhi: Bharatiy and Adimjati Sevak Sangh.
Bodding, Paul O. 1942. *Traditions and Institutions of the Santals*. Translated from the Santal: L.O. Skrefsrud "*Horkoren Mare Hampramko Reak Katha.*" New Delhi: Bahumkhi Prakashan.
Chaudhury, Roy P.C. 1961. "Bitlaha, A Santhal Ritual." LII *The Quarterly Journal of the Mythic Society* 1:1–5.
Cooke, Philip. 1990. "Locality, Structure, and Agency: A Theoretical Analysis." *Cultural Anthropology* 5: 3–15.
Darian-Smith, Eva 2012. *Legal Anthropology: Culture, Custom, Power and Law*. London: John Wiley and Sons Ltd.
Das, Uttam Kumar. 1996. "Ethnic Communities of North Bengal Face Uncertain Future." *Earth Touch 2*: 37–40.
Datta, Kalikinkar. 1940. *The Santal Insurrection of 1855–57*. Calcutta: University of Calcutta.
Devalle, Susana. 1980. "Multi-ethnicity in India: The Adivasi Peasants of Chota Nagpur and Santal Parganas." IWGIA Document. Available at http://www.iwgia.org/iwgia_files_publications_files/0180_41_India.pdf Last accessed 1 November 2012.
Ekka, Alex. 2000. "Jharkhand Tribals: Are They Really a Minority?" *Economic and Political Weekly*, 30 December 2000, p. 4610.
Falzon, Mark-Anthony. 2009. "Introduction: Multi-sited ethnography." In *Multi sited Ethnography: Theory, Praxis and Locality in Contemporary Research*, edited by Mark-Anthony Falzon. London: Ashgate.
French, Jan Hoffman. 2005. "Personal encounters with the work of Laura Nader." *Law and Society Review* 39:957–963.
Golder, Ben and Peter Fitzpatrick. 2009. *Foucault's Law*. London: Routledge.
Griffiths, Anne. 2009. "Anthropological perspectives on legal pluralism and governance in a transnational world." In *Law and Anthropology: Current Legal Issues*, edited by Michael Freeman and David Napier, 164–186. Vol. 12. Oxford: Oxford University Press.
Gutmann, Amy and Charles Taylor (eds.) 1994. *Multiculturalism: Examining the Politics of Recognition*. Princeton: Princeton University Press.
Hossain, Kazi Tobarak. 2000. *The Santals of Bangladesh: An Ethnic Minority in Transition*. Paper Presented at the Sixth Workshop of the European Network of Bangladesh Studies (ENBS), Oslo, May 14–16.
Hossain, Kazi Tobarak and Syed Zahir Sadequ. 1984. "The Santals of Rajshahi: A Study in Social and Cultural Change." In *Tribal Cultures in Bangladesh*, edited by Mahmud Shah Qureshi, 158–167. Rajshahi: Institute of Bangladesh Studies.
Hunter, W. W. 1868. *The Annals of Rural Bengal*. Calcutta: West Bengal District Gazetteers, Government of West Bengal.
Jenkins, Richard. 1996. *Social identity*. London: Routledge.
Kabeer, Naila. 2002. "Citizenship and the boundaries of the acknowledged community: Identity, affiliation and exclusion." *IDS Working Paper* 171, Brighton: Institute of Development Studies.
Kochar, V. K. 1966. "Village Organization Among the Santals." *Bulletin of the Cultural Research Institute* 5: 11–19.
1964. "Attributes of Societal Status Among the Santals." *Bulletin of the Cultural Research Institute* 3: 20–29.
Kochuchira, John. 2000. *Political History of Santal Parganas From 1765 to 1872*. New Delhi: Inter-India Publications.
Kymlicka, Will and Norman Wayne. 2000. "Introduction." In *Citizenship in Diverse Societies*, edited by Will Kymlicka and Wayne Norman, 1–41 Oxford: Oxford University Press
Lam, Janice H. 2006. "Rise of the NGO in Bangladesh: Lessons on improving access to justice for women and religious minorities." *George Washington International Law Review* 38: 101–130.
Madan, Triloki N. 1998. "Coping with ethnicity in South Asia: Bangladesh, Punjab and Kashmir compared." *Ethnic and Racial Studies* 21: 970–989.
Mallick, Somar Kumar. 1993. *Transformation of Santal Society: Prelude to Jharkhand*. Scottish Church College, Calcutta: Minerva Associates (Publications) Private Ltd.
Maniruzzaman, Talukder. 1983. "Bangladesh politics: Secular and Islamic trends." In *Islam in Bangladesh: Society Culture and Politics*, edited by Rafiuddin Ahmed, 185–219. Dhaka: Bangladesh Itihas Samiti.

Mishra, Asha and Chittaranjan Kumar Paty (eds.) 2010. *Tribal Movements in Jharkhand 1857–2007*. New Delhi: Concept Publishing.
Mitchell, Timothy. 1990. "Everyday metaphors of power." *Theory and Society* 19: 545–577.
Mohsin, K. M. 1983. "Trends of Islam in Bangladesh." in Rafiuddin Ahmed (ed.), *Islam in Bangladesh: Society Culture and Politics*. Dhaka: Bangladesh Itihas Samiti.
Nader, Laura. 2002. *The Life of the Law: Anthropological Projects*. Berkeley, Los Angeles and London: University of California Press.
1990. *Harmony Ideology: Justice and Control in a Zapotec Mountain Village*. Stanford: Stanford University Press.
O'Malley, L. S. S. 1910. *Bengal District Gazetteers: Santal Parganas*. Calcutta: Bengal Secretariat Book Depot.
1916. *Bengal District Gazetteers: Rajshahi*. Calcutta: Bengal Secretariat Book Depot.
Prakash, Amit. 2001. *Jharkhand: Politics of Development and Identity*. Hyderbad: Orient Longman Limited.
Ray, Pramode C. 1975. *Socio-Cultural Process and Psychological Adaptation of the Santal*. Calcutta: Anthropological Survey of India. Government of India.
Risley, Herbert H. 1891. *The Tribes and Castes of Bengal, Vol. II.* Calcutta: P. Mukherjee
Sachchidananda. 1969. "Bitlaha: Analysis of a Santal Institution." *Man in India* 49 (3): 281–228
1955. "Bitlaha." *The Eastern Anthropologist* 9: 42–47.
Sadique, Mahfuz. 2005. "Rights of Santals trampled, land looted." *Holiday*, Internet Edition, 4th March 2005. Available at http://www.weeklyholiday.net/2005/_040305/advoc.html Last accessed August 11, 2005. 11/08/05.
Sattar, Abdus. 1983. *In the Sylvan Shadows*. Dhaka: Bangla Academy.
Scott, James. 1985. *Weapons of the Weak: Everyday Forms of Peasant Resistance*. New Haven and London: Yale University Press.
Sen, Nadini. 2002. *Citizenship as Practice: Meanings and Identities of Citizenship Amongst Santals in Jharkhand, India*. Dumka: PRIA/Agrarian Assistance Association, Conference paper, 14 March 2002.
Sen, J, Sinha, S.C, and S. Panchbhai. 1969. "The concept of diku among the tribes of Chotanagpur." *Man in India* 49(2):121–138.
Shah, Alpa. 2010. *In the Shadows of the State: Indigenous Politics, Environmentalism, and Insurgency in Jharkhand, India*. Durham and London: Duke University Press.
2007. "The dark side of indigeneity: Indigenous people, indigenous rights and indigenous development in India." *History Compass* 5: 1806–32.
Shariff, Fauzia. 2013. "Establishing Field Relations through Shared Ideology: Insider self-positioning as a precarious/productive foundation in multi-sited studies" *Field Methods* Vol 25 (4) (forthcoming November 2013)
2008. "Power Relations and Legal Pluralism: An examination of "strategies of struggles" amongst the Santal adivasi of India and Bangladesh" *Journal of Legal Pluralism* Vol. 57 pp.1–43
Siddiqui, Ashraf. 1976. *Bangladesh District Gazetteers: Rajshahi*. Dacca: Government of Bangladesh Press.
1972. *Bangladesh District Gazetteers: Dinajpur*. Dacca: Government of Bangladesh Press.
Singh, Abhishek and Faujdar Ram. 2006. "Jharkhand since independence: a demographic analysis." *Social Change* 36(4): 19–47.
Sinha, S. K. 2000 "Bihar." In *Status of Panchayati Raj in the States and Union Territories of India*, edited by George Matthews, 77–89. New Delhi: Concept Publishing Company.
Sinha, S. P. 1990. *Santal Hul (Insurrection of Santal) 1855–56*. Ranchi: Bihar Tribal Welfare Research Institute for the Government of Bihar Welfare Department.
Singh, Amar K., Ramesh Sharan, Meera Jayaswal and Shriti Chaudhary. 1999. "Status of tribals in Jharkhand." *Social Change* 29 (3–4): 59–107.
Somers, George. 1977. *The Dynamics of Santal Traditions in a Peasant Society*. New Delhi: Abhinav Publications.
Starr, June and Jane Collier (eds.) 1989. *History and Power in the Study of Law: New Directions in Legal Anthropology*. Ithaca: Cornell Univ. Press.
Timm, Richard W. 1991. *The Adivasis of Bangladesh*. London: Minority Rights Group International 92/1.
Troisi, J. 1979. "Social organisation of a Santal village: Expanding socio-economic frontiers." *Social Action* 24/4, reproduced in *The Santal: Readings in Tribal Life*, edited by J. Troisi, 293–303. Delhi: Indian Social Institute.

Tuck, Donald R. 1976. "Santal religion: Self-identification and socialization in the Sohrae-harvest festival." *Man in India* 563: 215–236.
Westergaard, Kirsten. 1986. *State and Rural Society in Bangladesh: A Study in Relationship*. New Delhi: Select Book Service Syndicate.
Whitaker, Ben. 1982. *The Biharis in Bangladesh*. London: Minority rights group, 4th edition.
Wood, Geoffrey. 1994. *Bangladesh: Whose Ideas, Whose Interests*? Intermediate Technology Publications.

Legal pluralism in discourse: justice, politics and marginality in rural Rajasthan, India[1]

Tommaso Sbriccoli

SOAS, University of London, London, UK

This paper explores juridical and political practices and conceptions of justice and authority in Rajasthan, India, outlining a discursive approach to legal pluralism. The presentation and the analysis of the narrative of a Rajasthani woman will be the focus of the present work. By providing her 'internal' perspective on a case study concerning a village dispute the aim of the paper is both to clarify how legal pluralism can be seen to work in a region of rural Rajasthan, and to prove the usefulness of the method here adopted for the identification and comprehension of the modalities through which different levels of organization are produced and structured within discourse. Indeed, the attempt is to show how legal pluralism can be analyzed not only according to the postulated presence of different normative systems or access to diverse legal forums, but also in relation to the capacity of social actors to build, in a (semi)autonomous way, their position within a discursive order characterized by the potential production and multiplication of legal and political planes.

Introduction

Only that which narrates can make us understand.

Susan Sontag, 1973, 21

This paper explores juridical and political practices and conceptions of justice and authority in Rajasthan, India, outlining a discursive approach to legal pluralism. By 'discursive' I mean to focus on the way in which subjects build themselves, their relations with others and their inter-relationship with 'facts' within discourse, which can shed light on the constitution and working of the legal and political fields at work in rural Rajasthan. The importance of the 'subject' is here recognized not so much as the point of articulation of strategies of action (as the 'social actor' in the classical processual approach in social and legal anthropology). Rather, here, the 'subject' is understood as an analytical construct through which it is possible to unpick and thereby clarify the complex functioning of a field constituted by social practices, power relations, legal and political institutions, state law, 'un-official' normative orders, and discursive and institutional devices.[2] The subject is understood simultaneously as the point where all these technologies of power and their devices 'catch on', and thus as the standpoint from which to look at the possible reconfiguration of the overall system through practices of resistance and translation.

The presentation and the analysis of the narrative of a Rajasthani woman will be the focus of the present work. By providing her 'internal' perspective on a case study concerning a village dispute my aim is both to clarify how legal pluralism can be seen to work in a region of rural Rajasthan, and to prove the usefulness of the method here adopted for the identification and comprehension of the modalities through which different levels of organization are produced and structured within discourse.

The necessity to give attention to the "internal" perspective[3] of social actors when dealing with the relation between law and society has been stressed by many scholars. Chiba (1998) has been presenting what he calls "law in subjectivity" as an important turn in socio-legal studies toward a more nuanced understanding of the relation between subjects as recipients of law on one side, and as active agents on the other.

In a similar fashion, Vanderlinden looks at legal pluralism from the standpoint of the individual or, better, the "sujet de droits", redefining it as

> the condition of the person who, in his daily life, is confronted in his behaviour with various, possibly conflicting, regulatory orders, be they legal or non-legal, emanating from the various social networks of which he is, voluntarily or not, a member. 'Legal pluralism' is pluralism limited to the legal regulatory orders with which the 'sujet de droits' can be confronted. (1989, 153–54)

Further insights on these matters can be obtained by looking at the debates on the relation between 'law and society', which have been central in the last decades in legal and socio-legal studies[4]. I will draw mainly on two of the approaches to this problem.

Comaroff and Roberts (1981) have explored the normative background as that in which litigants develop their 'paradigm of arguments' while negotiating value and meaning in disputes as "predicated on shared symbolic categories and ideological assumptions". For the authors, though, these categories and assumptions "become analytically comprehensible only by virtue of their relationship to the constitution of the socio-cultural order at large" (ibid, 20). This interpretative approach establishes a clear connection between society and normative orders. It identifies the analytical necessity to look at social order at large in order to understand how arguments are built by social actors in specific cases and further, in general, to make sense of the legal practices and ideas in a given society. Law and practices related to it become thus understandable only if linked to wider cultural horizons and form a substantial part of ideological systems. Another productive way of looking at the question is that developed by Moore, who starts from identifying the semi-autonomous social field as an appropriate subject of study (1973). In Moore's words, "the semi-autonomous social field is defined and its boundaries identified [. . .] by a processual characteristic, the fact that it can generate rules and coerce or induce compliance to them" (ibid, 722). The object of analysis thus selected draws attention "to the connection between the internal workings of an observable social field and its points of articulation with a larger setting" (ibid, 742). The analytical proposal of Moore has met with enormous success in studies of legal pluralism, as it allows for the identification of a space of enquiry which is shaped by the relations that constitute it rather than by prior definitions of law.

While Comaroff and Roberts offer the chance to reason on the discursive relation between diverse levels of semantic pertinence, Moore identifies different levels of organization along which to analyze the production and enactment of rules. By trying to keep both these perspectives together in a comprehensive model, I here propose to start from the narrative of a subject and consider it as the field of analysis upon whose surface to identify the traces of the relations constituting it. The 'internal' perspective here is neither utilized as a way to look at how social actors relate to legal systems that remain external to them, nor to identify the appropriate field of enquiry by searching for what is defined as 'law' by people (Tamanaha 2000). Rather, it is the analysis of the construction of oneself within a narrative, that is, the way a subject produces her subjectivity within discourse – and so relations of control over things, relations of action upon others, and relations with oneself (Foucault 1984, 48) – that allows for the identification of what I will call here the various 'systems of (legal) pertinence'.[5] The concept of governmentality as formulated by Foucault (2007) will prove useful to disentangle this system of interdependences and strategic reconfigurations. The structure of the system cannot in fact be defined once and for all, as it acquires its features through continuous processes of redefinition, negotiation and resistance enacted by subjects caught in multiple networks of power relations (see also Shariff, 2008).

The concept of 'semi-autonomy' as developed by Moore keeps thus its analytical usefulness, but it no longer concerns a social field (at the same time capable of generating rules and vulnerable to the ones generated outside it) as much as a subject. Semi-autonomy becomes thus an attribute of the capacity of the subject to articulate different subsystems through processes of translation within constraints posed by discursive and institutional devices and by the relations of power that constitute them. It can thus only be identified starting from the analysis of the relations that a subject builds within discourse. From a theoretical point of view, in fact, two different legal/normative systems must be considered as equivalent and their interaction can occur only as far as they manage to establish a plane of inter-translatability. It is only when we come to the empirical level that we can detect how such translations enacted by subjects are constrained by peculiar discursive and institutional devices and power relations that force subjects into a narrower field of action.[6]

Narratives, the selected field of enquiry for the approach proposed, shall thus be constructed as complex texts for the analysis in order to show how different planes of legal and political pertinence are articulated by social actors. The concept of text, here used, differs greatly from the one developed in its analytical interdependence with a context in hermeneutic theory (Ricoeur 1971, 1974), which has been re-elaborated by Bentley (1984) in his approach to disputing and dispute resolution as cultural processes. The concept of 'text' here adopted is in fact that of structural semiotics, understood as "the semantic representation of discourse" (Greimas 1979, 359). In this way, text not only concerns language but also comprises all the semiotic forms through which sense becomes manifest (see Greimas 1979, 1983; and Fabbri 1998). In this respect ethnography helps in delineating such texts and drawing them out in all their complexity. By carving texts out in this manner, they are elaborated on their discursive levels, thus permitting an analysis of the devices that lead to the affirmation of subjectivity. Spatial organization, temporality, relations between subjects, objects and field of values, the emergence of voice and of the subjectivity that lie behind these: all these will be the main elements of inquiry. The analysis of these textual functions and devices leads to the description of the diverse planes of semantic pertinence and of their relation to the subjectivity projected on them[7].

At the methodological level, the choice of the narrative for the analysis poses some further problems to be addressed. The fact that the narrator is a woman, in fact, raises some interesting questions related to the position from where the subject speaks. As Nader (1986, 2006) has rightly stressed, the position of women in different societies has to be analyzed in the terms of those same societies in order to fully understand the way and the extent to which they are subordinated and the kind of practices of resistance enacted (1986, 378). Through the analysis of a Rajasthani woman's narrative I will thus test the capacity of the method proposed to identify how marginality and resistance practices are constructed and enacted in the process of production of one's own subjectivity.[8]

In the following paragraphs I will identify the strategic acting of the subject within a narrative and point out how she narrates. This will permit both the identification of the ways in which the diverse planes of legal and political pertinence are built, and to show how they relate to the position of the subject and to the wider discursive order.

The context of the research and the story of Durga

The region of study lies in South-western Rajasthan. From 2003 to 2010 I spent 18 months in the area on various visits, focusing my research on the traditional caste *panchayat* of the Raika pastoral community. Raikas, also known as Rabaris, are a caste spread mainly in the states of Rajasthan and Gujarat[9]. They occupy a middle range position in the local caste hierarchy and their traditional occupation is sheep and camel breeding. Historically linked to Rajput rulers and to villagers as suppliers of camels for war and agricultural work, and as herders of village cattle, in the last 30 years Raikas have been facing a big crisis in their pastoral system. Only a small percentage of them are now practicing pastoralism as a main occupation (Köhler-Rollefson 1992; Robbins 1998, 2000; Sbriccoli 2009). They are divided into three subcastes that do not intermarry, but can eat together and have common names for their *gotras*. The latter are exogamous divisions, and each village hosts usually one or two main *gotras*, to which others have been attached in the course of time through practices such as adoption or migration. *Gotras* are important both in villages' social and ritual life and for selecting spouses. Beneath *gotras*' divisions are *kuthoms*, which are lineages including three to four generations and could be defined as corporate groups in matters related to marriage, death, and disputes. When conflicts arise within the community, in fact, people belonging to the same *kuthom* usually act together, supporting the other members' interests, and can be punished as a unique 'juridical person'. Raikas still manage their internal questions mainly through their caste *panchayat* (*jati panchayati*), which deals with conflicts related to property, marriage, divorce, fights, and other minor issues[10]. It is sometimes activated even for inter-caste disputes (Sbriccoli 2009, 2010). *Jati panchayats* should not be confused with statutory *panchayats*, official elective bodies at village level with executive tasks and judiciary competence in minor penal and civil offences. Both the personnel and the normative references of these two parallel but separated institutions differ, the first being composed only of members of one caste, the latter by elected members (in some cases, though, other influential villagers can participate in it, as described for instance by Mayer, 1960). Furthermore, while *jati panchayats* usually take decisions according to normative systems based on "custom" or "tradition", statutory *panchayats*, like state courts, should act in accordance to state norms and laws.

Raika *jati panchayat* is structured according to a series of inclusive layers – from village level up to encompass the whole region – with the upper ones sometimes functioning as 'courts of appeal' for decisions taken at lower levels. *Paragna* level – which is the one immediately above village and usually includes five to 20 villages – is the more important and more frequently activated one. *Paragnas* are ritual unities as well, and when a *mausar* (a funeral party usually held on the thirteenth day after the death of an old man or woman) is organized, all families from the *paragna* must be invited and fed. Even if authority is generally considered as equally held by all caste males, in practice a few old men, called *panches*, are told to be those who actually take decisions in the *panchayat*. General consent is however considered the right way to decide about caste issues, and *panches* are those people whose wisdom, knowledge of caste rules and past cases, and skills in talking allow for correct and shared decisions to be taken.

An important concept to be introduced here is that of *holba*. This is the term used to indicate the sanction given by *panchayat* to anyone who is proved to have broken community rules and is thus considered both as guilty and as 'polluted'. Interactions with other caste members are forbidden to people who are *holba* to a variable extent according to the seriousness of their actions (from the prohibition to share opium and smoke together with caste fellows, to that of commensality, to a radical and complete exclusion from caste). Even if it bears resemblance to the concept of *eli* discussed by Hayden in relation to Nandiwalla traditional *panchayat* (Hayden 1999), *holba* differs from it in the fact that it also conveys an idea of punitive power: a person is *holba*, but *holba* can also be given[11].

Recent changes at the economical, political and social levels are pushing more and more people into challenging traditional authority, and looking toward different ways of settling their disputes. For example, people are beginning to resort to state courts both against *panchayat* decisions and as a supplementary choice to increase chances of success in personal cases. Youth associations have recently strongly increased in number and have become important actors in community political and social life. They are one of the channels through which village community politics is connected to the wider political field; the others being represented either by religious figures who have attached themselves to political parties, sometimes even running for election at district and state level, or by individuals personally connected to politicians. Chandilal, one of the two main characters in Durga's narrative (the one I am going to present), is one of the latter. His political career began thanks to his links with an MLA of the region, a Rajput who had historical patron–client relationships with Raikas in the area due to the large amount of pastures he controlled and made available to herders. When in 2005 *panchayat samiti* (block level) elections came and in Kharan constituency the *pradhan* seat was reserved to a woman, Chandilal's wife, Gita Bai, was given the ticket and eventually won. It is within this context, with a Raika elected for the first time as *pradhan* in the area, that the following narration took place.

During my fieldwork I regularly visited village families in the evening, when all the members gathered at home after a day of work or school. While talking with men it often happened that women, usually sitting aside and preparing dinner for the family, intervened in the conversation. They would say what they thought on the topics we were discussing and many times even corrected their husbands. It was on one such occasion, while I was asking her husband about caste *panchayats*, that Durga cut in on our discussion by stating that *panches* are not people to rely on. She knew very well about those matters, she continued, because of what had happened to her brother and her family. Intrigued by her words, and always open to narrations of *panchayat* cases, I thus replied by asking what she was talking about. At that point her husband told me it was not an interesting story. Durga went back to preparing chapattis mumbling something about the fact that it was too long a story to be told. By then I knew too well that there was no point in keeping on asking Raikas something they deemed unsuitable for sharing with a stranger, and so I just let it go. A few days later, while walking around the village, I came across Durga at the village well. After greeting her, she whispered to me, in the typical way Rajasthani women address men, that if I still wanted to know her brother's story I could go to her house that evening: she would tell me everything. That evening I went to her house where, in the presence of her husband and with the help of a local friend for the translation of terms in the local dialect, a variant of Marwari, I started transcribing her words into my notebook as she narrated. I did not use a recorder, as they would not allow me. I came back two times more to Durga's place in order to collect the entire story, and to clarify some points. The narrative thus produced cannot be seen as Durga's 'original' told story, because of the process of translation, mediation, and partial restructuring it has gone through in the way from (her) 'mouth' to (my) 'notebook'. But it still preserves the overall tone it had, and both the style and the narrative passages have been respected as much as possible so as to maintain the causal connections as they have been elaborated by Durga[12].

I have opted to present the story by splitting it into various chapters. The accounts that I shall narrate concern episodes of violence and corruption, to the point that Durga was apprehensive about recounting them to me. Consequently, I have modified the names of places and persons and been vague about the exact locations of my research. Furthermore, even if the major events related here were corroborated by a majority of the interviewed informants, the fact that I had neither access to official sources (i.e. police and courts files), nor I assisted personally to any of the episodes, could appear to some as a flaw in the ethnographic material. As the focus of this paper is the investigation of how different normative and political orders are produced and characterized within discourse through practices of subjectification and translation, the 'factuality' of the story will not affect the veracity of the analysis.

Subject, marginality and village politics

Durga is a woman in her thirties. Her husband works in a big city in Maharashtra and comes back home only twice a year, each time for two to three weeks. Their house is in the same plot of land as four of the husband's cousins. They all belong to a *gotra* that is attached to the principal one of the village. The five families live thus separated from the main Raika hamlet. Even if they participate actively in the community's ritual and political activities, the fact that they do not completely belong there is still noticeable. Durga has to take care of her daughter and two sons almost alone and, being the younger wife of her husband's kin group, she has little inclusion in the neighbourhood's common activities. She thus participates less than other women in the daily late morning chats, which occur in one of the houses of the village. She is not often to be seen around beyond collecting water at the village well. Her relatively young age and her still uncertain place within the village, compounded by her being alone most of the time, means she maintains quite a close and frequent interaction with her parents' family. This is also because her village of provenance is not far from the one where she lives, allowing for frequent visits on both sides. Her knowledge, interest and involvement in family matters are thus still substantial. This can be inferred from her narrative, the first part of which follows:

> Everything started at Holi 2006. A big party was being held in Ramnagar, and all men from the eighty Raika families in the village were taking part in it. The atmosphere was nice and everyone was enjoying. At some point, Chandilal got up and announced to those present that the Panchayat Samiti had made a 3 lakhs rupees fund available to the village thanks to the work of Gita Bai [his wife and *pradhan* of Kharan's Panchayat Samiti], and to the commitment of BJP. But they don't do any work, they have only built their own house. You should see it, it's like a temple. Chandilal intended to use that money for building a meeting-place for Ramnagar's Raikas. The village already had a meeting-place, close to the shrine of a Raika *Jhojhar*[13]. It had been built by fifteen families, eight of which belonged to the same *gotra* of the *Jhojhar*. Yet, all the community used to gather there for specific events.

Chandilal's idea was to give money to those fifteen families to buy the place and formalise in this way its collective ownership. Many of those present, though, disagreed with such a proposal and left the party after having made explicit their dissent. In the days following Holi, a heated debate arose within the community around the issue. Due to the great opposition met by Chandilal's proposal, even the fifteen families which owned the existing meeting-place and were at the beginning enthusiastic about it, slowly changed their mind. Some of them stated they were not disposed to sell their God. Money was not a sufficient condition. Some days later, a caste meeting was called where the fifteen families publicly declared they were not willing to sell their God to the village. As soon as the first plan had been discarded, Chandilal, in accord with his supporter families, put forward a new proposal: to build a new meeting-place on the field adjacent to the *Jhojhar*'s shrine. In fact, there was nearby a plot of land belonging to a Meghwal, Kishor, who lived out of the village and neither used it nor rented it to anybody. Chandilal proposed to buy the land and the whole community agreed with the new plan. It was decided to ask Kishor for the land. The next week the deal was made by paying to him 500 rupees as *sahi paise.*[14]

At this point all seemed to run smoothly, when Chandilal set new conditions for managing the affair. All the families in the village had to make a collection for the construction of the new meeting place, participating with 10,000 rupees each. On the top of the 3 lakhs provided by the Panchayat Samiti, 8 lakhs more would have been raised, bringing the total to 11 lakhs of rupees. This money had to be utilized both for buying the plot of land and for paying building expenses. Many people disagreed, and unrest and quarrels spread over the village. Young men were the more fierce opponents, since they deemed the amount to be given well beyond their means. At this point, two opposite factions [*palti*] began to emerge. The first one [from now on 'the forty families'] was composed of the fifteen families allied to Chandilal and of twenty-five more families, mostly belonging to Chandilal's *gotra*. The second one [from now on 'the thirty-five families'] was formed by the remaining thirty-five families, which stood out against the decision to invest such an amount of money and challenged even the fact that the meeting-place had to be built where Chandilal had proposed. In the following months, the two factions had minor conflicts and, consequently, their division sharpened. During Holi 2007, one year after everything had begun, the village was celebrating the *dand utsav* ritual [a ritual in which the whole community is supposed to pay a visit to each of the houses where a new child has been born in the last year]. The forty families organized their own ritual and did not invite the opposite faction. The latter met then together to perform the ritual. After some discussion, they decided to send someone to speak to the other families, deeming such situation as negative for the future of our sons' relationships. As soon as the delegation arrived on the spot, those present hid the *prasad* so not to have to offer it to the guests. Members of the thirty-five families, surprised by such behaviour, asked to the people sitting on the *jajam*[15] why they were acting like that. They said: "We are not low caste people, nor beggars or untouchables; we are Rabaris as you are. But we, the Rabaris, when beggars or untouchables arrive at our homes, even to them we give something, since it is our *dharam*. Why, thus, are you acting like that with us?" A fight soon arose, and Chandilal and his followers told to the visiting families that they did not need them in the village, and that they could go away. The delegation left thus the meeting and went back to the other families. Few days later, Chandilal's younger brother had planned his son's marriage. Chandilal decided not to invite the thirty-five families to the collective functions. When the latter came to know that, they thought the time was come to call a caste *panchayat* at the *paragna* level in order to discuss village matters. When the *panchayat* convened, the thirty-five families explained to the assembly the issue, complaining that they were being excluded from village ritual and social life as if they had been excommunicated. Chandilal, required by the *panches* to provide an explanation of what was going on in the village, told the whole story, claiming that if he had not acted in that way, the families now complaining would never have contributed financially to the construction of the meeting-place. At the end of the *panchayat*, *panches* agreed with Chandilal's position and gave *holba* to all the thirty-five families, deeming it right that they should contribute with their share to the construction of a collective meeting place.

I will focus here on three main problems this part of the narrative invites me to address: the position of the subject; the articulation of different planes of pertinence in relation to politics and legal orders, and the problematization of the relation between state and non-state levels of organization (this latter I will do by referring to the concept of 'governmentality').

The position of the subject

With regards to the first problem, Durga almost never places herself within her own narrative. There is no linguistic marker that could have us guess she is an internal actor of the dispute, except for the fact that she displays a detailed knowledge of the events narrated and their context. Indeed, her ability in reconstructing the story within clear spatio-temporal coordinates and a coherent causality, and to describe what happened by inserting it in a framework capable of highlighting actors' choices and roles, produces the effect of a sort of journalistic report. However, as the case involved her own family directly, we should rather see here at work one of the ways through which marginality is discursively produced and enacted. First person pronouns are completely missing, as well as explicit personal considerations and evaluations, and all that occurs is referred to via male actors. Indeed, the only moment when Durga explicitly expresses a personal evaluation of what is happening, and when she breaks the linearity of the narration by directly addressing the interlocutor (in this case, the anthropologist), is when she points to the fact that Chandilal and Gita Bai have done nothing good for the community and only use their position to make money. It is no coincidence that the only occasion when Durga appears in this first part of her narrative is in relation to a judgement concerning another woman, whose way of acting is contested and criticized. This is also the only passage when Gita Bai is referred to. The only woman who could possibly have some power in this case, and who should be the official and institutional promoter of such initiative, appears here and then disappears from Durga's story[16].

The paradoxical overall stylistic effect is thus that of a narrative that could only be produced by an actor internal to the dispute, but whose personal point of view on the events is almost completely absent. Voice, understood as the capacity of the subject to produce her own features autonomously within discourse, appears here as neutralized.

Raika women, indeed, never participate in community meetings, nor do they have any direct involvement in public decision making processes. They are invited to *panchayats* only as witnesses in particular cases, and even then their marginality is made particularly and explicitly evident through spatial and procedural practices. During my research on Raika *panchayats* I found only two instances of women attending them. The first concerned a widow whose husband was killed by some Rajputs of her village and directly and individually addressed some *panches* to ask for support in her attempt to be given at least some money as a compensation from her husband's killers. The second woman was called to bear witness to the fact that her daughter-in-law, before running away from her husband, had stolen some valuable jewellery. In both cases the two women had to wait to be heard sitting alone and silent, far from the men. When they were finally called to testify, they did so covering their faces completely with the veil and whispering in an almost inaudible way. However, women often actively contribute to family discussions on community problems and cases and, through their cyclic returning to their home villages, they are a good source of information on what happens elsewhere for village Raikas.

The neutralization of the subject's voice and her position in the narrative as they can be inferred through the analysis seem thus to substantiate the marginal position of the women in community political life and its juridical field, whilst highlighting their knowledge of the legal and institutional mechanisms from which they are mostly excluded. The only exception confirms this point. Gita Bai's appearance in the narrative, in fact, produces the only space where Durga's voice can emerge – as critical of what is considered inappropriate conduct for a woman.

Translation and planes of pertinence

This brings us to the second problem, that is, the articulation of the political/legal field into two opposite but strictly related sub-systems. Durga never explicitly establishes such a division, whose features can nevertheless be reconstructed through analysis of her narrative.

There are two turning points in the story. Both concern the rupture of a situation of harmony and collective peace and both are induced by the proposals put forward by Chandilal regarding how to spend money made available thanks to his wife's position as Pradhan. Opposite factions articulate along lines of kinship (*gotra*) and age (young family heads vs. older ones). Chandilal is the point of articulation of these emerging oppositions and comes to represent the symbol around which a specific system of values gravitates and is produced. The narrative theme informing his actions is that of self-interest and division in opposition to an ideal of unity and harmony. This motivation will recur throughout the whole story and establish the changing and contextual division between symmetric systems discursively produced around various couples of structural oppositions, as self (economic) interest vs. public interest, oligarchic vs. collective decision making, division vs. unity, true vs. false. At first sight, one system could appear as built around 'traditional' local institutions, normative order and values, and the other around state institutions and their correlated governmental practices. As an example, we could recall the lines where Durga points to the fact that as politicians Chandilal and Gita Bai have done nothing for the community and only used their position to grow rich: a clear assessment of the public uselessness of state politics. But the way in which Durga constructs her narrative shows how from the internal point of view the overall system does not have clear-cut borders between its internal subdivisions. Instead, their opposition is built through the attribution of differential values to specific actions, institutions, relations, events, and subjects in specific contexts. Thus, *panchayat* and its way of dealing with the situation is here coupled with Chandilal's way of acting as a politician, and the relations of kinship along which factions are produced refer both to alignments to political parties and to matters regarding the place of worship of a lineage. They structure a field where state and village politics on one side, and community jurisdictions and internal divisions on the other, 'speak the same language', so to say, and are on the same side. There is continuity, rather than rupture, between the actions of Chandilal and the final sanction of the *panches*. What I have called a system of pertinence is drawn here as a field of continuities that cuts through legal and institutional levels supposedly divided. Durga's ideas about *panches*, that they are all corrupted and take decisions without taking care of justice, hints at the perception of this very articulation between state and non-state jurisdictions and/or institutions. As shown by Moore for instance (1993, 1995) for a different part of Rajasthan, this articulation is dominated by the powerful within a strong patriarchal framework which prevent marginal categories from making their voice heard. This field is built around structural oppositions within a system of values and a network of relations between subjects, and it is in turn contrastable with a symmetric, but by now only virtual, field of continuities: the field that should have been activated in order to achieve a just outcome to the dispute.

In this process Chandilal acquires a prominent role. He is neither simply the external agent of an external power impinging on a traditional and valued order, nor is he a man playing the same game with two different teams. He is rather the 'border' along and across which Durga identifies and translates at the same time the two systems of pertinence one into the other through the play of categories of value. It is the act of translation that produces the two systems and, at the same time, the border dividing them, and not the other way round. It is in fact only through translation that something new can be inserted within the horizon of meaning of subjects.[17]

To illustrate this point briefly I report a brief extract from another case involving Durga's family and Chandilal, occurring some time after (and as a consequence of) the one I am analysing in this essay:

> Suraram owns six bigas of land, and they were registered in our father's name. Thanks to his contacts with the *patwari*, Chandilal managed to change the owner's name to that of a Sargara[18] widow of Ramnagar. [...] Once she accepted [to collaborate], he provided her with the documents proving her ownership of the land, and told her to occupy it as soon as possible. She began saying all around in the village that that plot of land was hers. Then she brought to the field a *Ramji ka ghoda* and started to build a shrine for Baba Ram Deo.

The *Ramji ka ghoda* is a horse symbol of Baba Ram Deo, a god often depicted on horseback and who is worshipped mainly by low castes in Rajasthan. By making a place of worship for the god in the field, the Sargara woman has ritually taken possession of the plot of land. Ritual action, if considered in its performative character, could be seen here as a legal way of asserting and proving one's property within the local normative framework. The widow's ritual and Chandilal's production of false documents for the property of the land are coupled in Durga's narrative without any discontinuity. They are paired as two faces of the same coin, the one signifying the other in a sort of perfect translation between two different legal systems[19]. Here again, the system of pertinence established by Durga seems to encompass in its internal relations what is usually considered separate.

This way of looking at the relation between different normative and political orders allows one to overcome the often-posited and rigid distinction between state and non-state legal and political levels. In this way rather, one may investigate more accurately the different ideas and practices associated with these competing paradigms, in terms of their mutual articulation and intermingling, rather than as opposed or contra-distinct.[20]

The Government and the subject

Durga's narrative raises another important question: what kind of relation between the 'traditional' political/legal system and the state system is identifiable? The previous analysis shows indeed that a linear relation is not traceable. As in the cases described by Moore (1973) while developing her concept of semi-autonomous social fields, there is not a direct correspondence between legislative intents to shape society and effective results. It seems here that state practices of governing populations are caught within existing local political networks that reconfigure them at the same time as they are reconfigured by them. Looking at the institutions, laws and resources connected to the contemporary discourse about development (the field triggering the dispute) through the lenses of the concept of governmentality developed by Foucault could here prove useful.

Governmentality could be described as that practice of governing that, by producing the concept of population as an 'object of government' rather than as the 'sujet de droits', develops both a specific apparatus for governing (procedures, institutions, tactics, etc.) and a series of knowledges ('savoirs') on it. This model is opposed both to classical liberalism's juridical concept of power as contract and sovereignty, and to the institutional paradigm that sees power as emanated from the state apparatus (understood as a 'warlike' field). For Foucault, to govern is "to structure the possible field of actions of others" (Foucault 1994, 341). Power is thus to be analyzed in terms of a force that links macro levels of strategic elaborations with micro practices of tactical penetration that involve processes of subjectification.[21] Power does not exist 'in itself', but only as an economy of relations. Power relations become thus the focus of the study of power, and, as stated by Shariff (2008, 9)

> they are perpetuated through cultures and customs and disciplinary technologies, which shape the way we constitute ourselves as individuals with collective identities. They direct the way we perceive, think, act and react.

This penetration of government practices triggers processes of subjectification and re-elaboration mediated by already existing social networks and the power relations constituting them. It thus cannot be linear. Rather, it forces the reconfiguration of such networks through both processes of resistance and, as I proposed before, translation.

In the case under scrutiny, intermediate networks formed through party affiliation have shaped the direction and modality of resource distribution and reconfigured the discourse on development in strictly local terms. At the same time, the very 'hybrid' form of such networks has allowed for a space to be opened to the further penetration of models of governing into the system of localized power relations and institutions.

The fund, in fact, was directed specifically to Chandilal's village – his place of residence and thus community of belonging – appearing thus as a sort of compensation/reward for his success in having his wife elected through the mobilization of his pool of voters in the area. Chandilal's strategy, in turn, appears as explicitly directed toward the redistribution of this money to a specific section of the village community, that is, the families who were directly engaged in the political campaign in favour of Gita Bai. These were linked to Chandilal through kinship ties, demonstrating how kinship networks still play an important role in local politics. Furthermore, the consequent division of the Raika village community has interestingly taken place within an institutional framework, the *jati panchayat*, which belongs to a political order that is supposed to be external to that of the State.

Raika village community meetings have been working both as an institution for the implementation of projects and the management of external funds, and as a judicial body. As soon as the divergence of opinions on what to do became patent, the behaviour of Chandilal's faction displayed the features of both a judgement and a sanction. By not inviting the opposite families to a village ritual and a marriage, and by not even sharing food with them, the forty families were affirming the exclusion of the other side from village ritual and social life, that is, the condemnation of what they believed to be sinful and guilty behaviour. It is exactly at this point, when the other faction began to understand that it had received a silent *holba* ('excommunication') that it decided to activate the formal caste forum that encompasses the village. It could even be said that the *paragna* level *panchayat* was here acting as a court of appeal for dealing with a matter whose first judgement had already been given through the activation at village level of social practices of exclusion and boycotting. The *jati panchayat*, giving credit to Chandilal's moral understanding of what was happening, simply sanctioned an exclusion that was already there[22]. At the same time, the *panchayat*'s judgment can be read as the acceptance of the way in which Chandilal had managed the money coming from the block. This decision clearly shows how traditional jurisdictions on the one hand, and governmental patterns on the side of state institutions and political parties on the other hand, interweave within a unique field of action.

Durga's idea of *panches* – their corruption and contempt of the good of the community – shapes this field in its internal constitution of value. Many people in the region share with Durga such a vision of *panches*' way of acting, and consider them as more interested in money than in settling disputes in a rightful way. Some of the criticisms I collected in the field concern *panches* as being "people who just want to eat" (alluding to the meals the party calling a *panchayat* has to offer to all those convened), "people who can turn false into truth by being paid", "people who just like to speak, but then do nothing for the community and stand out against community's development [*vikas*]".

Interestingly such negative features are also attributed by the same people to lawyers and judges operating within the official state legal framework. The local discursive practices do not apparently juxtapose the two fields in absolute terms. Rather, they build them by translating their contextual relations in terms of a common system of values while referring to specific events, persons and institutions. The concept of 'governmentality', with its focus on modes of penetration of practices and forms of control and subjectification at all levels of society (from the general one of institutions to the micro level of subjects' bodies) seems to be a productive way to look at the processes of mutual constitution and continuous negotiation between these different levels. Furthermore, it allows the identification of both the forces and devices that constrain a subject's field of action, and the space of freedom left to them and within which they can resist and/or reorganize the overall system along complex, and often apparently contradictory, lines.

The last statement above reported, for instance, "*panches* stand out against community's development", is often heard when speaking with young men. In this context, it acquires a peculiarly paradoxical flavour. In fact, rather than opposing development, we could here say that the *jati panchayat* has sanctioned as appropriate a specific way of managing development projects, which has in itself been rather problematic for the people involved in it in Ramnagar.

The political and administrative functions of state institutions affect local systems of decision making in complex ways, so that a matter of managing state development funds can activate juridical processes of sanctioning according to local normative orders, systems of values, and power relations. These local institutions act both in continuity and discontinuity with state ones within a unique multi-layered system. The internal subdivisions of this field are not clear-cut, but contextually produced by actors both in their discursive practices and in their way of acting.

Ideal models and effective strategies

Eight of the thirty-five families belong to the same *gotra* and lineage and are economically well off. They all run small businesses in various cities of Maharashtra, which are managed by some of their members. The informal leader of this group, thanks both to his economic resources and his skills, is Suraram, who owns a small shop in Mumbai. He is the brother of Durga and, according to her, he is the only person in the village whom Chandilal is afraid of. The second part of Durga's narrative:

> After receiving *holba*, the thirty-five families decided to ask Suraram to come back from Mumbai and help them in dealing with the issue. My family did not completely agree with the decision, since we feared it would have turned a village matter into a personal one for us.

> But in the end, they agreed and called him back. So he came back to Ramnagar. The very evening he arrived, the thirty-five families organized a meeting in order to discuss the situation. Suraram spoke to the families, asking them not to be angry with the other families, because the important thing was to live all in peace like in a big family. He promised that the day after he would go to talk to Chandilal, who was his friend since when they were children and with whom he had never fought before. The next morning, Suraram came to know that a sheep-shearing was going on in the house of one of the rival families. He thus went there, where he found some of the Raika village elders. He spent some time discussing with them about village matters. Suddenly, while he was talking, a young man came waving a stick and tried to hit him. Suraram managed to avoid the stroke, grabbed the guy and threw away the stick. Suraram was astonished and asked those present why they wanted to hurt him. He said he had just arrived and only wished to talk about the situation. Someone thinks that the boy had been sent by Chandilal, who decided the evening before to frighten my brother as soon as possible so that he would have gone back to Mumbay immediately. In the evening, Suraram went directly to Chandilal's house because he wanted to understand what was going on. As soon as he arrived, Chandilal's brother approached him with a stick and was ready to hit him when Chandilal himself stopped him. After that, Suraram was so shocked that he said to Chandilal he did not want to have anything to do with him and his family anymore. He went away saying to him to make sure to be at Thakur's house next morning, because he wanted the Thakur to set definitively the issue. The day after, Suraram, Chandilal, and most of Ramnagar's Raikas went to Thakur's place. In the end only one decision was taken: the deal with Kishor, the Meghwal owner of the land, was broken. This was a victory for us, since Chandilal was now forced to start all over again. Outside Thakur's house, Chandilal began to shout at Suraram, threatening him by saying that he would have killed him within two days.

This part of the narrative is important as it illustrates what authority and the right way to take decisions are or should be in Durga's terms, at the same time as identifying the risk of the situation becoming a matter between families rather than a community issue. Regarding the latter point, we can identify in Durga's narrative a tension between individual families' strategies and concerns, and the will to find a solution to a village problem. The dialectic between these two attitudes is significant as it displays social actors' awareness of the fact that disputes can evolve by unfolding along the various potential fractures that articulate the social field.

This is further stressed by the presence, for the first time, of linguistic markers that position the subject of the enunciation, Durga, within the narrative. Once her brother appears in the story, Durga is able to articulate her own presence on the scene. Expressions such as "my family", "my brother", "this was a victory for us", project Durga within her own narrative and display the workings of the progressive and discursive fragmentation of the social field. Once the level of pertinence of the family enters the narrative, Durga can insert herself within the story as participating in a collective autonomous subjectivity. If Chandilal is built as the operator of the translation between, and of the production of, two different systems of pertinence, Suraram comes to represent the point of articulation of Durga's presence and of her point of view on the events narrated[23].

In this respect, Suraram's speech to his faction offers indeed a model of authority and justice to which Durga seems to completely adhere. The speech is interesting as it articulates the system of value already met in its ideal positive form. Indeed, Suraram tries explicitly to ignore or overcome divisions by stressing the importance of dialogue and consent. These two features are linked to the statement that, in the village, all Raikas should consider themselves as being part of the same family and act accordingly. The paradigm of consensus, in opposition to that of 'the majority' (in matters related to governance) and 'truth' (in legal matters), is often presented both locally and in anthropological literature on India as the main characteristic of the traditional decision making system vis-à-vis the modern/Western one. Even if I believe this stance to have a certain correspondence to empirical reality, still, in my opinion, 'traditional' is often here used instead of 'ideal'. By this, I mean to emphasize how such vision about how things should go either shapes actual social practices or interacts with other models in specific situations rather than considering it as the principle actually informing legal and political practice[24]. For example, it is interesting to look at how, among Raikas, kinship is utilized in discussing about *panchayat* in a twofold, opposite way. On the one hand, as in Suraram's speech, the rhetorical device of stating that everybody is part of one and the same family is that through which Raikas found the very possibility for a common institution to exist and take decisions on matters related to its members. On the other hand, at the practical level, when young Raikas are asked why they almost never speak during caste meetings and have no voice in making decisions, answers are mainly framed within a kinship idiom: they refrain from speaking as a form of respect to the elders, as the latter are their grandfathers, fathers, and uncles. Equality and hierarchy, consent and the power of the few, are principles present and opposing each other already in the 'traditional' conceptions of authority and justice. The fact that, as often happens in local narratives such as Durga's, they are respectively attributed on one side to the 'old and golden' times, and on the other to the 'modern and decadent' ones, must thus be problematized rather than taken at face value.

This ideal of 'traditional government' manifests itself in two ways in the story. First, the attempt made by Suraram to find a consensus in the village and re-establish peace through dialogue with the opposite faction. Then, after the failure of this strategy, the activation of another legal forum available in the village: the mediation of the *Thakur*. *Thakur* (literally meaning 'Lord'), is the title assumed by those, usually Rajputs in the area, who in pre-Independence Rajasthan had control of the political and economic life of villages granted to them by the king. At present, *thakurs* still informally hold part of their traditional authority, and are often addressed by other communities for settling disputes. Suraram's move was in this case effective, to the extent that it completely nullified what Chandilal had managed to obtain until then. In fact, the decision of the *Thakur* to rescind the agreement with the Meghwal affected the substantial part of Chandilal's strategy, rather than a minor procedural issue. Suraram played in this occasion one level of organization (village 'super partes' authority) against the other (inter-village caste authority), and succeeded in temporarily stopping his rival.

This configuration shows how access to, and activation of, different forums pertaining to different normative and organizational levels cannot simply be understood as a 'shopping strategy'. We are here witnessing complex ways of dealing with conflict, which play one level against the other and overlap rather than juxtapose the normative frameworks they refer to. In this part of the narrative, indeed, Suraram forces the rival to submit their case once more to a supposed neutral authority. The interesting thing is that Chandilal, in Durga's narrative, never appears able to avoid such new judgement, and has at the end to comply with the decision. At this point, even if Suraram and his faction are out of the community, the Thakur's decision disrupts Chandilal's strategy. The latter's use of violence on two occasions against Suraram seems thus aimed at interrupting any attempts by the rival toward a reconfiguration of the field of forces in his favour. Which eventually occurred.

There is not so much here a straight opposition between different levels of organization and jurisdictions, but a field of intersection where, within specific constraints and disparities of power (and the use of violence as a means toward the production or reinforcement of such disparities), social actors can elaborate peculiar strategies that activate specific configurations of the forces at play. The effectiveness of such strategies lies indeed not only in the capacity of a subject to move along different legal orders (with all its corollary of economic, political, and 'intellectual' capital necessary to do so), but also in his ability to articulate the overall system in a way favourable to himself by playing with the categories of values, the power relations and the institutions of the social field, so as to force the compliance of the other actors in the game into his desired outcomes.

State vs. Panchayat justice and new political subjectivities

In the last section of Durga's narrative, which I omit for reasons of space, we are presented with a personal and unscrupulous use of public resources and agencies by Chandilal. His response to the defeat is massive and dramatic, and hits Suraram as the person responsible for the failure of his 'development' plans. The scale of the reaction is indeed impressive and involves the utilization of conniving policemen and the silencing of state courts through the concealment of police files and the bribing of witnesses. According to Durga, Chandilal gave 40,000 rupees to a group of Raikas for hitting his enemy, and 130,000 rupees ca. to the police station of a nearby village in order to help him in covering up the case. Suraram spent almost one month in a hospital after the attack. When he was released, in Durga's words,

> the whole Raika community of the *paragna* welcomed him at Ramnagar. The *panchayat* immediately removed the *holba* from him and my family, and gave it instead to Chandilal and to the families of his faction.

> Afterward, my family has organized some demonstrations, to which also some of Congress local politicians have joined. The first was in front of Rudrapur police station. We asked them to re-open the Suraram case, and to make the file public. Until then nobody had been interrogated or charged. After some time, we organized a new demonstration in front of Kharal Court. A lot of people came, Raikas and even *panches*, and Congress party and some Raika Youth Associations too. We made some puppets personifying Chandilal and the policemen involved in the case, and then we burnt them.

I would like now to focus on the peculiar relation between State Courts and *panchayats* as can be inferred from such an episode.

Durga's account is impressive for the detailed precision with which she reconstructs what happened, even reporting the amount of the alleged bribes paid by Chandilal to his 'accomplices'; a knowledge of facts that sharply contrasts with the silence and incapacity to proceed on the side of state courts. It looks as though, at the local level, facts were well known by many. This would explain why, as soon as Suraram comes back home, the *jati panchayat* welcomes him, removes his *holba* and gives it instead to Chandilal and his supporters. The gap between local awareness of what happened and state courts' incapacity to even partially reconstruct the 'truth' of the events is at the root of a frequent narrative *topos* in people's discussions on justice, this time completely in favour of *panchayats*. This stance is usually framed in the following terms: "Courts are not even able to ascertain facts, and you can easily either find or pay some witnesses who will testify what you want. But *panches* always know what happened, and if courts will not find the guilty one, *panchayat* will. *Panchayat*'s justice is certain and tough. Courts' justice is uncertain and can be easily manipulated." If compared to statements previously reported about *panches*' and *panchayats*' faults, these claims clearly indicate that we are once more facing complex and often contradictory ideas about justice, which cannot easily be paired up exclusively with either one kind of forum or the other.

The *panchayat*'s removal of the *holba* from Suraram shall be understood within a legal paradigm that sees justice as a matter of punishing the rupture of, and preserving, an order which is at the same time religious and social. It provides in turn space for expiation on the side of the culprits, so as to reintroduce them within that very order.[25] Suraram's suffering and the way it was produced, which was well known to everybody in the region, could be here considered as a process of expiation allowing him to be reinserted within the community, at the same time as providing the reasons to excommunicate Chandilal and his followers. *Panchayat* is not here admitting a previous mistake, as much as reorganising the balance of right and wrong according to new events.

So, one might wonder, why do Durga's family and other Raikas demonstrate against state justice for the case to be decided when a sanction against Chandilal has already been taken? It looks as if the field of forces whose configuration was triggered in the first place by Chandilal's actions cannot be further disarticulated. As in the above reported case of the "theft" of Suraram's land, subjects seem to mirror one system and to translate both within a unique and complex system of pertinence. Within the latter, performativity of legal actions toward the fulfilment of ideals of justice is looked for in ways appropriate to the new relations established.

Thus, even if the two legal systems might appear opposed in subjects' statements, dichotomies between state and non-state jurisdictions, at the local level, are built by reconfiguring continuously and in contextual ways both their mutual relations and the overall discursive framework, rather than by linearly juxtaposing two contrasting paradigms.

The final public demonstration represents indeed the projection on the political field of such legal articulation. Here, at the end, a sort of unity is finally achieved. Raikas, politicians, Youth Associations and "even *panches*" all participate in the event and deploy a common and shared political position. The latter goes beyond both the village level and the encompassing structure of Raika *jati panchayat* and produces new lines and fractures along which potentially novel political subjects and ideas about authority and justice could develop. The suffering of Suraram has allowed for the reconfiguration of the system of affiliations and organization and opened a space for the creation of new solidarities and a new kind of unity: a subjectivity that is now able to inhabit the new plane of pertinence produced. The 'we' Durga articulates at this point differs greatly from the one she used when the level of pertinence of her family first entered the narrative. This 'we' presupposes a direct action enacted by the subject in a collective political situation: "*We made* some puppets personifying Chandilal and the policemen involved in the case, and then *we burnt them*." This 'we' projects for the first time an active 'I' within the narrative and an autonomous subjectivity within the discursive space opened by a new political articulation.

Conclusion

In this paper my aim was to outline a discursive approach to legal pluralism in order to understand how social actors make sense of and build their legal and political world in a region of Rajasthan. Rather than focusing on the differences between specific normative orders and their 'content' and procedures, I gave attention to their relations to other organizational levels and to the way all these layers are established and differentiated by subjects within discourse. This has meant analysing a woman's narrative concerning a village dispute thereby bringing the traces of the relations constituting it to its surface. Reasoning in terms of systems or planes of pertinence has proved appropriate in defining the portions of epistemes that intervene as the condition for the generation of meaning in specific situations. These situations – sets of practices that also comprise language as a form of expression – can be described as texts. By focusing on the way an axiological system is put to work in the process of 'mise en discourse', I thus highlighted how translation and the consequent setting of borders are fundamental practices enacted by a subject in selecting the continuities and discontinuities along which to think and act in the world. In this way, there is no need to postulate from the beginning two or more distinct systems, to be later analyzed in their different features. Rather, the point of departure is the analysis of a text in order to see how different levels are produced within discourse, always by means of a translation that makes use of specific markers of value and narrative topoi.

The socio-political-legal field of Raikas has thus appeared as a complex system contextually divisible into subsystems that are interwoven in ambiguous and unexpected ways. The same division between political and legal fields manifests itself as weak when confronted by the discursive constructs that articulate them together in subjects' enunciations. Governmentality is a useful analytical tool in order to identify the processes of interpenetration between different levels of organization and the way they trigger reconfigurations of the overall system. The subject, as the centre of processes of subjectification, resistance and translation, constitutes therefore a privileged standpoint to analyze such dynamics and to measure the extent to which she is able to negotiate or challenge the power relations she is inserted in. Legal pluralism, from this perspective, is indeed strongly linked to the position the subject occupies in a social field structured by complex networks of power relations (see also Shariff 2008).

The case of Durga is illuminating from this point of view. While able to articulate the legal and political fields in her narrative through processes of continuous translation, which involve the construction of the characters of the story as points of articulation of sets of practices within wider systems of values – demonstrating thereby a detailed knowledge both of facts and of their social and legal construction – her position, as shown by the analysis, varies considerably according to the way different planes of pertinence are built. While her position within the overall legal-political field appears as marginal along most of the narrative, she is able on one side to articulate her presence and point of view on the events through those of her brother when the level of pertinence of family comes to the fore and, on her other side, to express a personal critical judgment on state village politics by directly addressing another woman's way of acting. At the end, she appears as a political subject provided with autonomous competences in the new discursive space opened by the unfolding of the events and by the constitutions of new political strategies and subjectivities.

At a more general level, thus, Durga, by telling her own version of the story, had the chance to participate in the local discursive production that configures the model for the right and the wrong, the legal and the illegal, the true and the false. In elaborating a narrative in her own terms, Durga could activate her own strategic position and point of view within the field of forces described, as it has been inferred by the analysis of the roles – charged with opposite, and often contradictory, values – of the other characters in the story. The will of Durga to talk about her story lay indeed in the possibility to 'change the world' through telling it; something Raika women are mostly prevented from doing both in local forums and state courts.

By giving attention to the way subjects build themselves within narratives and to the devices through which their voices become perceptible within them, we can identify contextually how marginality and subalternity is discursively produced at the same time as we are able to grasp the perspectives of the marginal and the subaltern[26]. Though, to have the chance to produce oneself autonomously within discourse does not mean in any way to automatically produce an autonomous subjectivity for oneself within it. Our discursive productions are deeply entwined with the overall discursive order we are inserted in, and often subaltern subjects re-produce the very 'ideologies' that found their marginality. This notwithstanding, Durga's narrative offers an instance of how the ones whose access to forums where making public their problems and suffering is mostly impeded, are still able to elaborate their own structuring of events within complex frameworks.

Indeed, even though Durga's way of structuring the different levels of her story and the different conceptions about authority and justice proved to be not so dramatically different from other more hegemonic stances, the very fact that she is here the point of articulation around which discourse unfolds, opens fruitful fractures for the analysis. It allows a way of looking at how legal pluralism can be analyzed not only according to the postulated presence of different normative systems or access to diverse legal forums, but also in relation to the capacity of social actors to build, in a (semi)autonomous way, their position within a discursive order characterized by the potential production and multiplication of legal and political planes.

Notes

1. I wish to thank Livia Holden, Patricia M. Jeffery, Adrian C. Mayer, Edward Simpson, Pier Giorgio Solinas, and the anonymous reviewers for their very helpful criticisms on earlier versions of this article. I also want to thank Stefano Jacoviello and Tarcisio Lancioni for their useful comments. The article is based on field research funded by the Doctoral School "Metodologie della Ricerca Etno-Antropologica" at the University of Siena.
2. It might be useful to briefly discuss what it is meant here by the terms "state law" and "un-official normative systems" or "non-state law". The first term refers to that corpus of norms and rules emanating directly from the state and mainly enforced through its institutions and agencies. The second, whose field of definitions has been much more controversial (see for instance Dupret 2007; Griffith 1986; Merry 1988; Moore 1973; Tamanaha 1993), refers to a variety of normative/legal orders, which may range from social norms regulating people's lives to more systematized normative systems emanating from multiple sources and enforced to different degrees by various kinds of non-state institutions. In what has been defined as "strong" or "deep" legal pluralism (Griffith 1986, Merry 1988), state and non-state laws coexist and overlap without being unified under any single legal system, both exerting authority on social life.
3. For a discussion of the internal/external distinction in legal and socio-legal theory see Tamanaha 1996.
4. See among the others Benda-Beckmann and Benda-Beckmann (2006), Galanter (1981), Griffiths (1986), Merry (1988) and (1999), Moore (1973), and Tamanaha (2000). For a discussion of how law is conceptualized by different authors and in different theoretical approaches see Tamanaha (1993).
5. Here I am selecting the pertinent field of enquiry by partly reformulating what Foucault had called 'practical systems' and defined as follows:

   > "Here we are taking as a homogeneous domain of reference not the representations that men give of themselves, not the conditions that determine them without their knowledge, but rather what they do and the way they do it. That is, the forms of rationality that organize their ways of doing things (this might be called the technological aspect) and the freedom with which they act within these practical systems, reacting to what others do, modifying the rules of the game, up to a certain point (this might be called the strategic side of these practices)." (Foucault 1984, 48).

6. For an interesting analysis of how relations of power structure the field of action for marginal subjects in a context of legal pluralism see Shariff (2008).
7. For previous works conducted with a similar approach see Sbriccoli and Jacoviello (2011, 2012).

8. For works developing approaches akin to this by utilizing women's narratives in India, see Wadley (1995) and Holden (2004, 2008).
9. In the last 20 years many scholars have been doing research with Raika community. Among the most interesting studies are those by Prevot (2007), Sharma (2005), Srivastava (1991, 1997, 2000) and Agrawal (1999).
10. Hayden titled the final paragraph of his book on Nandiwalla's panchayat (published in 1999 and drawing on ethnographic material collected in the late seventies) "Requiem for the panchayats." In contrast the Raika panchayat I have documented is still healthy; its reconfiguration of itself within new political conditions, as will be made clear throughout the article, gives substance to a disagreement with Hayden's obituary.
11. For a detailed discussion of the concept of *holba* see Sbriccoli (2009). See Holden (2003) for a discussion of how concepts of punishment and expiation are not mutually exclusive in rural legal practices and conceptions in Madhya Pradesh.
12. For some reflections on the collection of life stories by anthropologists as processes of cultural translations and on the concept of causality, see Sbriccoli and Jacoviello (2011).
13. *Jhojhars* are deified heroes. They were usually people who died fighting to protect village animals from robbers. They are worshipped in the place where they are supposed to have died, and mainly by members of the same lineage see also Srivastava (1997).
14. *Sahi paise*, literally 'the right money', is a symbolic advance serving as guarantee for both parties.
15. The *jajam* is the mat on which *panches* sit during *panchayats*. It is said, among Raikas and other communities in the region, that in *panchayat* "*jajam devi, panch parmeshwar*", that is "*jajam* is the Goddess, *panches* are God", clearly hinting to the linga-yoni image and referring to the superior and almost divine authority *panches* are held to possess in traditional justice forums (for similar conceptions of traditional authority in other parts of Rajasthan see also Moore 1993).
16. Indeed, Gita Bai is often referred to as "Chandilal's wife" by most of the people in the area (men and women), rather than by her name, and she is explicitly seen only as proxy for her husband, the true *pradhan*. For a discussion on such matters and women acting as proxy for the men of their families see Nolle (2008).
17. For a discussion on the relation between the constitution of borders and translation in situations where different cultural or legal systems meet, see Sbriccoli and Jacoviello (2012).
18. Sargaras are inserted within Scheduled Castes in Rajasthan.
19. It is this kind of translation which many anthropologists are requested to assist Western Courts in comprehending. Here however this translation is plainly and easily enacted by a subject who sees no discontinuity between the two legal orders. See Good, Holden, and Sbriccoli & Jacoviello, all collected in Holden (2011), for a series of contributions on such issues.
20. Holden (2003) and Michelutti (2007, 2008) offer other instances of analysis in such direction.
21. For explicit reference to the concept of governmentality and techniques of the self see Foucault (1984, 2007), Dreyfus and Rabinow (1982). For detailed discussions on the concepts of governmentality and power in Foucault see Senellart (1993) and Agamben (1998).
22. I am here referring to the framework of analysis of Indian traditional *panchayats'* procedure vs. that of Western courts as elaborated by Hayden (Hayden 1983, 1984, 1987). Hayden here makes the point that in Indian *panchayats* the task at hand is not one of fact-finding, as in Western courts, but rather of the normative evaluation of known facts. This way of looking at *panchayat* 'justice' and procedure will be useful in the understanding of other events reported by Durga.
23. It is important to stress that here I am not stating that Durga makes her brother say what she would have said in the same situation. Rather, as the prince in a fairy tale, what he does and says is constructed in the narrative, through textual functions, as the model of what people should do and say in particular situations. In this sense, the whole structure of Durga's narrative recalls that of a tale.
24. The concept of 'vernacularization' of democracy by Michelutti (2007, 2010) is a good instance in such direction. For instances of how the Indian Government has addressed dispute settlement forums other than its own by trying to subsume them within new official paradigms that were intended as a formalisation of local and traditional ones see the literature on *Nyaya Panchayats* and *Lok Adalats* (Galanter 1972, 1978; Galanter and Krishnan 2004; Baxi and Galanter 1979; Meschievitz and Galanter 1982; Hayden 1984).

25. In order to be freed from *holba*, usually a family has to call a *panchayat* in their house and be ready to comply with any of its decisions (even if, of course, room is given to everybody to restate his own reasons and negotiate an outcome). At the end, fines (money to be given to the *panchayat* and then used for the community), compensations (money to be given to the other party, if any and if asked), and practices of expiation (usually involving feeding one or more times either village or *paragna* Raika families) are established and a collective meal is offered to all those present. For further discussions on such issue see also Hayden (1983, 1999), Holden (2003), and Sbriccoli (2009, 2010).
26. Here voice in not understood as 'what one says'. Rather, it is the point of surfacing within narrative of a subject's successful strategic action. See Sbriccoli and Jacoviello (2012) for a detailed discussion of such issues. The works of Ranajit Guha (1982, 1983a, 1983b) and of other scholars belonging to the school of subaltern studies provide critical reflections on the relation between historical sources, subaltern subjects, voice, and the production of subjectivities. For an important discussion of this issue, also see Spivak (1988).

Notes on contributor

Tommaso Sbriccoli is Post-Doc Research Assistant at the School of Oriental and African Studies (SOAS, University of London), where he is involved in a research project on rural change and anthropological knowledge in postcolonial India. He is a political and legal anthropologist and has been doing field research in Northern India since 2003, working mainly with rural and pastoral communities in Rajasthan and Madhya Pradesh. In 2008 he opened a new fieldwork research in Italy on refugees and the Italian process of claiming asylum, developing together with Stefano Jacoviello, a semiotician, an interdisciplinary methodological framework of text and discourse analysis.

References

Agamben, Giorgio. 1998. *Homo Sacer: Sovereign Power and Bare Life*. Stanford California: Stanford University Press.

Agrawal, Arun. 1999. *Greener Pastures: Politics, Markets, and Community among a Migrant Pastoral People*. Durham NC: Duke University Press.

Baxi, Upendra and Marc Galanter. 1979. "Panchayat justice: an Indian experiment in legal access." In *Access to Justice, Emerging Issues and Perspectives*, edited by Mauro Cappelletti and Bryant Garth, 341–389. Alphen aan den Rijn: Sijthoff and Noordhoff *III*.

Benda-Beckmann, Franz von and Keebet von Benda-Beckmann. 2006. "The dynamics of change and continuity in plural legal orders." *Journal of Legal Pluralism* 53–54: 1–44.

Bentley, Carter G. 1984. "Hermeneutics and world construction in Maranao disputing." *American Ethnologist* 11(4): 642–655.

Chiba, Masaji 1998. "Other phases of legal pluralism in the contemporary world." *Ratio Juris* 11(3): 228–245.

Comaroff, John L. and Simon Roberts. 1981. *Rules and Processes: The Cultural Logic of Dispute in an African Context*. Chicago: University of Chicago Press.

Dreyfus, Hubert. L. and Paul Rabinow. 1982. *Michel Foucault, Beyond Structuralism and Hermeneutics*. Chicago: Chicago University Press.

Dupret, Baudouin. 2007. "Legal pluralism, plurality of laws, and legal practices: theories, critiques and praxiological re-specification." *European Journal of Legal Studies* 1(1). Available at www.ejls.eu/1/14UK.pdf, last downloaded January 30, 2013.

Fabbri, Paolo. 1998. *La svolta semiotica*. Bari: Laterza.

Foucault, Michel. 1984. "What is Enlightenment?" ("Qu'est-ce que les Lumières?"). In *The Foucault Reader*, edited by Paul Rabinow, 32–50. New York: Pantheon Books.

Foucault, Michel. 1994. "The subject and power." English translation from 1982. In *Power: Essential Works of Foucault 1954–1984*, edited by James D. Faubion, 326–343. Vol. 3. London: Penguin Books.

Foucault, Michel. 2007. *Security, Territory, Population. Lectures at the College de France 1977–78*. Edited by Michel Senellart. New York: Palgrave Macmillan.

Galanter, Marc. 1972. "The aborted restitution of indigenous law in India." *Comparative Studies in Society and History* 14(1): 53–70.

Galanter, Marc. 1978. "The displacement of traditional law in modern India." *Journal of Social Issues* 24: 24–65.
Galanter, Marc. 1981. "Justice in many rooms." *Journal of Legal Pluralism* 19: 1–47
Galanter, Marc and Jayanth K. Krishnan. 2004. "Bread for the poor: Access to justice and the rights of the needy in India." *Hastings Law Journal* 55: 789–834
Good, Anthony. 2011. "Witness statements and credibility assessments in the British asylum courts." Pp. 94–122 in Livia Holden (ed), *Cultural Expertise and Litigation. Patterns, Conflicts, Narratives*. London: Routledge.
Greimas, Algirdas J. 1983. *Du Sens II, Essais Sémiotiques*, Paris: Seuil.
Greimas, Algirdas J. and Joseph Courtés. 1979. *Sémiotique. Dictionnaire raisonné de la théorie du langage*. Paris: Hachette.
Griffiths, John. 1986. "What is Legal Pluralism?" *Journal of Legal Pluralism* 24: 1–55.
Guha, Ranajit. 1982. "On Some Aspects of the Historiography of Colonial India." In *Subaltern Studies No. 1.*, edited by Ranajit Guha, 1–8. Delhi: Oxford University Press.
Guha, Ranajit. 1983a. *Elementary Aspects of Peasant Insurgency in Colonial India*. Delhi: Oxford University Press.
Guha, Ranajit. 1983b. "The Prose of Counter-Insurgency." In *Subaltern Studies No.* 2, edited by Ranajit Guha, 1–42. Delhi: Oxford University Press.
Hayden, Robert M. 1983. "Excommunication as everyday event and ultimate sanction: The nature of suspension from an Indian caste." *The Journal of Asian Studies* 42(2): 291–307.
Hayden, Robert M. 1984. "A note on caste Panchayats and government courts in India. Different kinds of stages for different kinds of performances." *Journal of Legal Pluralism* 22: 43–52.
Hayden, Robert M. 1987. "Turn-Taking, Overlap, and the Task at Hand: Ordering Speaking Turns in Legal Settings." *American Ethnologist* 14 (2): 251–270.
Hayden, Robert M. 1999 *Dispute and Arguments amongst Nomads. A Caste Council in India*. New Delhi: Oxford University Press.
Holden, Livia S. 2011a. *Cultural Expertise and Litigation. Patterns, Conflicts, Narratives*. London: Routledge.
Holden, Livia S. 2011b. "Expert report writing: professional commitments and legal outcomes." In *Cultural Expertise and Litigation. Patterns, Conflicts, Narratives*, edited by Livia Holden, 195–211. London: Routledge.
Holden, Livia S. 2008. *Hindu Divorce: A Legal Anthropology*. Aldershot: Ashgate.
Holden, Livia S. 2004. "Official policies for (un)official customs: The hegemonic treatment of Hindu divorce customs by dominant legal discourses." *Journal of Legal Pluralism* 49: 47–74
Holden, Livia S. 2003. "Custom and Law Practices in Central India: Some Case Studies." *South Asia Research* 23 (2): 115–134.
Köhler-Rollefson, Ilse. 1992. "The Raika dromedary breeders of Rajasthan: a pastoral system in crisis." *Nomadic Peoples* 30: 74–83.
Merry, Sally E. 1999. "Pluralizing paradigms: From Gluckman to Foucault." *PoLAR: Political and Legal Anthropology Review* 22 (1): 115–122.
Merry, Sally E. 1988. "Legal pluralism." *Law & Society Review* 22 (5): 869–896.
Meschievitz, Catherine S. and Marc Galanter. 1982. "In search of Nyaya Panchayats: The politics of a moribund institution." In *The Politics of Informal Justice: Comparative Studies*, edited by Richard L. Abel, 47–77. Vol. 2. New York: Academic Press.
Michelutti, Lucia. 2007. "The vernacularisation of democracy: popular politics and political participation in North India." *Journal of the Royal Anthropological Institute* (N.S.) 13: 639–656.
Michelutti, Lucia. 2008. *The Vernacularisation of Democracy. Politics, Caste and Religion in India*. New Delhi: Routledge.
Moore, Erin P. 1995. "Moral reasoning: An Indian case study." *Ethos* 23 (3): 286–327.
Moore, Erin P. 1993. "Gender, power, and legal pluralism: Rajasthan, India." *American Ethnologist* 20 (3): 522–542.
Moore, Sally F. 1973. "Law and social change: The semi-autonomous social field as an appropriate subject of study." *Law & Society Review* 7(4): 719–746.
Moore, Sally F. 1977. "Individual interests and organisational structures: Dispute settlements as 'event of articulation'." In *Social Anthropology and Law*, edited by Ian Hammet, 159–187. New York: Academic Press.
Nader, Laura. 1986. "The subordination of women in comparative perspective." *Urban Anthropology and Studies of Cultural Systems and World Economic Development* 15 (3–4): 377–397.

Nader, Laura. 2006. "Orientalisme, occidentalisme et contrôle des femmes". *Nouvelles Questions Féministes* 25 (1): 12–24.

Nolle, Louise. 2008. "The two-sided family. The impact of the family and everyday life on women's political participation in Rural Karnataka." *Working Papers in Contemporary Asian Studies* 22, Centre for South-East Asian Studies, Lund University, Sweden.

O'Connor, Richard A. 1981. "Law as indigenous social theory: A Siamese Thai case." *American Ethnologist* 8 (2): 223– 237.

Prevot, Sandrine. 2007. *Les nomades d'aujourd'hui. Ethnologie des eleveurs raika en Inde.* Montreuil: Aux lieux d'être.

Ricoeur, Paul. 1971. "The model of the text: Meaningful action considered as a text." *Social Research* 38: 529–562.

Ricoeur, Paul. 1974. *The Conflict of Interpretations: Essays in Interpretation.* Evanston, IL: Northwestern University Press.

Robbins, Paul. 1998. "Authority and environment: Institutional landscapes in Rajasthan, India." *Annals of the Association of American Geographers* 88 (3): 410–435.

Robbins, Paul. 2000. "The rotten institution: corruption in natural resources management." *Political Geography* 19 (4): 423–443.

Sbriccoli, Tommaso. 2010. "Una questione di villaggio: analisi di una disputa inter-castale nel Godwar (Rajasthan)." Pp. 392–410 in Maria Angelillo (ed.), *Asiatica Ambrosiana* 2. Roma: Bulzoni.

Sbriccoli, Tommaso. 2009. *I Raika: Spazio, Parentela, Politica. Etnografia di una Comunità Pastorale del Rajasthan.* PhD Dissertation, University of Siena.

Sbriccoli, Tommaso and Stefano Jacoviello. 2012. "The voice in C. The Creole attitude of a Bangaldeshi refugee in Italy". In *Shifting Borders. European Perspectives on Creolisation*, edited by Tommaso Sbriccoli and Stefano Jacoviello, 83–109. Newcastle upon Tyne: Cambridge Scholars Publishing.

Sbriccoli, Tommaso and Stefano Jacoviello. 2011. "The case of S: Elaborating the 'right' narrative to fit normative/political expectations in asylum procedure in Italy." In *Cultural Expertise and Litigation: Patterns, Conflicts, Narratives*, edited by Livia Holden, 172–194. London: Routledge.

Senellart, Michel. 1993. "Michel Foucault: gouvernementalité et raison d'État". In *La pensée Politique, Situation de la démocratie 1*, edited by Marcel Gauchet, Pierre Manent, and Pierre Rosanvallon, 276–303. Hautes Études, Paris: Gallimard-Le Seuil.

Shariff, Fauzia. 2008. "Power relations and legal pluralism: An examination of "strategies of struggle" amongst the Santal *Adivasi* of India and Bangladesh." *Journal of Legal Pluralism* 57: 1–43

Sharma, Pragya. 2005. *Tribal Society in a Flux. An Anthropo-Sociological Study of Raika.* Jaipur: Panchsheel Prakashan.

Sontag, Susan. 1977. *On Photography.* New York: Farrar, Straus and Giroux.

Spivak, Gayatri C. 1988. "Can the subaltern speak?" In *Marxism and the Interpretation of Culture*, edited by Cary Nelson and Lawrence Grossber, 271–313. London: Macmillan.

Srivastava, Vinay K. 1991. "Who are the Raika/Rabaris?" *Man in India* (Special Issue) 71(1): 279–304.

Srivastava, Vinay K. 1997. *Religious Renunciation of a Pastoral People.* Delhi: Oxford University Press.

Srivastava, Vinay K. 2000. "The Raika Jāti and its Dharmic order." *Journal of Human Ecology* 11 (4): 281–298.

Tamanaha, Brian Z. 1993. "The folly of the 'social scientific' concept of legal pluralism." *Journal of Law and Society* 20 (2): 192–217.

Tamanaha, Brian Z. 1996. "The internal/external distinction and the notion of a 'practice' in legal theory and sociolegal studies." *Law & Society Review* 30: 163–204.

Tamanaha, Brian Z. 2000. "A non-essentialist version of legal pluralism." *Journal of Law and Society* 27 (2): 296–321.

Vanderlinden, Jacques. 1989. "Return to legal pluralism: twenty years later." *Journal of Legal Pluralism* 28: 149–157.

Wadley, Susan S. 1995. "The 'Village Indira': A Brahman widow and political action in rural north India." In *Women in India. Two Perspectives*, edited by Susan S. Wadley and Doranne Jacobson, 225–250. Delhi: Manohar.

Index

Note: Page numbers followed by 'n' refer to notes

abandonment 84
Abu Talal 34
academic discourse: daughters' inheritance 115–17
actant 113
Action India: *mahila panchayats* 90–2
Actor Network Theory 113
adivasis: denial of rights 130
agency: political naming 16
agnatic theory 117
Agnes, F. 20n
Ahmadis 48; custom 50; diaspora 49; Pakistan law 51, 52, 53
Algeria: French citizenship 71n
All-India Democratic Women's Association (AIDWA) 87
All-India Muslim Women's Personal Law Board 89
all-woman courts 77, 88–90
all-woman police stations 84–5
Allah Rakha v Federation of Pakistan (2000) 51
alternative dispute resolution (ADR) 76, 77, 79, 95
alternative dispute settlement venues: women 84
An-Na'im, A. 62
Ananda Margis 28–9, 31, 33, 36
Anderson, P. 25
Anderson, W. 33
Anglo-Pakistani law 36
angrezi shariat concept 56n, 64
Arab Spring 59
Arbitration Acts: (1940) 78, 94; (1996) 64, 66–7
Arbitration and Mediation Services (Equality) Bill 66, 67
Arendt, H. 44, 45
arranged marriage 48
Asad, T. 59, 62, 70n
Australia: indigenous peoples 11, 13, 20n; *Native Title Act* (1993) 13
Balagangadhara, S.N. 59, 61–2, 67, 70n
Ballard, R. 43, 68
Bangladesh: Chakma 140n; Dhanban 133–8; Thakurban 133–8; tribal peoples 130–1
Bannerji, H. 16
Barak, A. 28
Basu, M. 95
Batei Din (Jewish) 64
Baxi, U. 2
Benda-Beckman, F. 2, 120
Benda-Beckman, K. 2, 120
Bentham, J. 27
Berman, H.J. 61, 70n
Between Oxus and Indus (Schomberg) 115
Bhopal Gas Leaks Case (1984) 33
Biddulph, J.: *Tribes of the Hindu Koosh* 115
Birmingham Shari'a Council 63
Bleach, P. 29, 37n
blood money 36
Bowen, J.R. 64, 68, 72n
Brahmins 7
Breivik, A. 59
British colonialism 6–7
British immigration law 52
British Indian law 25

C Masilamani Mudaliar v Idol of Sru Swaminathaswami Thirkoil (Supreme Court of India, 1996) 9
Canada: Family Statute Law Amendment Act (Ontario, 2006) 64; multiculturalism 16; Muslims 63
canon law: Gregorian reforms 61
cartoon crisis: Muhammad 30
Caste Disabilities Removal Act (1850) 8
Caste Panchayats 15, 20n, 78
Catholic Tribunal (Wales) 63
Chakma (Bangladesh) 140n
Chaudhary, A.: and Holden, L. 3, 104–23
Chiba, M. 2, 145
Child Marriage Restraint Act (1929) 8

Christian religiosity 58
Christianity 62
colonialism 6–7, 16, 19n
Comaroff, J.L.: and Roberts, R. 144–65
common law judges 55
community: identity 17; practice 15
Comparative Science of Cultures 59
contestability 37
cooperation: international 34
corruption 155; Indian justice 82
Cotterrell, R.: *Politics of Jurisprudence* 20n
courts 28, 65; all-woman 77, 88–90; domestic 54–5; European Court of Human Rights (ECtHR) 64; matrimonial 8; *shari'at* 83–4, *see also* Indian courts; Indian Supreme Court
Cox, Baroness C. 66
Criminal Procedure Code (CrPC): dowry harassment 79
Crovetto, H. 29, 37
cultural identity 17
cultural practices 16
custody 72n
custom 14, 72n; Ahmadis 50; Hindu Law 20n; inhumane 15; as practice 116; religion 112; religion and governance 119
customary law 37, 94

Daniel Latifi v Union of India (Supreme Court of India, 2001) 9
daughters' inheritance: academic discourse 115–17; Bibi Sitara 115–17; case study one: Mavara, Khadija and Mandan 106–8; case study two: Awais Bibi (Shado) 108–9; case study three: Shahnaz 109–11; methodological remarks 105–6; Misalpur 106; Nimrah Begum 113–15; Pakistan 104–23; stereotype threat 118; temporalization of claims 111–13
Davis, R. 25, 35, 36
Davy, K. 35
deaths: dowry 80
decision-making process 55
Declaration on the Rights of Indigenous Peoples (UN) 130
deep legal pluralism 43
definitions: acceptance 13
Delhi Commission for Women 91
democracy: funding for implementation 1; vernacularization 163n
Denmark 30, 35; *Ombudsmand* institution 32
developmental terrorism 32
Dhagamwar, V. 15
Dhanban (Bangladesh) 133–8
dharma 6
Dharmashastra 6, 7, 9
dictatorship: anti-pluralist 44
discourse: power of 14–18
discrimination: gender 14, 17
discursive approach: legal pluralism 144–65
discursive narrative 160
dispute resolution: alternative 76, 77, 79, 95; minorities 138; Santal 125–8; women's alternative venues 84
disputes: transnational 47
diversity 16, 37; legal 36; super 43
divorce 47, 98n; Muslim women 63
domestic abuse: India 79, 81
domestic courts: foreign laws 54–5
domestic violence 84, 91, 99n
Douglas, G. 63
dowry deaths 80
dowry harassment 84, 90; Criminal Procedure Code (CrPC) 79
Dowry Prohibition Act (1961) 80
Durga 147–65; government and the subject 153–5; ideal models and effective strategies 155–8; position of the subject 151–2; state v panchayat justice 158–9; translation and planes of pertinence 152–3

East London Muslim Centre 60
Emergency (1975–7) 90
empirical legal pluralism 12
English law 56; Arbitration Act (1996) 64, 66–7; Muslim law 58–75; Turkish law 43
equality: Indian law 28
Equality Act (2010): amendments 66
equity formulae: justice, equity and right 8
Europe: Muslim immigrants 58–9
European Convention of Human Rights (ECHR): Article 3 torture 30; religious freedom 58
European Court of Human Rights (ECtHR): *Refah Partisi* case (2003) 64
excommunication *see holba*

Family Courts Act (FCA, 1984) 80, 98n
family law 19n; gender just 19n; governance and governability 42–57
family problems: privacy 81
Family Statute Law Amendment Act (Ontario, 2006) 64
fatwa: anti-woman 83; guidance 68
Fazilet Partisis case (ECtHR, 2006) 65
feminism 79
feminist literature 13
Fitzpatrick, P. 2
folk law 36
foreign laws: domestic courts 54–5; interpretation 55
formal law 48
Foucault, M. 2, 120, 124, 153, 161n
fractured sovereignty 25
Fraser, N. 18
Fuller, C. 119
fundamentalists 43

Galanter, M.: and Krishnan J.K. 78
Gandhi, I. 90
Gandhi, R. 33
gender discrimination 14, 17
gender just 19n
gender justice 93; India (independent) 10; religious personal laws 5–23
Gilgit Baltistan (Pakistan) 115–17
global legal monism: calibrating 31–5
global legal pluralism 25; innovative 35–6
global normativities 43
globalized messiness 42–4
governability: family law 42–57; law 120
governmentality 151, 155, 160, 162n; Foucault 124, 153; power 124
Gregorian reforms: of canon law 61
Griffiths, A. 2, 11, 12, 36
Griffiths, J. 12, 94
Grover, S. 91–3
Grundnorm 24, 28

harassment: dowry 79, 84, 90
Hardin, G. 37
harmony: ideology 124–43; justice 79
Harmony ideology (Nader) 124
Hastings, W. 7
Hayden, R.M. 148, 162n
Himmelfarb, G. 27
Hindu Inheritance Act (1928) 8
Hindu Law: custom 20n; description 6–8; gender discrimination 14; marriage 9; Marriage Act (1955) 15; reform 9; Religious Personal Law 5–23; Succession Act (amendment 2005) 9–10, 19n; Widows' Remarriage Act (1856) 8
Hindu marriage: breakdown scenario 47–50
Hinudttva movement 17
holba: Raikas 148, 150, 154–5, 158–9, 162–3n
Holck, N. 25, 28–33, 36
Holden, L. 1–4, 15, 81; and Chaudhary, A. 104–23
honour 52; killings 83
Hukook-e-Niswan Mahila Sanghatana: Women's Federation for Women's Rights 90
human rights: fundamentalists 43; implementation funding 1
husband-wife relationships 77

identity 17, 128, 131
immigrants: Muslim 58–9
immigration: British law 52; Netherlands abuse 49; status 52
incest 84
India: British colonialism 6–7; contemporary interloper 28–31; and Denmark 30, 35; domestic abuse 79, 81; gender justice 10; justice corruption 82; minority rights 10; Muslim rights 10; Rajasthan 144–65; reservations for Scheduled Tribes 130; women's treatment by traditional dispute-resolution 82–3
India (British colonial): colonial interloper 26; equity formulae 8; Regulation II, Article 23 (1772) 7
Indian Constitution (independent) 8–13; Uniform Civil Code 8
Indian courts: distrust in 78; people's (*lok adalat*) 78, 85–8, 98n; treatment of women 82; women's 76–103, *see also* Indian Supreme Court
Indian law: British 25; divorce 47; equality 28; marriage 47; Protection of Women from Domestic Violence Act (PWDVA, 2005) 79–80; Public Interest Litigation (PIL) 25, 27–8, 31; Religious Personal Laws 5–23; right to life 28; Terrorist and Disruptive Activities Act (TADA) 37n; unification and reform 26–8
Indian Penal Code (IPC) 25–8; rape 79
Indian Supreme Court 9, 32; *C Masilamani Mudaliar v Idol of Sru Swaminathaswami Thirkoil* (Supreme Court of India, 1996) 9; *Daniel Latifi v Union of India* (Supreme Court of India, 2001) 9; *Mary Roy v State of Kerala* (1986) 9; Muslim Women's Act (1996) 9; *Nandini Sundar and others versus State of Chhattisgarh* (Supreme Court of India, 2011) 32; *State of Bombay v Narasu Appa Mali* (1951) 9
indigenous peoples 19n, 139n; Australia 11, 13, 20n; United Nations 130
individual view 145
informal law 48
inheritance: daughters 104–23
institutionalized superiority 18
intelligibility: secular state 62
international cooperation 34
Islam: characterization 71n
Islamic law: divine 18–19n
Islamic marriage contract (*nikah*) 63
Islamic Shariah Council (Leyton) 68
Ismaili Conciliation and Arbitration Boards 71n
Israel Supreme Court 28
Iyengar, S. 93, 95
izzat 52, 54

Jahrkhand: Madhura 133–8; Pahara 133–8
jama'at 89
jati panchayat: Raikas 147, 154, 155, 159
Jayaram, N.: and Saberwal, S. 24, 35
Jenkins, R. 128
Jharkhand 131
jirga 120
Judaism 62
judges: common law 55
judicial populism 28

juridical legal pluralism 12
justice: gender 5–23, 93; harmony 79; Indian 82; *panchayat* 158–9; Rajasthan 144–65

Kandiyoti, D. 92
Kapaku Papuans 2
karewa 112
Khan, A. 65, 113
killings: honour 83
Kolsky, E. 25, 35, 36; *White Peril: Law and Lawlessness in early colonial India* 26
Krishnan J.K.: and Galanter, M. 78

Lady Judges of Pakistan (project) 113, 121
laiklik (secularism) 62, 65
law: fog of 36–7; governability 120; social institutions 2
Law and Society conference (Honolulu, 2012) 1
law in subjectivity (Chiba) 145
Legal Aid 86
Legal Aid Services Authorities Act (LSAA, 1987) 8
legal diversity 36
legal monism 2; white violence 24–41
legal neo-positivism 44
legal orders 119
legal pluralism 2; defining 13, 18; discursive approach 144–65
legal positivist philosophy 12
Lemons, K. 92–3
lived practice 14
living law 15, 44
local normativities 43
lok adalats (people's court): women 85–8, 98n
London Beth Din 63
Lubin, T. 6
lumberdar 113–14

Macauley, T.B. 25–8, 37n
madar sangam 85, 87
maddhab 63
Madhura (Jahrkhand, India) 133–8
Madsen, S.T. 2, 24–41
mahila adalat/mahila mandal see women's courts
Mahila Aghadi 87
mahila panchayats (women's councils) 90–2
Mahila Samakhya: *nari adalats* 92–3
mahila samiti (women's committee) 87
mahila shakti mandal (women's power circle): Women's Research and Action Group (WRAG) 90
mahr (dower) 68
maintenance 98n; law (post-divorce) 45
Malik, M.: *Minority Legal Orders in the UK* 60
Manjhi (headman): Santal 126–8, 132–3
marriage 47, 68, 72n; arranged 48; document (Nikah Form) 49; Hindu 9, 47–50; Muslim law 49; prohibition with Holy Quran 105, 111; registration in Pakistani law 50; registration problems 63; religious/legal 48; Santal 133; to a tree 112; Urdu exchange 111
Mary Roy v State of Kerala (Supreme Court of India, 1986) 9
matrimonial courts 8
mediation: peer 77
Mehdi, R. 114
Menski, W. 2, 14, 16, 19n, 42–57, 56n; and Pearl, D. 62, 64
Mexico: Talean Zapotec community 124–5
migrants 42
minorities: dispute resolution 138
minority cultural identity 17
Minority Legal Orders in the UK (Malik) 60
minority rights: India (independent) 10
modern state: development 11
Modood, T. 58
money: blood 36
monism: global legal 31–5; legal 2, 24–41
Moore, E. 82, 145–6, 152–3
Moore, S.F. 44
Muhammad cartoon crisis 30
Mujib, Sheikh 130
Mulla: ultra-orthodox 17
multiculturalism 16
Muslim Arbitration Tribunal (MAT) 55, 63, 64, 66, 68, 71n
Muslim Family Laws Ordinance (1961) 48
Muslim immigrants: Europe 58–9
Muslim law 20n; English context 58–75; marriage 49; reconstruction in diaspora 63–5
Muslim Personal Law 78
Muslim Personal Law (Shariat) Application Act: (1937) 62, 104; (1961) 104
Muslim rights: India (independent) 10
Muslim women: divorce 63
Muslims: Canada 63

Nachol insurrection (1948) 129, 139n
Nader, L. 79, 139n, 146; *Harmony ideology* 124
naming: power of 17
Nandini Sundar and others versus State of Chhattisgarh (Supreme Court of India, 2011) 32
nari adalats 91; Mahila Samakhya 92–3
nari nyaya samiti see women's courts
narrative: women 146
National Secular Society 66
Native Title Act (Australia, 1993) 13
Naxalite 31
Nelson, M.J. 119
neo-positivism: legal 44
Netherlands: immigration abuse 49
Nichols, J.A.: and Witte, J. 63
nikah (Islamic marriage contract) 48, 49, 63, 68
nomic din 55

non-state laws: religious personal laws as 5–23
Norway: foreign law 54
nyaya panchayats (judicial councils) 78

Occam's razor 31
Okin, S. 17
Oklahoma: *shari'a law* 67
Ombudsmand institution (Denmark) 32
One Law for All (campaign group) 60, 66, 70n
Ontario: Family Statute Law Amendment Act (2006) 64
ordering devices 24
other: Santal 128–32

pagans 58–75; pursuing 65–9
Pahara (Jahrkhand, India) 133–8
Pakistan: daughters' inheritance 104–23; Gilgit Baltistan 115–17
Pakistan constitution: *Prevention of Anti-Women Practices (Criminal Law Amendment) Act* (2011) 104–5
Pakistani law 37, 48; Ahmadi 51, 52, 53; Ahmadis 51, 52, 53; Family Courts Act (1964) 50; marriage registration 50; Penal Code 35; Special Marriage Act (1872) 50
panchayats 89, 120, 148, 157, 162n; caste 78; justice and state 158–9; media critiques 83–4
panches 155
pandits 7
paradigm of arguments (Comaroff and Roberts) 145
Parashar, A. 2, 5–23
parcellization of sovereignty 25
Parker, Mrs Justice 53, 54
patriarchal bargain 92
Pearl, D.: and Menski, W. 62, 64
peer mediation 77
people's court (*lok adalat*) 78, 85–8, 98n
personal law 118; unification 44
Phillips, Lord N. 60
plural legalisms 19n
police: women 111
police stations: all-woman 84–5; women's cells 84
political naming: agency 16
Politics of Jurisprudence (Cotterrell) 20n
pop (plurality of pluralities) 45
populism: judicial 28
Pospisil, L. 2
power 124, 154
Prabhakaran, V. 33
Prevention of Anti-Women Practices (Criminal Law Amendment) Act (Pakistan, 2011) 104–5
private international law 45
proselytization 59
protection: RPLs 18
Protection of Women from Domestic Violence Act (PWDVA, 2005) 79–80
Proutist Universal 28
Public Interest Litigation (PIL): India 25, 27–8, 31
punishment 15
Purulia Arms Drop case (2011) 25, 29–31

Quran 105, 111

R v M (2011) 46, 49, 50
radical legal pluralism 43
Raikas (Rabaris) 147; *holba* 148; ideal models and effective strategies 155–8; *jati panchayat* 147, 154; Rajasthan 145–65; subject, marginality and village politics 149–55
Rajasthan: Durga context and story 147–9; justice 144–65
Randeria, S. 25
rape 83, 84; Indian Penal Code (IPC) 79; Santal case 125–8
recognition 18
Refah Partisi case (ECtHR, 2003) 64
religion 2, 61, 112, 119
religious freedom 58
religious fundamentalists 43
religious identity 17
religious marriage 48
Religious Personal Laws (RPL): concept 6–8; non-state laws 5–23
resource curse 32
Riaz Javed v Sheraz Ahmed (2010) 50
right to life 28
rights: denial 130; minority 10; Muslims 10
Roberts, R.: and Comaroff, J.L. 144–65
Rohe, M. 65
Rosen, L. 118
Roy, O. 60, 62, 68, 70n
Rudd, J. 13

Saberwal, S.: and Jayaram, N. 24, 35
sabla mahila sanghs (associations of empowered women) 91
Salwa Judum case (2011) 28, 31–2
Santal: alcohol 130, 139n; dispute resolution 125–8; harmony ideology 124–43; identity 131; locality of oppression and resolution of disputes 132–3; *Manjhi* (headman) 126–8, 132–3; marriage 133; micro politics of struggle in four villages 133–8; origin 128–9; other: rebels, benefactors, subalterns 128–32; relations with modern state 130–2; uprising against British 129; violence of settlement 128–30
Santal *Hul* (1855) 129
Santal Pargana Tenancy Act (1949) 131
Santos, S. 117
Sarkar, P.R. 28–9
Sbriccoli, T. 3, 144–65
Schomberg, R.C.F.: *Between Oxus and Indus* 115

Scott, J.: *Weapons of the Weak* 124
secular age 59
secular state 62
secularism (*laiklik*) 62, 65
secularization 59, 60; Westernization 71n
semi-autonomy 146
September 11th terrorist attacks (2001) 30
sexual violence 52
Shah, P. 2, 43, 58–75
shame 111
shari'a: councils 60, 63, 64, 66, 68, 71n; demand for recognition in Britain 64; fora and principles 65; law 36, 37; Oklahoma 67
shari'at courts 83–4
shariatization 61
Sharifa Khanam, D. 89
Shariff, F. 3, 124–43, 154
Shirkat Ghar (NGO) 114
Shiv Sena party 87
Siddiqi, Faiz ul Aqtab 68
Sitara, B. 115–17
slavery 16
Sobhraj, C. 33
social engineering 1
social institutions 2
social relations 124
social subordination 18
soft legal pluralism: PIL 31
Somers, G. 125, 128
Sousa Santos, B. de 2, 117
sovereignty: fractured 25; parcellization 25; state law 11
State of Bombay v Narasu Appa Mali (Supreme Court of India, 1951) 9
state law 2, 161n; sovereignty 11
status 52
Steele, C.M. 118
STEPS Women's Development Organization: Tamil Nadu 89
stereotype threat: daughters' inheritance 118
super diversity 43
superiority: institutionalized 18

Talean Zapotec community (Mexico) 124–5
Tamanaha, B. 2, 20n, 44
Tamil Nadu: State Legal Aid Authority 85; STEPS Women's Development Organization 89
terrorism: developmental 32; September 11th attacks (2001) 30
Thakurban (Bangladesh) 133–8
thakurs (Lords) 157
Tickborne, J. 25
torture 30
Torture Convention (UN, 1984) 30, 35
totalism 28
transnational dis

tribal peoples: Bangladesh 130–1
Tribes of the Hindu Koosh (Biddulph) 115
Trier, T. 30, 34
Turkey: Constitutional Court 65
Turkish law 43

Uddin v Choudhury (EWCA, 2009) 68
ulema (learned men) 63
unification: personal law 44
uniformity 37
Union Carbide 33
United Nations (UN): Declaration on the Rights of Indigenous Peoples (2007) 130; Security Council resolution 1373 (2011) 34; Torture Convention (1984) 30, 35
United States of America (USA): Establishment Clause of the First Amendment (1789) 67
unity of law 24
universal history 59
universalization 59

Vanderlinden, J. 94, 145
Vatuk, S. 3, 76, 103
Vienna Convention on Diplomatic Relations (1961) 35
violence: domestic 84, 91, 99n; sexual 52; white 24–41; women 79

Wales: Catholic Tribunal 63
watta-satta (Urdu exchange marriage) 111
Weapons of the Weak (Scott) 124
Weber, M. 24
Westergaard, K. 33
Westernization: secularization 71n
White Peril: Law and Lawlessness in early colonial India (Kolsky) 26
white violence 24–41
Wieber, M. 3
Williams, Dr R. (Archbishop) 60, 63, 70n
Witte, J.: and Nichols, J.A. 63
women: alternative dispute settlement venues 84; committee (*mahila samiti*) 87; confederation 92; *jama'at* 89; *lok adalats* 85–8; Muslim divorce 63; narrative 146; police 111; violence 79; wing of political parties 87, *see also* daughters' inheritance
Women's Counselling Centre 84
women's courts (India) 76–103; all-woman court 77–8, 88–90; historical background 78–80; low rate of resort to 81–2; treatment of women by traditional bodies 82–3
Women's Federation for Women's Rights (Hukook-e-Niswan Mahila Sanghatana) 90
Women's Research and Action Group (WRAG): *mahila shakti mandal* 90, 99n
Woodman, G. 2, 120